# IN THE PRESENCE
# OF AUDIENCE

# IN THE PRESENCE OF AUDIENCE

## The Self in Diaries and Fiction

Deborah Martinson

The Ohio State University Press
*Columbus*

Library of Congress Cataloging-in-Publication Data

Martinson, Deborah, 1946-
  In the presence of audience : the self in diaries and fiction /
Deborah Martinson.
       p. cm.
Includes bibliographical references and index.
  ISBN 0-8142-0952-1 (hardcover : alk. paper) — ISBN 0-8142-9022-1
(CD-Rom)
  1. English diaries—Women authors—History and criticism. 2. English
prose literature—20th century—History and criticism. 3. Women and
literature—Great Britain—History—20th century. 4. Authors and
readers—Great Britain—History—20th century. 5. Women authors,
English—Biography—History and criticism. 6. Lessing, Doris May, 1919-
Golden notebook. 7. Mansfield, Katherine, 1888-1923—Diaries. 8.
Woolf, Virginia, 1882-1941—Diaries. 9. Hunt, Violet,
1862-1942—Diaries. 10. Women in literature. 11. Self in literature.
I. Title.
  PR908 .M37 2003
  828'.9103099287—dc21
                                    2003007467

Cover design by Dan O'Dair
Printed by Thomson-Shore, Inc.

The paper used in this publication meets the minimum requirements of the American
National Standard for Information Sciences—Permanence of Paper for Printed Library
Materials. ANSI Z39.48-1992.

9 8 7 6 5 4 3 2 1

*For the Stewarts and the Martinsons*

# *contents*

# *acknowledgments*

Many people have made this book possible. Early readers and advisors Vincent Chang, Tania Modleski, Jim Kincaid, Hilary Schor, and Pat C. Hoy showed keen interest. Later readers encouraged and edited: Ashley Opp, Lynn Dumenil, and Cecilia Fox. Others continued reading, thinking, and critiquing with me as the book took shape: Gloria Mazzella, Darsie Bowden, Lika Miyake, Jacqueline O'Connor, Sandra Chrystal, Arthe Anthony, and the Occidental Writers Network. I thank Elias Rodriquez for technical advice. Through it all, Jay, Hope, and Barry Martinson patiently supported my endeavors. Institutions have had their role, too, and I wish to thank the libraries and librarians at the University of Southern California and Occidental College. Special thanks to Occidental for granting me leave and research funding from the Brown Fund.

*Introduction*

# In the Presence of Audience

*The Self in Diaries and Fiction*

"Women have to be cautious in any century . . . husbands may expect diary privileges"(Blodgett 1988, 57). The male "privilege" of reading, judging, and perhaps even amending diary entries makes women vulnerable to their control, makes them "cautious" of exposure, and makes them talented in both writing and concealing themselves and their lives in text. Whereas men often write diaries of their public lives, and often for publication, women historically wrote from the personal sphere of their lives,[1] making all the more risky their depictions of themselves on the domestic front. In both American and British culture, even in the twentieth and twenty-first centuries, dominant culture holds that the husband wields not only domestic and economic power but inhabits the center of his wife's social and sexual life. Any woman's refutation of those suppositions, especially in a diary, which traditionally, though not accurately, has been deemed both private and true, places the writer in the precarious position. "'What could a poor fellow do with a wife who kept a journal but kill her?'" (Buller in Simons 1990, 18).[2]

With husbands and lovers as audiences, it can hardly be news to women readers and writers that the diary obscures much. My early interest in this study was to examine diaries of women writers whose husbands did indeed read their diaries to find the effects of such scrutiny on their process, their style, their textual production of self in the diary. What in their more public fictions seemed sublimated in the so-called private text? To choose the diaries to explore, I read many wonderful modernist British diarists, seeking women writers who shared similar cultural and literary contexts but who also exhibited various diary-writing strategies and fictional explorations. Most important, I looked for diarists who knew that their husbands had access to their diaries and read them at least occasionally.

To examine the important issue of audience effect on diary texts, I analyze diaries written by three exceptional women writers living in Britain

1

at the turn of the twentieth century: Virginia Woolf, Katherine Mansfield, and Violet Hunt. All three of these women were published, respected writers, and all three wrote diaries that their husbands read.[3] In my probing, however, I found that audience presence was not simple. Because I necessarily researched diary texts written by published writers, I found that their fame in the literary circles of modernist Britain brought them additional audiences—and they knew it. Each woman at some point in the diary worries that her journal will find a public place in years to come, instincts borne out by eventual publication. To illuminate the difficulties women writers face in relation to male readers at home and in publishing houses, I chose Doris Lessing's fictional *The Golden Notebook* to provide the conclusion for this study of women's diaries. Her use of diary fiction structurally and thematically deflects her own authorial presence through Anna Wulf, a diarist narrator, powerfully exposing what a woman confronts when she seeks to write about herself and her experience in ways that threaten her masculine audiences. Closing so dramatically, I hope Lessing's experimental dispersal of diaries and selves will emphasize the powerful leverage an audience has on autobiographical writing, diaries in particular, and the difficulty of drawing "strict demarcations between autobiography and fiction" (Hetata 2003, 125).

## Audience and Publication Details

The risks of exposure were real for these writers, as the husband/editor ensured the publication of these "private" diaries. Indeed, Woolf, Mansfield, and Hunt all had their diaries published, edited, and amended by their husbands, "destined to play in autobiography the Cinderella to the literary prince, the heroine to the editorial hero" (Personal Narrative Group 1989, 37). With regard to these three women, only Hunt's 1917 diary was published by someone other than her mate, though his name as coauthor ensured its publication. Woolf's and Mansfield's diaries were published posthumously, and Hunt's *The Desirable Alien* was written at her "husband's" request with publication in mind. Thus, men exercising editorial control partially shaped the women's accounts, especially at the initial publication. By writing a fiction about diaries, Lessing sublimates her own voice in favor of Anna Wulf's, therefore dispersing her authorship in narrators and fictionalizing the dilemma and the consequences of writing a diary sought out by male readers and editors. Lessing thus far has avoided a husband/editor's shaping and defining her diary texts, planning to have her own diaries published posthumously.

Death makes diaries available to more public audiences, unless diarists choose publication in their lifetime. Only Hunt agreed to the 1913 publication of her travel diary with Ford Madox Ford, her disputed husband but definite lover. Woolf's diary was first published thirteen years after her death in 1954, edited by Leonard Woolf and called *A Writer's Diary*. The five-volume *The Diary of Virginia Woolf*, edited by Anne Olivier Bell, is considered complete and is the text I primarily used. Woolf's early diaries, edited and published in 1990 by Mitchell E. Leaska under the title *A Passionate Apprentice*, were also useful. Katherine Mansfield's diary, called *Journal of Katherine Mansfield*, much expurgated, was first published by her husband, John Middleton Murry, in 1927, just four years after she died. In 1954 Murry offered what he called the "definitive edition" of *Journal of Katherine Mansfield*.[4] The huge mass of papers that comprised Mansfield's private writings had not until recently been published in their entirety, but I was able to analyze both Murry's *Journal* and Margaret Scott's *Complete Notebooks*. My study of Violet Hunt's diaries depends primarily on two very different texts: *The Desirable Alien at Home in Germany*, a travel diary "coauthored" and edited by Ford Madox Ford, and *The Return of the Good Soldier: Ford Madox Ford and Violet Hunt's 1917 Diary*, edited by Robert and Marie Secor and published in 1983.[5] The latter, even though Ford receives authorial credits, is entirely Hunt's diary, written in the waning days of their relationship. Each husband edited and wrote as his lifework. Editing their wife's work, even her "personal" work, seemed a given.

With readers in mind, Woolf, Mansfield, and Hunt create diaries that simultaneously erase and multifoliate selves, that evoke shifting images of the world as the persona herself shifts and recedes, vanishes and reappears. The writers break what Woolf calls the "moulds" of autobiography and fiction and enable readers to find, but not confine, the deviser of the diary. These women aim to protect themselves and have their say: The "protests were not silent. Many were subtle, many tentative . . . there was a price to pay" (Schenck 1989, 211). Each writer cleverly negotiates the terms of her own self-text. Because the women write adeptly, their manipulation of language contrives to personate their conventional roles as women, yet to speak "between the acts," as Woolf would have it.

The diary text then acts as a site for the writer's tension, rebellion, and remaking of self. Though the writer carefully constructs the self on the page, she gives herself power through the act of writing.[6] As "'that shrewdly innocent breed, those secret exhibitionists'" (Godwin in Simons 1990, 2), diary writers bare and cloak themselves in diary text. With an audience certain on the domestic front and potential on the literary front, these diarists use their talents to rhetorically shape self-identities in literary production. All four diarists—including Anna Wulf—write texts that conform to traditional expectations of diaries, yet all four writers—five if we include Lessing—also write fictions within the diaries: practice fictions, fictionalized autobiographical stories, literary characterizations, and prosaic musings.

The proliferation of genre within the diary, as well as the contested literary definitions of the diary, necessitate some theoretical grounding as to the traditions and more current thinking about this subset of autobiographical writing. After laying the groundwork for the presence of audience as a paramount concern, I introduce the diarists within these theoretical contexts. I close the introduction by brief suggestions as to the ways of reading diaries to uncover the strategies diarists use. *In the Presence of Audience* then properly begins, letting the diarists have their say, create themselves textually, and elude the dominion of others who seek to define them.

## Traditional Conventions of the Diary Genre

By looking first at the traditional literary understanding of diaries, more mythical than borne out by experience, then at actual writers' rearrangement of conventions, we see the diary not as a factual document but as "liquid literature" (Marcus 1988, 118).

Autobiography traditionally was seen as a masculine genre designed to record the public lives of important men.[7] From St. Augustine's and Jean-Jacques Rousseau's classical and historical definitions of autobiography as "confession" to Georges Gusdorf's more recent work defining autobiography as self-narrative, critics tend to divide diaries into categories of "private" for women and "public" for men. The literary public historically saw a man's diary as more historical than psychological, a subgenre, important only as a precursor to the published work or a factual record of a man's public experience. Women's diaries, "private, domestic, and psychological, were thought to conform to the . . . banal elements" (Raoul 1989, 58–61) of a woman's life.[8] Thus, "girls" in their adolescence were encouraged to keep "nonproductive" diaries as an accomplishment, something like needlepoint, that did not take away from their femininity but could embellish their routine domestic duties. This traditional denigration of the diary as a genre of men's rough drafts or young girls' unsophisticated craft limited the study of diaries as literary or social texts and promoted traditional myths about diaries.

Although no two critics perceive the diary genre in precisely the same way, traditional definitions support notions of writers with authentic fixed identities writing diaries in private with no sense of audience, who nevertheless write with a sense of historical realism. William Matthews's 1977 article on diaries notes their critical neglect and attempts to define them as a "daily record," "normally formal and regular in style" though lacking in "pattern and design" and "personal . . . in that it envisages no external audience" (286–91). In 1999 Edward Seidensticker insists that the diary is "self-centered writing . . . different from both autobiography and memoir. . . . By virtue of being a record of daily events it is obviously more detailed. Much of it is by nature trivial . . ." (47). He, like many endeavoring to theorize the diary, operate under assumptions more personal than critical. Current and astute theorist Lawrence Rosenwald also defines the diary too narrowly, but his definition does serve to acknowledge the generic assumptions traditionally made about diaries, the form of "personal" writing that "in form . . . is a chronological ordered sequence of dated entries addressed to an unspecified audience" (Podnieks 2000, 29).

Critics understandably face problems of definition because of the sheer diversity of kinds of diaries—their varying degrees of privacy, fictionality, and reflexivity. Formulaic definitions do not stand up well when applied to specific diaries. But in an effort to bring autobiography, and by extension diaries, to some degree of respect as a literary genre, critics define forms, terms, and writing circumstances, however erroneous. Elizabeth Podnieks says, "The issue of genre authenticity is linked to the question of whether the self can ever be known and whether it can be rendered accurately, if at all, in words (5).

## Current Trends in Theorizing Diaries

Of course, claims of authenticity and the knowable "self" seem outrageous to those of us well versed in poststructuralist theories. A full historical mapping of the way the "self" and "text" have both undergone scrutiny and dispersion is outside the focus of this introduction. It is important to note, however, that what Eakin calls "possessive individualism" has increasingly shifted in favor of more relational, cultural, and communal constructions. Early diary critics such as Elizabeth Bruss suggested that diary texts acted as "mirrors" of experience, but in seeking to formulate "constitutive rules" for a diary to "count" as literature (1976, 8) destabilized the self by emphasizing its variable and creative possibility. Bruss attacks the "faulty or naive assumptions" that compromise autobiographical understanding; she emphasizes the way the diary's language distorts self-images as the writer reimagines the self on the page. The diary writer's multiple readings of herself, fixed and unfixed, fill the diary pages; she tweaks images of the self as she imagines the shadow reader rifling the diary's pages. Thus, although

Bruss conflates writer and self, it is performative, constructing a form with aesthetic possibility, not an iconographic image of the writer.

Endeavoring to work through the paradox of autobiography as "self-expression," a site where identity and narrative too often function as whole, Barry Olshen proposes that critics distinguish between subject as "center of awareness," "persona" as that "entirely constituted by discourse," and the difficult term "self," which is "connected to both the subject and the text" (1995, 8–9). Theoretically astute, Olshen's careful definitions rely on shared assumptions about autobiography and the self. Given the critical debate, these shared assumptions are all but impossible. The self as lived experience in specific contexts continues to flourish, even for the wary scholar who mistrusts "[t]he ideas of truth and judgment, [which] are, perhaps, more radical, enduring, and valuable than late-twentieth-century postmodern theory has credited them with being" (Parke 1996, 91).

The debate surrounding autobiographical criticism of all types is political—related to self and cultural definition, to class, race, and gender—the ontological state of being. Noting the issues surrounding "both the form and content of diaries," Suzanne Bunkers and Cynthia Huff enter "those debates by highlighting a genre that challenges boundaries and enhances transdisciplinary thinking" (1996, 1–2). Diary criticism suggests that many women from medieval days to our own twenty-first century write diaries that interrogate self and culture and "break all the rules" (Walters 1987, 90).

## Theorizing Audience

The diary labors under the continuing assumption—even among sophisticated readers—that it is primarily private, a claim about which I am skeptical. Even in "private" autobiography, the question of narrative cannot be separated from the question of audience. But many theorists only reluctantly acknowledge the profound effect of audiences, potential or real, on diary writers. Bernard Duyfhuizen continues to assert that diaries are "assumed to be private texts written only for the writer's eyes" (1986, 175) but acknowledges that diaries are "culturally coded" (ibid.). Theorists increasingly note the existence of diary readers but more generally point to the writer's "conformity to the dominant ideology" (Davis 1987, 8), on one hand, and her topics "muted, masked, or ignored" (Chevigny 1983, 77), on the other. Yet the diary writer's conformity (or not) may dictate that she "mask" the contradictions in so-called private text. Gradually critics of autobiography have, though sometimes reluctantly, acknowledged the audience of so-called personal writing. But so often the audience imagined is ambiguous and general.

Judy Simons argues that women often imagined audiences but still wrote to "unburden themselves . . . informed by seclusion and their response to it" (1990, 6–8). Except in her analysis of Fanny Burney's work, Simons assumes an audience only vaguely imagined. Blodgett notes in her *Centuries of Female Days* that many diaries were made available to readers but directs her own study, paradoxically, to those she assumes were truly private (1988). Both Simons and Blodgett include Mansfield and Woolf in their excellent studies of diaries, but make the similar assumption that Mansfield and Woolf wrote in privacy to produce art in diary form.

Acknowledging very real audiences of many diary writers, Lynn Z. Bloom interrogates the "popular perception" that "privacy" is implicit in the genre. Bloom writes: "Indeed, it is the audience hovering at the edge of the page that for the sophisticated diarist facilitates the work's ultimate focus" (Bunkers and Huff 1996, 23). Bloom emphasizes the diary's becoming a "public document" saying "once a writer, like an actor, is audience oriented, such considerations as telling a good story, getting the sounds and the rhythm right, supplying sufficient detail for another's understanding, can never be excluded" (25). In this instance Bloom turns the perception of the audience into a positive force necessary to change personal chroniclers into writers. The aesthetic qualities of the diaries under study certainly point to that function.

Many critics of the autobiographical see art as incidental to the personal. Georges Gusdorf, for example, sees autobiography as a "a work of personal justification" (1980, 115) but assumes a masculine writer in his studies. Nancy Miller notes that for women autobiographers "justification" is an added trap. A woman who writes about her unorthodox life doubly violates "masculine turf" (1980, 263).[9] Thus, the limitations a writer imposes on her text and the fictions she inserts may be a direct result of the need to be cautious in relationships with another who maintains an authoritative stance. In essence, any woman writing against the grain of social conformity writes a hazardous political diary. Political diaries can be dynamite, presumably because the text makes the aberrant writer vulnerable to exposure. And what wife can doubt that marriage is one political staging ground in the battle between the sexes?

## Husband

I do not see husbands as the enemy, certainly. In the diaries under consideration, only Lessing's fictional husbands and lovers act like looming spies and dominating controllers. But husbands nearly always hold more power than the wives would willingly concede, and this is certainly the

case for Woolf, Mansfield, and Hunt. Not least, the pressure of the marriage and the husband does not come from the husband's impositions but
from the wife's internalized desire to be a more ideal wife than is actually
possible. Still, it would be foolhardy to deny the real risk of a husband's
reading diaries for evidence of his wife's true and personal life.

To a husband (or father) who reads a diary, an entry detailing the
smallest indiscretion may seem unorthodox and radical, a violation that
warrants censure or punishment. This reading makes diaries dangerous
documents indeed.[10] A woman writer, who for a myriad of reasons may
seek approval from the men in her own domestic and literary sphere,
writes in peril when she writes a diary. As Bloom persuasively argues,
"When such readers [as husbands] lurk at the writer's elbow, welcome or
not, there is no way to rule out self-censorship" (1996, 24). Each diarist
writes experience and performance in the context of deeply ingrained cultural impositions of the proper role and behavior for women. More directly, tension escalates when someone else who ironically assumes that diaries
are private and self-revealing reads the diary to discover the "truth" of the
writer's experience. Diaries are rarely safe from intrusion. Most diary writers learn to be cautious.

Mansfield, Woolf, and Hunt (even in her 1917 diary) all admit sharing parts of their diaries with the men in their lives; in each case, the ever
present "husband" who had "diary privileges" was enough audience to
caution them to a careful construction of their diary configurations of
identity. Lessing's Anna Wulf dramatizes this struggle. In becoming aware
of an audience who reads—or might read—her text, each woman confronts limitations by using writing strategies to deflect the reader's gaze, to
"drop a safety curtain over ones [sic] private scene" (Woolf 1984, 323), yet
to write creatively of resistance.

The invisible enemy in the diaries of Hunt, Mansfield, and Woolf is
not really man but man's disapproval, which inevitably results in loss for
women. These women fear exposure because of the consequences, both
imagined and real, of revelation. As Lessing points out in her later fiction,
what women experience in patriarchy is confined neither to one literary
or historical period, nor to one country. Women, automatically outside
the symbolic order, are vulnerable to the power of masculine erotics and
economics. The outside place of women inflects their texts: "What is
expected of this individual, as manifested in this self-narration, for him or
her to 'count as' a person?" (Eakin 2001, 117).

Women of talent especially find they must maneuver carefully to
achieve in a world of men quick to judge, quick to take offense. If they
are writers who privilege their writing over feminine roles of nurture and

conciliation, their very articulation becomes a trespass on masculine privilege and control. But in heterosexual or bisexual women, the pressure of culture is intensified by their own desire. The strength of those largely unequal cultural ties becomes the pressure of audience when those men are readers, or potential readers, of the diary that is inevitably but inaccurately perceived as the "true" text of self-identity.

This pressure from male audiences who wield various kinds of power urges women writers to shape fictional selves that conform to dichotomous cultural expectations. Diary writers, as autobiographical subjects, find themselves "on multiple stages simultaneously" (Smith 1995, 110), caught in an ideological double bind, as it were, to maintain modes of social and moral conformity as well as to speak out and assert themselves. In this interplay between a woman's particular perspective on truth and her imaginative interpreting of material (i.e., her design), woman diarists both defend themselves against the possible censorious displeasure of her reader or readers and also create personae she wishes to present to the world and to herself.[11]

## Literary Coterie:
## Competitive Presence Who Looks for Female Weakness

Because of the importance of audience on discursive practice, I examine within the studies themselves the shaping presences of husband/audience/editor and the literary world of men who write "the avalanche of books" about women (Woolf 1929, 28) in the "red light of emotion and not in the white light of truth" (33). In response to these critical audiences, each diarist writes, but each within a different set of social conditions that determine the varied audiences in her purview. As educated women they must have been aware of Rousseau's call to "girls" to ask themselves "*How will your discourse be received?*" (1979, 11) Certainly they shied away from sharing their diaries with people other than their husbands. Modernist literary rivals traded diaries, asked for sections of diaries, and the like. Mansfield, for example, told Woolf she would send her part of her diary, and when she didn't, Woolf asked her again. Woolf apparently read portions of E. M. Forster's diary on a regular basis and regularly read portions from diaries of others in her world. Woolf was reticent about sharing her own diary with friends, however, and Mansfield resisted, too, never sending Woolf her diary. Nevertheless, the care these diary writers take intimates their awareness of diary "discourse" as "received" texts. "The importance of the audience, real or implied, conscious or unconscious, of what is usually thought of as a private genre cannot be overstated. . . . Friend, lover, mother, God, a future self—whatever the role of audience assumes for the writer—that presence becomes a powerful 'thou' to the 'I' of the diarist" (Culley 1998, 218).

Internal dramas arise from the ethical propriety to write "authentically" while all the time knowing that as women they operate within institutional, cultural, and discursive categories. As literary women they occupy positions as both the writer and the subject, narrator and character of the diary. In each case the writer feels the stakes of self-revelation are high, thus they compose proliferations and evasions, maneuvering and creating the performance of self, "[t]he woman, protective, secretive, plac[es] the needs of others before her own, accustomed to her mysteries which man has feared; and the creator, no longer able to contain her discoveries . . . people so ardently pursued," negotiating the "battle" between the "impulse to give and the impulse to hide" (Nin 1983, 381). In the process the diarist constructs "a one-woman show" (Miller 1988, 261).

Annette Kolodny argues that Virginia Woolf, for example, "anticipated the male reader's disposition to write off what he could not understand" (1985, 155); this anticipation of skewed male reading may have encouraged the subtexts within the diaries. These subtexts surface more clearly in fiction, within the more public scenes that dominate the diary entries.

Because of the importance of Hunt, Mansfield, and Woolf as literary figures, the stature of their husband/editors, and the availability of their published diaries, I am able to look for the threads of audience pressure and intrusion in these diaries. I compare the stories told there to the stories of their lives published in biographies, memoirs, and their other literary works. Although the group under study is small and select, the influence of audience on their diaries suggests that women—or men under someone's power—take great care with depictions of the self. Those that don't should exercise caution. Who wants trouble? Who wants to be controlled? Better deflect the taboo, the unauthorized, to fiction.

## The Place of Fiction and Biography

The writerly design of Woolf's diary prompts questions as to whether Woolf's diary is not entirely fiction disguised as autobiography, something we might ask of Mansfield and Hunt as well. The mixing of fiction and autobiography illuminates the imaginative perception of selves, what Lessing's Anna calls "one's self direct . . . one's self projected" (Lessing 1973, 571). Inevitably, with readers in mind, projection and direction of selves combine, fancifully.

Because these writers alter the diary form, projecting the self to accommodate their potential audience intrusions, readers of diaries must look beyond the diary itself to edify the life of the diarist. In Woolf's case and in Mansfield's and Hunt's, we can widen our search for a full textual rendering, if not the "truth," of their lives. This broadened search must include published writings juxtaposed to the diary in order to locate the marks of erasure and censure, the fictional posturings, the imaginative renderings. For example, adjoining Woolf's autobiographical renderings in the diary to her published fiction, essays, and memoirs permits readers to discover the gaps in the diary text, the misleading cues of Woolf's speech in the diary compared to the subtle but articulate voice elsewhere. By using Woolf's other works to gloss the diary, we discover the emotionally charged rendering of "dark recesses" that Woolf writes in "fiction, making up my scenes again—however discreetly" (1982, 145). Woolf writes in her diary: "I wonder . . . whether I too, deal openly in autobiography and call it fiction?" (1978, 7) She asks the question rhetorically, knowing her proclivity to "break every mould & find a fresh form of being, that is of expression, for everything I feel & think" (1978, 233). This search for form and expression of feeling and thought brings Woolf, Mansfield, and Hunt together in a shared cultural literacy and literature.

In each body of works, diaries included, these writers negotiate the artist's elaborative and imaginative portraits of personality within specific historical and cultural contexts. Their quests for expression as "modernist" writers and their reticence and inhibition as women in early-twentieth-century culture create pressure within their text.[12] Each woman thus negotiates art and experience in imaginative fictions, gaps, masks, and sites of "reservation" (Woolf 1982, 178). This art of mediation is adjusted in ways that suit her own literary practices and her own perception of how she wishes her readers to view her. The gaze of her audience intensifies her awareness of "cultural context" as she strives for agency in difficult social and literary contexts. Both Woolf and Mansfield at times observe a fragmenting self and use the diary to build an illusory wholeness. Less radical, Hunt subverts the writer's conflict through a carefully constructed persona in carefully devised narratives or "stories."

## Virginia Woolf

I begin the book by investigating the diaries and fictions of Virginia Woolf, who performs in her diaries not as actress but as stage manager—directing spectators to images of her world, to characters she creates. She positions herself within the managed stage, always trying for an external focus. A picture of Woolf emerges as a woman searching for the perfect articulation of a reality both aesthetic and real, in the full knowledge that any such rendering will be wanting. Woolf notes that "the only exciting life is the imaginary one" (1980, 181). She eloquently describes her world in artful images, recounting and fictionalizing simultaneously, perhaps willfully dispersing a representation of herself in the process.

Woolf represses much of a Virginia she disparages, choosing to negate as well as to "remake" the self. She glosses over the pain of her childlessness, for example, and the terror of her madness, which she calls "these curious intervals in life" (1980, 214), shying away from her own images of self and the multiple contradictions of character. In her diary she asks: "But how queer to have so many selves—how bewildering!" (1982, 329). Woolf knew she created plural selves in a diary spanning so many years, but Leonard created one presentation of Virginia in his one-volume edition, *The Writer's Diary;* in the many diary books themselves, Virginia composes a series of carefully chosen self-portraits of many selves, one of whom is narrator of the diary.

When Woolf says, "I like masks. I like the disorientation they give my feelings . . ." (1982, 139), she acknowledges her proclivity to hide, to disperse herself into the "impersonality" she sought throughout the diary. Leonard's role of husband/reader and "nurse" (Ozick 1990) may have encouraged Virginia's strategies of hiding and dispersing the narrative "I." Leonard encouraged Virginia to keep a diary early in their marriage, when recurring bouts of madness beset her. Virginia documents and seems to approve of Leonard's "diary privileges," but his sometimes oppressive presence accounts for many of the silences within the diary. As she aged she exhibited a heightened sensitivity to writing a diary that others would possibly scrutinize. Her increased fame widened the scope of audience interest in the diary she kept for more than twenty-five years. Yet in all those years of diary writing Woolf admits she employs "reserves & subterfuges" (1982, 277). "For Woolf, human nature is a hidden nature . . . human nature figures itself female—misread, misused, taken for granted . . ." (Benstock 1988, 11). Woolf writes knowing, as do other diarists, that a reproachful reader painfully cuts off thought and disclosure. Woolf's particular audience included a concerned but controlling husband and potentially the scornful literary scions of the age. When as early as 1920 she writes, "I can't help suspecting that both Mr & Mrs Woolf slowly increase in fame" (1978, 80), she hints at a future audience that may increase to include a reading public. Shortly before her death in 1941, for example, Woolf writes a series of rather superficial descriptions of unimportant events, then says, "A psychologist would see that the above was written with someone, & a dog, in the room" (1984, 351). Even though she learns to write "around" an audience, she feels the weight of the burden of an audience quick to criticize.

A question difficult to answer, of course, is how much repression and inhibition in a woman's diary is conscious and how much is an unconscious product of her upbringing? Leslie Stephen, Virginia's father, read and judged all she wrote as a child and adolescent, prompting Virginia to write anything remotely personal in the diary under a pseudonym of "Miss Jan." Lyn Lifshin notes: "Those who had diaries violated when they were children . . . tended to express few personal feelings in the diaries they keep now, let alone sharing them"(1982, 17).[13] Indeed, even as an adult Woolf questions: "[H]ow far it is permitted to go here in indiscretion[?]" (1978, 77).

Early experiences with her father's supervision did not actively inhibit the act of writing the diary, but rather taught her techniques to have her say while protecting herself too. Certainly her willingness to share her diary with Leonard in the early days of their marriage seems straightforward, Virginia having learned to use language and story in her service. Thus her diary, written over a span of twenty-five years with various audiences in mind, endeavors to give form to that which she perceives at the expense of self-depiction.

Woolf's artfulness in both style and content cleverly and engagingly deflects attention away from herself and onto the artifact of the diary itself. Many critics see Woolf's diaries as primarily an experiment in writing.[14] Podnieks notes, however, that "for Woolf there was little distinction in her conception and execution of the myriad of genres she employed, including the diary, memoir, biography, essay and fiction. . . . Woolf emerges from her diary as one who, in the spirit of modernisms, made her life and work 'new'" (2000, 98).

The great critical acclaim accorded Woolf's diary is due primarily to her images, her portraits of others, and her witty depictions of the antics of Bloomsbury. "It was the canvas on which she painted her self-portrait of an artist" (Podnieks 2000, 99). Of course, just as the diary transcends simple personal renderings, Woolf's diary transcends simple "rehearsal" and artistic portrait. Woolf's ability to impart a fictional quality to the diary's reality, to use language to construct and deconstruct meaning simultaneously overturns traditional readings of the self as authentic and unified. We can therefore see Woolf's construction of the diary as a site for an artful structuring of both autobiographical and fictional selves.

## Katherine Mansfield

Unlike Woolf's controlled and aloof performance of self, Katherine Mansfield's performance runs the gamut in her diary: She's a mimic, ingenue, prima donna, tragedian, and comedian. She turns personal flamboyance and malaise into theatrics; she channels experience and emotion into fictions, sometimes losing herself in the process. She says: "I positively feel, in my hideous modern way, that I can't get into touch with my mind. . . . I can't 'get through'" (1954, 133). Mansfield's separation from a secure sense of self comes about from a sense of exile and a consequent eagerness to please at the expense of self. A strongly rebellious and cunning personality, she refuses to conform to cultural dictates but insists on the appearance of conformity. This insistence further complicates Mansfield's sense of the woman she is. She relies on performance to gain audience approval using her exhibitionism to mask the insecure woman circulating within the text.

Consisting of pages replete with partial fictions, scattered fictional autobiographies, poems, and drafts of letters, Mansfield's chaotic mass of papers seems a reckless obfuscation of the woman who writes the entries. Far more than Woolf or Hunt, Mansfield makes use of textual fragmentation and unstable generic discourse to obscure the self and critique culture. Yet all of Mansfield's manipulation and self-negotiation take place in full view of her audience. Mansfield early grasped the importance of the diary text as controlled self-exposure and opened her diary to several lovers. Ultimately, her lover/husband Murry became her primary audience, and his presence contributed to her rather artfully performed shadow play within the journal.

Rather than repress the staged self as Woolf and Hunt do, Mansfield mimics male expectation, and her posing leads to an expressed anxiety about her identity. She, like many women before her, "'ventriloquates' male ideologies of gender while allowing alternative discourses of 'experience' to erupt at the margins of meaning" (Nussbaum 1988, 149). The spaces Mansfield's personae inhabit most comfortably are those of writer and wife. Her greatest sense of achievement comes as a writer, yet she guiltily measures that achievement against what she perceives as a failure to care properly for her husband, Murry. However, her many fictions within the text strongly depict women's confrontations with the cultural expectation of marriage. Her insistent writings and reconstructions of herself as the women and the men in her fictions point to her resistance to containment, her desire to be more, to exert more power. She feels outside the culture she inhabits, but she feels she must beguile her colonizers, and she does.

The roles Mansfield chooses to play in her life and in her diary demand a degree of self-censorship in her journal. She writes in February 1922: "I am a *sham*. I am also an egoist of the deepest dye—such a one that it was very difficult to confess to it in case this book should be found" (294). Mansfield vacillates within the diary about the degree of audience intrusion she allows. She sends diary entries to Murry, writes him letters within the diaries, gathers parts together for publication, and writes to "plant cuttings of futurity" (179). She still insists, however, that her notebooks are "*really private*" (255). Her heightened sense of self-drama leads inevitably to her public sense of the journal; she adopts the role of actress to hide her performances. But hide she does, noting in June 1919, "Often I reproach myself for my 'private' life—which . . . *would* astonish even those nearest to me" (165). Certainly she ignores much of this "private" life in the journal, conforming rhetorically to cultural expectation as far as she is able; precisely because Mansfield sees her journal as public in some sense, she creates fictions to confront the culture that wishes to limit her. She chooses to censor and masquerade rather than to rebel openly. The price of difference is too high for Mansfield.

Mansfield's experiments in self-production couple with Murry's editorial censorship to manifest a textual Mansfield who conforms to the social codes for women of her world, a conformity that her published fiction, her letters, and her biographers overturn. In reading Murry's edition of his wife's *Journal*, it might seem that Murry, even more narrowly than Leonard Woolf, sought to present his wife in texts of strict social conformity. Murry's choices for publication present a tightly focused Mansfield, one closely conforming to the brilliant writer, the idealized woman of Edwardian England, beset by illness but little else. But Mansfield textually creates such poses, shaping herself. Murry chooses representative diary entries in what is now fully published in fifty-three volumes. But he does not edit her sense of herself, and critics who earlier implied that he did "were cruelly unfair to him," or so says Scott, the editor of the complete manuscripts (2002, xvii).

In my study I find it was indeed Mansfield who practiced those censorships, fictions, and elaborations in her diary aimed at producing a conventional rendering of a woman surrounded by controversy and change. Mansfield searched for innovative ways to insert less conventional selves within the diary without exposing herself to censure, disrupting her text in innovative fragments and unpublished fictions and poems to confront the very culture, and sometimes the man, she was intent on seducing.

This need to simultaneously seduce and undermine her male audience points to Mansfield's acquiescence to an identity that, as for many women, depends on her relationship to men. Though we see a profound bisexual presence in early diaries, she succumbs to the heterosexual cultural "overvaluation of Love" (Horney 1967, 209). She says, "I live upon old made-up dreams; but they do not deceive . . ." (70). In her diary Mansfield writes her dreams, and to some extent they do deceive. Even in her "private" journal Mansfield twists in the wind between self and male perception.

## Violet Hunt

Though Mansfield seems overwhelmed by the "ideal" of love rather than an actual obsession with a man, Violet Hunt's narrative tells the story of a woman who willingly displaces her sense of self in her life and her text to reinforce the masculine dominance of her lover/"husband" Ford Madox Ford. Whereas Woolf represses sexual suggestiveness in her diary and Mansfield sentimentalizes "love," Hunt seems to lose an elemental part of herself in creating a textual persona Ford can dominate. The Violet in the text acts out the role of young wife under the tutelage of a stronger, more vital, man. "Love, along with domesticity and beauty, creat[e] the traditional boundaries that mold and define women" (DuPlessis 1985, 126). Hunt in many ways seeks to break through the "traditional boundaries" confining women. But in 1911, when she writes *Desirable Alien* with Ford, Hunt boxes herself in by obsessively loving Ford; as her later 1917 diary shows, she nearly eradicated her sense of selfhood in her desire for marriage. Their travel diary serves as an ideal text for Hunt's uneasy self-displacement in her life with Ford. She creates a persona of a rather naive storyteller, pleasing Ford and other audiences, yet penetrating the plot with a subtext of doubt and alterity using the external details of nature, history, and anecdote to do so. Using her artistry as a writer in this diary, Hunt exposes the ambivalent role of a woman who supports and subverts prevailing mythologies about love and romance and marriage.

Hunt closely follows the conventions of both Victorian travel diaries and modernist impressionism in *Alien,* acting on Ford's suggestion that she record their travels in Germany. Travel diaries differ considerably from traditional generic definitions of diaries; consequently Hunt's early diary varies significantly in form from Woolf's organized, carefully chronological diary and Mansfield's chaotic and sporadic diary. Still, like the two of them, Hunt uses her travel narrative to structure her experience enigmatically, to write impressions with various audiences in mind and yet have her say as well. She makes use of the conventions of narrative to create a text of the ideal that collides with actual experience. Travelers wrote Victorian travel diaries—for specified audiences; with publication in mind; as a metaphor of exterior and interior voyages; as juxtapositions of experience and emotion. Given the odd circumstances of Hunt and Ford's travel in Germany, Hunt follows the Victorian honeymoon travel diary conventions as well. "Expectations of transformation for both men and women were played out against, and worked through, in terms of specific geographical sites . . ." (Michie 2001, 232). Hunt's diary endeavors to satisfy these generic expectations, enjoying her playful role as "wife," while subtly exploring the darker aspects of the journey.

Much of the charm of Hunt's text arises from her "surrender" to experience while maintaining an appropriate independent stance tempered by her husband. Hunt's persona bows in a double surrender to a foreign culture and to a patronizing husband, while Hunt herself adeptly controls the conventions of the text to assert a feminist apostasy. In *Alien* she maintains a dual allegiance, writing to woo Ford and to mount her own subtle insurrection. She succeeds in writing within these conventions a humorously engaging text of idyllic marriage and adventure in a foreign land, with subtexts that critique both English and German patriarchies. Even as she charms her readers, her ironic, playful persona violates the panegyric overlay of the journal. Deflecting criticism, she speaks through a comic, resistant, and disobedient persona that seemingly allows correction by a higher, Germanic and masculine authority.

By creating a persona who both is and is not Hunt, much as Mansfield creates many personae who are and are not Mansfield, both women challenge "the assumption that honesty lies in personal revelation"(Gilmore 2001, 24); rather, their integrity as writers demands that they become more, or larger, than life. Negotiating the course of multiple audiences, Hunt tells her own story within a text of contradictions, gaps, and uneasy juxtapositions. As a unified narrative, *Alien* is quite different from the form and content of Woolf's and Mansfield's diaries. *Alien*, however, conforms to audience expectations of a travel diary, yet, in ways similar to the texts of Woolf and Mansfield, Hunt's text fictionalizes experience. When Edward Garnett says of Ford that "[f]acts never worry Joseph Leopold much!" Hunt responds, perhaps to her own writing method, as much as to Garnett's criticism, "And why should they? [Facts] were made for slaves not for gipsies; for policemen, not for authors. Truth and fiction are all one—part of the cosmoss . . . (Hunt 1926, 209). Writing in a modernist aesthetic, aware of similar literary and personal audiences, Hunt, Mansfield, and Woolf use "facts" to serve the fiction of their diaries, writing not self-texts so much as their "cosmos."

In writing her 1917 diary, however, with the promise of love gone, Hunt exhibits the "typical traits" of "repressed power and actual powerlessness . . . the bitterness of a person prevented from full fruition"

(DuPlessis 1985, 126). Hunt's two diaries, so different from each other in content, form, tone, and perception of audience, both constitute textual reproductions of a woman's complicity in social expectations. The latter diary documents the sometimes disastrous consequences of that complicity. In *Alien,* Hunt romances her readers to idealize a relationship and a journey. In a transitional text, a historical/autobiographical fiction coauthored by Ford and called *Zeppelin Nights,* Hunt further idealizes her Ford persona but also records the beginning of the end of their affair. Even though *Zeppelin Nights* is in no sense a diary, it becomes useful in tracing the progression of Hunt's depiction of her relationship with Ford and in introducing the tone of desperation that surfaces so monstrously in her 1917 diary. Because the 1917 diary differs dramatically from all the other diaries in this study, it functions to show a diary written with little interest in placating a husband or appealing to audiences.

Hunt's 1917 diary replicates in excruciating detail a text written at the expense of self, where fictions within the self-text no longer enliven, placate, or communicate. The power of the text comes from the depictions of fantasy, not pleasurable daydreams, but the "classic female fantasy—a jilted woman dreams of her lover's return" (Coward 1984, 204). Classic, too, are the fantasies of love turning to those of revenge. The harsh light of reality illumines the emptiness of these fantasies as Hunt vacillates between writing entries entirely for herself and writing excerpts to show Ford in order to woo him again or to punish him for his refusal. She writes to uncover man's inhumanity to woman, to justify her own ills. Like Mansfield, Hunt fluctuates between desire and hatred for the man who fades from her life. Unlike Mansfield, who sometimes uses her journal to shame Murry for his neglect, Hunt has lost Ford as an audience; he cares little for her or her writing. The stark, blunt "monodrama" of the 1917 diary exhibits the loss of a lover, the loss of her audience.

## Doris Lessing and Anna Wulf and Ella

I close this book with Lessing's metadiary, *The Golden Notebook,* because it amalgamates the plethora of techniques that constitute diary discourse and then explodes them all. The structure of Lessing's novel denies the reader's quest for "the real," questions the myth of privacy, and insists on a commonality of experience over individual experience. These themes emphasize the force of cultural imposition on women, not woman. Lessing sees individual experience as inevitably representative of culturally forced roles. In Lessing's subversions and obfuscations we find Mansfield's proliferating fictions that disallow reductive readings of personality, what Lessing calls "naming." In the yellow notebook we see Anna's rewriting in a fictional story her struggle as a writer and a sexual being; her blue notebook or "diary" evades such topics. Lessing thus textually plays out Woolf's practice of writing fiction to mediate autobiography. Lessing structures her novel to include autobiographical fragments, diary entries, fictions within fictions, and dream litanies—all in notebooks that overlap and compete in a reader's search for authentic identity and truth, forever withheld. And in Anna's libidinous complicity with men, with her desperation for their approval despite efforts to subvert them, we see Mansfield and Hunt.

Importantly for this study, Lessing/Anna/Ella's texts exhibit a heightened sense of audience, of women editing their own experience, and of textual fluctuations women design to conceal and reveal. Lessing thematically and structurally confronts women's fear of exposure and depicts their courage in writing texts conventionally read as revelations of their unmediated consciousness, "a vertical thrust from consciousness down into the unconscious" (Olney 1980b, 239). Lessing discloses the process of writing as inevitably mediating between experience and audience, between caution and revelation. The "I" fractures under Lessing's textual negotiations, refusing any notions of a wholly contained self. Her book interrogates the voyeuristic temptations of readers eager to limit meaning and confine the author. As Anna's narrative illustrates, inevitable tensions surface between cultural taboos and literary tact, between composing and exposing, and between otherness and complicity within culture. Lessing, as do the three diary writers within this study, finally lets the narrators speak their voices in contradiction, in fictions, in many-layered narratives—forcing the audience to abandon the search for the authentic woman and exhorting them to view the performance.

## Reading Strategically

Andrew Hassam writes that the publication of a diary changes its status from private text into literature.[15] We readers, however, enjoy "the feeling of the voyeur, peeping around pages as if they were curtains, searching out the secret thought and life recorded on the private page" (Duyfhuizen 1986, 175). This reading of diaries "as if the illusion that it is possible to communicate with an essential self through writing were not an illusion" (Hassam 1987, 442) limits the reading of a diary to a search for an authentic self that cannot be represented textually. To avoid our own hastening to judge and to give integrity to our own place as audience intent on the voyeuristic pleasure of personal text, we must try to be adept readers: hear the chorus of contradictory voices and see the kaleidoscopic images twist in the fictions, anecdotes, characterizations, poems, and other narratives within the diaries. These voices and images make art and perform the self in myriad ways, both before and behind the curtain of self-censure.

To avoid the control of others—rhetorically and otherwise—these diary writers write in counterpoint, each maintaining an integrity as a writer, as an artist, as a woman living in particular contexts. Whereas the men in this study read—and published—their wives' and lovers' texts in ways specific to their time and place and their relationship with the writer, I read these women's diaries as a woman reading other women's life experiences, ever mindful of the influence of actual flesh-and-blood male readers with diary "privileges" who also exercised editorial control over some of the editions. While we keep in mind that these diarists were important in their own right, inhabited a body, and lived life as a woman writing in particular cultural contexts, a feminist reading suggests that it is the "representative aspects of the author's experience rather than her unique individuality which are important" (Felski 1989, 94). Negotiating theories of self and representation in reading diary texts is tricky, but necessary.

Thus I suggest that as readers we can examine the diaries with critical, knowing eyes. Helen Buss insists that "a reading ethic that involves reader responsibility as well as reader pleasure, a sense of reciprocal activity of text and reader, a respect for the writer's subjectivity—in other words, an ethic of love—is essential" (1996, 88).[16] In reading ethically, we diminish rigidly engendered, culturally assigned meanings of what it is to be a person—man or woman—inhabiting the space of difference. Despite the textual discontinuity and fictionality written into diaries, particularly when anticipating a reader, the writer makes a self in text. The reader participates in this process.

The diary, then, invites the contemporary reader to investigate its narrative of self-discovery, its dynamic interaction of woman and her world, and its experiments in fact and fiction. Those who read diaries to perceive the dark, carnivalesque selves missing from other forms of autobiography face inevitable disappointment. "Once she knows you are listening" (Temple 1987, 44), she subtly shifts the diary from private to public text. When the listeners are husbands and rival writers, the writers perform in earnest. But within the performance, when the writers are conscious of the limitations of language, the drama of living can be enacted textually, splendidly, even in the presence of audience.

*Chapter 1*

# Virginia Woolf's Diary:

*"Whom do I tell when I tell a blank page?"*[1]

V irginia Woolf calls her audience "the pack—reviewers, friends, enemies—" (1984, 141), and they influence all her writing, all her life. Woolf keenly senses audience criticism and approval and works to free herself from their "poison and excitement" (1984, 141), even in her diary. Woolf kept a diary nearly her entire adult life, writing to experience her own sense of self and to experiment with her view of reality, but, as she says, "I can get that at moments; but the exposed moments are terrifying" (1984, 63). Writing increasingly exposed her to those avid for information; thus her worry increased. In May 1938, for example, Woolf, awaiting the publication of *Three Guineas,* writes in her diary: "I'm uneasy at taking this role in the public eye—afraid of autobiography in public" (1984, 141). Woolf's highly conscious rhetorical strategies enable her to write "in some queer individuality" (1978, 168), yet to repress and cover over those parts most vulnerable to criticism. Since she did not regard her diary as necessarily private, she utilized the experiments and manipulative techniques she used in her other works—to have her say and protect herself as well.

By looking at Woolf's audiences and her responses to them, readers see the ways she perceives herself in response to cultural and literary judgments. She produces a self comprised of multiple self-proliferations, foregrounding others to depict a choral protagonist, repressing and deflecting to fiction discussions of her sexuality, madness, and feminist politics. When her self-conception fervently opposes cultural definitions of femininity, she feels imperiled but not daunted. She works through the perils in text and prevails. Beginning with her adolescent diaries and ending with those written shortly before her death, Woolf in varying degrees declines candid autobiographical renderings that make her vulnerable. As she says, "Confronted with the terrible spectre of themselves, the bravest are inclined to run away or shade their eyes" (Woolf 1986, 165–66).

## Woolf's Diary Habit: "Early" Intrusions

A self-conscious and sensitive Virginia Stephen wrote her early diaries in response to a floundering self-esteem, a way to make order and "art" (1990, 139). But she was wary of her father's reading of them. Leslie Stephen actively perused his children's writings, took great pride in them, and then imposed his own authoritative responses on them. Woolf both loved and feared and wanted to please him. But she also felt a need to assert herself in writing. Because of the internal and external pressures on her life-writing, in 1897 she creates "Miss Jan," a "fictive mouthpiece to explore sensation" (DeSalvo 1989, 235).[2] Using Miss Jan as narrator, seventeen-year-old Virginia addresses her own responses and feelings at one remove, distancing herself from the words she feared could bring reprisals from others. To Miss Jan's musings she adds only rather academic essays, no overt self-analyses. Clearly she feels drawn to the self-portraiture inherent in diary writing, but anxiety about what she might expose haunts her as well.

Off and on for the next forty-four years of her life, long after she had left the strict confines of Leslie Stephen's household, Virginia Stephen Woolf continued the diary habit, writing to engage in self-definition and construction. Even as an adult, though she had long ago abandoned "Miss Jan," she often uses strategies in writing to avoid the "terrible spectre" of self as well as the censure and control of other audiences. Woolf perseveres, "terrified of passive acquiescence" (1984, 329), courageously examining and creating herself, putting her "life blood into writing" (1984, 120). Her diaries record in remarkable detail her relationships, her creative experiments, and the daily routines that make a life. They provide more than mere glimpses into the woman she was and all that her life entailed. But the diaries do not tell all; they cover over as much as they reveal of the conflicts and complexities within the writer who composes them, and no wonder.

Woolf's later audiences, chiefly Leonard Woolf and the coterie of literary Bloomsbury, carried with them the masculine power of censure and control that Leslie Stephen earlier wielded so well. Woolf's diaries permit later readers to see a woman who feared both what others thought of her and her own melancholy spirit. A woman under scrutiny, she writes as late as 1937, "I looked at my eyes in the glass once & saw them positively terrified" (1984, 63). The mirror's reflection overpowers the subtlety of the felt self, producing a stark image. Woolf avoids the direct gaze of self in her effort to control the intensity of her imagination and emotion; with others watching, she depicts a self that flickers and alters to assuage cultural and social pressures. Yet even as impersonally and carefully as Woolf seeks to write herself into the diary, she "set a flame to the effort & the grind of the day" (1984, 106). Woolf's diaries magically depict a life—but not the whole life, perhaps not even the "real" life, but the truth as she saw it emerges in the outline through careful reading.

## Woolf's Audience: A Husband's Gaze

*The Diary of Virginia Woolf, Volumes One through Five,* begins in 1915 and ends in 1941 with her death. When the adult Virginia begins her post-adolescent diary in 1915, she has been married nearly three years. She writes for six short weeks before she lets it lapse. Taking it up again in 1917, she writes for a few months until she "plunge[d] into madness" (Bell 1977, 3). Doctors forbad her to write during much of this episode, "and then she was rationed, as it was thought to excite her" (Bell 1977, 3). Following this trying period Leonard made a great effort to organize a serene and patterned life for Virginia and himself. This included his encouraging, even insisting, on her diary writing, an activity Virginia enjoys. It quickly becomes a habit that "suited the comfortable bright hour after tea," one that could lead later to "several good books . . . & here's the bricks for a fine one" (1978, 24).

Taking it up again at Leonard's behest, her diary project changes perceptibly: "& by the way . . . L. . . . has promised to add his page" (1978, 55). Woolf's diary, always open to her husband, includes two entries written by Leonard that year to affirm the diary's status. He writes: "I rashly said that I would occasionally write a page here & now V. calls on me to redeem my word" (1977, 74). He teases her in the same entry for talking "incessantly" (1977, 74). Rarely rash and consistently hypercareful, Leonard's partaking in his wife's diary probably relates to his fear of her mental illness, which brings with it the consequent necessity of his watchful care. Certainly his coauthorship is more mythic than real, as after 1917 he never writes in it again. But from that point to the day of her death, Leonard has access to her diaries, and his ofttimes declining interest revives in times of crisis. "Leonard made Virginia's illness one of life's works . . . he studied her he says, 'with the greatest intensity'" (Lee 1977, 174), even to the extent of his recording her menstrual periods (Spater and Parsons 1977, 69). Leonard's " 'rule' over her life, including regulating her bedtime and her social engagements" (DeSalvo 1989, 10), probably saved Woolf's life, but it also pushed and pulled the shape of their marriage in ways neither could control.[3] That Leonard still, if only occasionally, reads Virginia's diary throughout their lives together becomes clear in a February 1927 entry: "L. taking up a volume the other day said Lord save him if I died first & he had to read through these" (1980, 125). Leonard's presence as audience certainly is not lost on Virginia. His certain interest in reading it is yet another way to "watch" Virginia for signs of madness, fatigue, or depression. Leonard's vigilance is part of his project to protect Virginia from herself, and he thinks her diary will enable him to succeed in that project.

Her diary audience of self and caring but watchful husband demands a healthy, functional, optimistic Virginia on each diary page. She desperately wants to rid herself of the crippling mental despair that threatens her well-being, and she wants to put her husband's mind at ease. She therefore nearly always strives for a positive presentation, even when her life becomes marred by the "heartbreaking sensation that the page isn't there" (1977, 139). She writes, "I hear L. in the passage & simulate, for myself as well as for him, great cheerfulness" (1980, 110). Although in this instance she clearly doesn't expect Leonard to read her confession of simulated cheerfulness, the diary often records the spousal necessity of maintaining a philosophy of optimism and health. "To suppress one self & run freely out in joy, or laughter with impersonal joys & laughters—such is the perfectly infallible & simple prescription" (1982, 135).

As her health improves, Virginia habitually writes in the diaries, and as the years pass, she writes more expansively about many issues, less fearful of Leonard's discovery of the "uncertain fabric I am" (1982, 132). Perceiving the diary as a genre as malleable and alive to possibility as fiction, her subject matter is varied, witty, and analytical. She probes her world, her fantasies, and her experience with equal scrutiny; the diary's form invites change and spontaneity, an important part of her textual expression of conflicting identities. Importantly, she uses it as a site to elaborate on her profession of writing, embedding within her diaries a textual richness: portraits, stories, reviews, outlines, plans, rhetorical experiments, dialogue, dramas, theatrics, imaginings, domestic scenes, and political journalism. As Elizabeth Podnieks writes, "Woolf used her private diary to deliver certain 'truths' about herself in what either she wrote or withheld—which she intended others to discover or decode at some later date, and this was her "'slant'" (2000, 105). Nevertheless, a diary conceived with the idea that it records life, especially a shared life, rather than a private life of the mind, necessarily omits much. Woolf won't be caught out as a stable subject susceptible to opposition. She reflects: "Always write as if a cynical eye, doubting were on me" (1982, 357). In this respect Leonard's audience function encourages the quality of the prose.

Virginia placed considerable importance on Leonard's opinions of her writing. In 1913, for example, she writes to friend Katherine "'Ka'" Cox on publishing *The Voyage Out:* "[I]sn't it wonderful? It's all Leonard's doing" (Lee 1997, 321). Shortly after this she "became deranged and was ill again for most of the year. She would not see Leonard for eight weeks" (Lee 325). Woolf's eagerness to share her diary with Leonard when she took it up again in 1917 springs from her desire to win his trust and to solidify a marriage made precarious by her breakdowns. She feels strongly about Leonard's goodness, believing that his response to her constrains her excesses and gives form to her character. His opinion matters, always. After giving Leonard her manuscript of *The Waves,* for example, she "confesses" that she "shall be nervous to hear what L. says when he comes out . . . carrying the MS & sits himself down & begins 'Well!'" (1982, 36). Her need for his approval adds to her ambivalence about his reading her writing, extending to the diary. She says of Leonard in 1917, "[O]ne's personality seems to echo across space, when he's not there to enclose all one's vibrations" (1977, 70). The "echo," always Woolf's word for audience, validates a sense of her personality as reflected off Leonard. Leonard's "echo" assisted her and concerned her at the beginning of the diary project and throughout her career, saying much about the dynamics of power between them.

If Leonard's pressure on Virginia to keep a diary was an effort to control her, then Virginia's emphasis on the "impersonal" in the diary undermines that control. In the conflicting patterns of diary entries, her response to Leonard is sometimes guarded, sometimes candidly affectionate, only rarely critical. She is ever cautious. The complexity of her feelings about him, her respect and resentment, may eclipse her writing about him, something she acknowledges she rarely does. The Woolf marriage "reads like a marriage which is worked at: a working marriage; and a marriage which works. The key to its completeness, she often perceives, lies in its privacy. . . . For much of the time she keeps it hidden even from the diaries, as though its particular virtue lies in not being too fully analyzed" (Lee 1997, 315–16). Their affection for each other and the strength of their marriage, however, become a narrative thread in the diary: "But my God—how satisfactory after, I think twelve years, to have any human being to whom one can speak so directly as I to L.! (1980, 49). With the possibility of a husband reading the diary, this strategy probably was astute.

Because the concept of audience is a literary given and because she wrote her adolescent diaries under the gaze of her father, she readily accepts Leonard's role of diary reader, even when it limits her writing about him there. Her skill in textual manipulation to elicit audience receptivity thus extends to the shaping of her diary. Woolf says of Lady Ottoline Morrell's diary, "Ottoline keeps one . . . devoted however to her 'inner life'; which made me reflect that I haven't an inner life" (1977, 79). Woolf has an inner life as her writing shows, even in the diary, but she deflects her husband's watchful eye and designs writing strategies to gloss over raw feeling. Virginia's restraint is remarkable; her respect and fondness for him overcome the anger, an oddity given the strength of the anger and rage she exhibited during one of her bouts of madness that had as its "principal feature . . . criticism of others—of men in general, of Leonard in particular . . ." (Spater and Parsons 1977, 68). In 1923 she notes Leonard's too cautious care taking, writing that it "sapped" her "self reliance" (1978, 222).

The complexities of Woolf's life and marriage add to her own perfectionist writer's ethos in the care she exercises in writing a diary. She circumspectly writes a discourse that fluctuates between private and public, exposure and repression. She says in 1918, "but to take up the pen directly . . . shows I hope that this book is now a natural growth of mind—a rather dishevelled, rambling plant, running a yard of green stalk for every flower" (1977, 150). Perhaps because she sees the diaries as material similar to that which she writes for publication, Woolf considers its "dishevelled" quality as an early necessity. Even in the diary, however, the writer Woolf quickly turns the disheveled habits of mind into a coherent and manageable vision. Woolf's textual presentation overrides any sense of a rudimentary self—what she writes metaphorically represents who she is in the presence of others. She insists on an orderly and coherent book, organizing entries consecutively, writing in books she has bound for the project. She begins new books in January, makes corrections in the margins of previous diaries, and adds travel diaries written on plain pages to extant books. Never "disheveled" in their physical presence, her diaries—Woolf early decides—will represent embodied and circumscribed form. As Lawrence Rosenwald suggests, any analysis of diary should include the aesthetic presentation (1988, 65–83). Woolf's books suggest she intends them to be only indirectly self-revelatory, primarily precursors to fiction complete with potential readers.

She often acknowledges the semipublic status of her diary. For example, she questions in March 1939 whether in fiction the "diary form . . . wd . . . be too personal?" but says in the very next entry, "We go on Thursday. I'm of course for reasons I can't go into selfishly relieved" (1984, 210). Woolf thus vacillates between writing for herself and cannily composing for others' eyes. Leonard in particular occupies a double position in Virginia's oscillation between self-scrutiny and audience awareness. In one instance she writes to "discover her emotions" but abruptly remarks, "But as L. is combing Sally I cant concentrate. No room of my own" (1984, 303).

Woolf's rhetorical interests govern this pattern and purpose of revelation and equivocation. She thus performs diary writing with many varied voices, hoping to "achieve in the end, some kind of whole made of shivering fragments; . . . the flights of the mind" (Woolf, quoted in Q. Bell 1972, I 138). She writes, knowing her watchful husband may or may not read her diary entries. And she prepares her textual version of herself in diaries as much for him as for herself, knowing they share goals with regard to her well-being. Despite his honorable and fine intentions and their shared purpose, over the years she often finds his analysis of her galling. She writes in 1929, "Of course, Leonard puts a drag on, & I must be very cautious, like a child, not to make too much noise playing" (1980, 332). As Lee says of Leonard: "There is a narrow line between this careful watchfulness and a desire for control" (1997, 331). Leonard is always there, imposing, forever watchful. When she becomes aware of his actual physical presence as reader, she chafes under his gaze, writing occasionally of her uneasiness in writing with someone else in the room: "If someone comes in one writes differently" (1984, 301).

Indeed, her recurring fatigue may have been caused in part by her spending vast resources of creative energy validating Leonard and her marriage and crushing her "ungrateful" criticisms. In the diary Woolf articulates her great affection for Leonard, but her guilt over what she sees as her failures in their marriage inhibits her criticism of him. "Leonard thinks less well of me for powdering my nose, & spending money on dress. Never mind. I adore Leonard" (1978, 303). Virginia carefully excises any anger, only occasionally disturbing the even tone that covers over strong feeling and eruption. She writes a rare, irritable entry after Vita Sackville-West has visited the Woolfs: "L. (I say) spoilt the visit by glooming because I said he had been angry. He shut up & was caustic He denied this, but admitted that my habits of describing him, & others, had this effect often" (1980, 111). Clearly, Woolf recognizes both Leonard's strength and limitation as husband, perhaps as future editor of her work, saying with characteristic mildness, "L., I think, suffers from his extreme clarity. He sees things so clear that he can't swim float & speculate" (1978, 222). Grateful for his care, she avoids conflicts that trouble her and would trouble Leonard; she chooses to emphasize the acceptable, the positive. Any rage she covers, saying mildly, "But why am I tired? Well I am never alone" (1980, 253).

Their relationship becomes more comfortable and affectionate as the years pass, but his vigilance over her person ends only at her death. Torn between worry about others' criticism and her fear of creative aridity, she despairs ambiguously that she "must go on doing this dance on hot bricks till I die" (1984, 63). Shaping the diary text and the role of audience, Woolf performs her "dance" before audiences in all her texts, even the diary.

## Woolf's Growing Fame: A Wider Audience

As Leonard's interest in the diary wanes, Virginia's fame and involvement with Bloomsbury increases, adding force to her audience awareness as she writes her diaries. Whereas Leonard is probably her only early reader, as her literary place in Bloomsbury becomes fixed and her reputation spreads, so does the likelihood of a more public audience. In January 1936, for example, she begins her entry by writing: "I open this, forced by a sense of what is expected by the public . . ." (1984, 8).

Woolf's success brings her into fierce competition with male writers she respects and in some cases fears. Writing from within a coterie of masculinist modernist writers, Woolf approaches her diary with the knowledge that others watch and judge her according to literary conventions and expectations that seek to exclude her. Although her later diaries record her anxieties over relationships with literary women such as Vita Sackville-West, Elizabeth Bowen, and Rebecca West, her worries are personal and social rather than literary. Katherine Mansfield was the only woman whose writing Woolf viewed as equal to her own; yet even in this relationship Woolf seems as much concerned with friendship and the shared experience of writing as with Mansfield's opinion. Woolf writes, "A woman caring as I care for writing is rare enough I suppose to give me the queerest sense of echo coming back to me from her mind . . ." (1978, 61). When Mansfield openly criticizes her, Woolf feels stung rather than slapped.

The men in literary Britain, the Cambridge Apostles, and the group known simply as Bloomsbury, comprise the audiences that stir her impulse in writing. Her diary entries record her adulation of Lytton Strachey, her fear of E. M. (Morgan) Forster's criticism, and her close appraisal of T. S. Eliot's writing. These literary elites kept diaries and alternately shared them and kept them secret, according to personal whim. She says in January 1918, "The diary habit has come to life at Charleston . . . the sad thing is that we daren't trust each other to read our books; they lie, like vast consciences, in our most secret drawers" (I 95). Yet within this admission of secrecy lies the impulse to share with "Bunny" and "Duncan."[4] "Secret" they might be, but as Bloomsbury notoriously shared secrets and much else, the diary was at public risk.

E. M. Forster, for example, does share his diary with Woolf, and she compares his technique to her own: "[I]n his diary Morgan writes conversation—word for word, when the humour takes him" (II 27). Open literary and personal exchanges within Bloomsbury often extend to diaries, and Woolf's care not to share too much is understandable; the ones who want to look can be scathing in their gossip and criticism. Forster, for example, labels her "the Invalid Lady of Bloomsbury" (Rose 1978, xi). Reducing Woolf's talent and fame to a word connoting feminine weakness does not commend Forster as friend or critic but is typical. Such remarks show the masculine sense of superiority that characterizes literary snobs who too often deprecate a "lady" writer, even while they want to snoop in her diary.

Sensing male disapproval on many fronts, Woolf admits "I hate not to be liked" (1977, 262) and years later, as *To the Lighthouse* is published, says, "I am now almost an established figure—as a writer. They don't laugh at me any longer" (1980, 127). Both of these admissions point to Woolf's writing a diary while acutely conscious of others' responses. Thus, her awareness of the masculine, literary audience that both includes and excludes her in their literary clique influences the shape and content of much of the diary, particularly as time passes. She can be defensive, cruelly responsive, knowingly evasive in her diary, aware of their interest, imagining their reproach, and carefully managing her responses. When Lytton Strachey criticizes the "discordancy" of *Mrs. Dalloway*, for example, questioning its "genius," Woolf records his detailed objections, then defends her position in her diary, saying that the techniques he suggests would cause her "to lose touch with emotions" (1980, 32). The diary allows Woolf to respond to critics in her own defense, for her peace of mind, as well as to vent her more immediate anger. In a remarkable example of British understatement, she says, after a visit by Katherine Mansfield and J. Middleton Murry, "The male atmosphere is disconcerting to me" (1977, 265).

In the last years of her life, Woolf confronts this "atmosphere" more openly while at the same time acknowledging the diary as "semi public" (1984, 338). Coming to terms with Leonard's presence and the lack of privacy her fame imposes on her, she still chafes under them. Openly deviating from the masculine modernist aesthetic, she creates fictions and essays such as *A Room of One's Own* and *Three Guineas* to establish literary works more resonant with her own depiction of life and art. This same independence of spirit allows her more easily to resist others' snooping in the diary. "As I cannot write if anyone is in the room, as L. sits here when we light the fire, this book remains shut. A natural slimming process" (1984, 338). Reluctant to write under scrutiny, she here reminds us of the force of audience pressure on the shape of the writing. The last volume of the diary, "slim" though it might be, manifests a strong sense of Woolf's courageous and independent spirit.

Woolf struggles lifelong to keep in her writing "the right degree of freedom and reserve" (1982, 133), not until very late in her life gaining the confidence to write what she thinks without fear of criticism and reprisal. Even during her last days, with her madness returning, she writes elliptically, ever cautious. Because of Leslie Stephen's early interference, Leonard's watchful care, and Britain's arrogant male literary establishment, Woolf often sickens with anxiety even as she boldly experiments. Her obsession with perfection, necessarily resulting in some kind of failure, comes in part from feelings of insecurity and in part from her dialogic sense of audience. She writes her diary, as well as her fictions, intensely aware of the external influences on her writing process. In her diary she questions: "Do I ever write, even here, for my own eye? If not, for whose eye?" (1984, 107). Woolf sees Leonard's vigilant "eye" and modernist males' jealous, exacting "eyes" watching her when she sits down to write.[5] She mediates the private voice and the public acknowledgment in the diary text, her concurrent saying and unsaying exemplifying her lack of answer to her own rhetorical question: "Shd. one judge people by what they write? Shd. people show their naked skins?" (1984, 227).

## Response to Scrutiny: "Proliferating Selves"

Woolf eludes the watcher-critic by experimenting with the narrative "I" in all her texts, including her diary. She endeavors "a summing up of all I know, feel, laugh at, despise, like, admire, hate, and so on" (1982, 152). To "grasp the whole" (1982, 152) she refuses to represent a knowable and authentic selfhood that limits self-representation and makes her vulnerable to others' interpretations. Thus she proliferates her "I" to resist others' controlling visions of her and to deflect criticisms. Although she necessarily articulates an "I" that represents what she calls "her own point of view" (1978, 107) in "this egoistic diary" (1982, 47), this operational, narrative "I" changes and multiplies within the daily diaries Woolf writes for more than twenty-six years. With shifts in time and circumstance, she privileges one "I" over other "I's": the writer, the wife, the sister, the critic—all speak in fluctuating voices of convention and rebellion, aware of the expectations of others.

The young girl standing in awe of Leslie Stephen's mandates and the young woman grateful for Leonard Woolf's attention dominates many of the early diaries. Louise DeSalvo writes of young Virginia's diaries as full of fictions, silences, and pretenses, noting that "she is doing it to save her own skin; to keep herself from being medicated, at the very least to keep herself from being sent away from the family" (1989, 239). Woolf thus manipulates the narrative "I" as early as 1897 using Miss Jan's narrations. She notes in an October 16 diary entry that "Life is a hard business—one needs a rhinoceros skin—& that one has not got!" (1990, 132). The "hard business of life" continues in her relationship with Leonard. In January 1918 Virginia seeks to change Leonard's mind about a commission he was undertaking, "speaking really not in my own character but in Effie's" (1977, 22), only to have him turn "melancholy" (1977, 23). She responds, "All I can do is to unsay all I have said; & to say what I really mean" (1977, 23). Thus the problem of relationships prompts a shifting in voice to maintain harmony.

Woolf's desire to deflect the critique and manipulations of others and her awareness of her ever-changing subjectivity merge in her multiple self-representations. As with many women diarists, Woolf's life stories "move forward within a subtle sequence of relational cycles. Rather than playing the mannikin who arrives at multiplicity from chaos, a woman may see herself as multiplicity . . ." (Temple 1987, 42–43). Woolf clearly reviews past selves and sees someone other than her current self. At the age of fifty Woolf writes: "Yes, but what can I say about the Parthenon—that my own gray ghost met me, the girl of 23, with all her life to come . . ." (1982, 90). The double bind of choosing a life of both conformity and rebellion grips Woolf; the "gray ghost" of the conforming self often meets the "little wild ponies that tug me so many ways at once" (1984, 250).

Woolf's proliferation of selves marks her project to encompass the contradictions of identity and experience. In *To the Lighthouse*, for example, Mrs. Ramsay, Lily Briscoe, Mrs. McNab, and Minta speak the multiple voices of women responding to their culture in different ways. Woolf speaks simultaneously through all of these women characters. "One wanted fifty pairs of eyes to see with" (1927, 294), says Lily. Woolf's dispersal of the feminine consciousness also scatters her cultural critique, disrupting a unified vision of the "mirroring surface." All of Woolf's women respond to patriarchy differently, some conciliating like Mrs. Ramsay, some choosing "art" like Lily Briscoe. Each response limits the feminine subject, but all of the responses together represent an amalgamation of voices that together characterize Woolf's conception of the multiple feminine.

In her diary Woolf practices many representations of "the feminine": its intricacies and its subsequent critique of an ideology that limits its boundaries. Even though Woolf often adapts what Sidonie Smith calls "speaking postures" to speak as "representative woman" (1987, 55), Woolf's complexity and her willingness to experiment push her to reproduce these postures for multiple conceptions of the feminine. In the two entries Woolf writes in

January 1927, for example, she speaks of Ka Cox as "matronly, but substantial" (1980, 123); Nessa as "poor dear creature" (1980, 124); the "bountiful womanly Mrs. Rubens" (ibid.); and "Vita stalking in her Turkish dress" (1980, 125). Other entries designate women as "natural, juicy, unfettered" (1980, 199) and women writers as evidence of "the refinement; the clearness of cut; the patience; & humbleness" (1980, 62). The sheer number of descriptions of women provides multiple readings of feminine roles. She tries them on to discover her own feminine weaknesses and strengths. In one entry she writes of seeing her perceived strengths disappear only to become "rather an elderly dowdy fussy ugly incompetent woman vain, chattering & futile" (1980, 111). She often notes her "constant change of mood" (1980, 62) and promises herself she will "allow no rigid poses" (1982, 232). Her diary and fictional protagonists together depict representations of selves and other feminine designations. This strategy of diffusion powerfully and admirably defends Woolf against criticism and control.

The plethora of depictions gives her a means to criticize with seeming impersonality—as observer only. Her "I," then, serves "as mirrors, echoes, or respondents in an internal dialogue" (Watson 1988, 188). As Woolf says at one point, "I hardly know which I am, or where: Virginia or Elvira; in the Pargiters or outside" (1982, 148). A woman exploring consciousness and evading cultural hegemony, Woolf thus depicts the multiple facets of personality, of the feminine. She maneuvers in opposition to the exact definitions that an audience can interrogate.

Woolf's proliferation of selves not only advances her project to encompass the contradictions of identity and experience into a kind of communal reality; this strategy also saves her from categorical designations. By surrounding the narrative "I" in a chorus of other voices, Woolf directs audience attention away from "the delicacy & complexity of the soul—" (1978, 308) to "human life: this is the infinitely precious stuff issued in a narrow roll to us now, & then withdrawn forever" (1980, 95). Woolf sees life as synonymous with people; she describes them often in lieu of self-description.[6] When others shift their focus to the success of the Hogarth Press, for example, she says with relief, "Happily, . . . I am now very little noticed, & so can forget the fictitious self, for it is half so, which fame makes up for one" (1980, 222). Woolf's shy response to the world's gaze reminds us that even in her diary she surrounds self-conceptions within a larger community of others: other selves, Bloomsbury, her family, the Woolfs, the villagers of Rodmell. Woolf's genius flourished in these communities, which she exemplifies in astonishing detail as she weaves perceptions of her own subjectivity within a web of relationships, recountings of parties, and records of letters sent or received.

Woolf's use of the community is extraordinary in foregrounding others to convey plural values, social reproduction, and "libidinal ties among a collectivity" (DuPlessis 1985, 172). She deploys diary strategies similar to fictional ones to reiterate thematics at the expense of her own narrative. Yet within her chorus of voices and her gallery of portraits, Woolf defines a personal subjectivity that changes as her diary does: "Just as she can never be relegated to one self, so her diary cannot be reduced to one genre" (Podnieks 2000, 98).

In page after page, year after year, she assesses others, seeking correspondence to her own sense of shifting identity. Early in 1935 she compares herself to T. S. Eliot: "A religious soul: an unhappy man: a lonely very sensitive man, all wrapt up in fibres of self torture, doubt, conceit, desire for warmth & intimacy. And I'm very fond of him—like him in some of my reserves and subterfuges" (1982, 277). In studying those around her and positioning her diary personae within a larger network, she gathers a heightened sense of self-worth: "[B]ut with intimates, when talk is interesting, one sentence melts into another; heads & tails merge; there is never a complete beast" (1978, 163). As part of the "complete beast" she avoids accusations of self-obsession or egocentricity, although she mocks the "diariser" (1982, 291) self who confesses her husband thinks she has "too much ego in my cosmos" (1978, 191). By shifting others to the center stage of the diary text, she displaces her own personae. Steven Monte (2000) suggests that it is precisely Woolf's willingness to consider other points of view that permits her to range freely through alternative perspectives and positions within the self.

## Performing as a Writer: The Uses of Fiction

As Woolf directs the diary's chorus of voices, she consciously performs her view of life, what she calls "writing imagining" (1980, 74). Diary/fiction interplay functions importantly for all diary/fiction writers, especially when diary writers deflect unpalatable truth and observation into fictions to save them a personal scrutiny by a personal audience. Woolf, for example, turns to fiction to display her agonizing conflicts: "oh to be free in fiction" (1982, 145). Turning autobiography into fictions, diary writers also construct fictions within the diary itself, blurring imagination and observation, creating scenes and characters that record their lives and recreate their own histories.

Virginia Woolf's fictional sketch, "The Lady in the Looking-Glass: A Reflection," portrays the mind as stuffed, locked, and spreading: simultaneously illuminating and imagined, as multiple as refracted light. The sketch recalls a scene recorded in her 1929 diary of "Ethel Sands not looking at her letters" (Woolf 1989, 306). Woolf later turns this diary scene into a story. She says of Isabella, her fictional Ethel:

> Her mind was like her room . . . , she was full of locked drawers, stuffed with letters, like her cabinets. . . . One must imagine—here she was in the looking glass. (ibid., 225)

This fictional passage, first created in a diary entry, underscores connections of the mind/diary story, echoing also an earlier description of her intended diary. In April 1919 Woolf writes:

> What sort of diary should I like mine to be? . . . I should like it to resemble some deep old desk, or capacious hold-all, in which one flings a mass of odds & ends without looking them through. (1977, 266)

For Woolf, then, the diary both orders and replicates the writer's life in a supposedly indiscriminate mass of material. The reader of Woolf's diary finds that the "mass of odds & ends" includes fictions, versions of experience meant for future fictions, and intentional distortions. Woolf's talent as a writer enables her to relate versions of experience in various forms, blurring generic designations of fiction and autobiography. "If one writes only for one's own pleasure—I don't know what it is that happens. I suppose the convention of writing is destroyed" (1980, 201).

As early as 1906, with her first fictional publication of "The Journal of Joan Martyn," Woolf depicts the importance of a woman's voice in telling an alternate story to man's standardized versions of history. Woolf's vehicle, Joan's living diary, takes up "'Antiquaries' Quarrels'" of right and wrong, truth and fiction" (1989, 35). Joan recounts far more than the tombs of male ancestors or "the household book of Jaspar" (1989, 42), the strictly factual account so much preferred by the "fathers" of history. In this story Woolf fictionalizes her belief in the necessity of women writing their own experience of living, with "Joan Martyn" clarifying Woolf's belief. Woolf's fictionalizing "The Journal of Joan Martyn," however, points to her impulse to write a diary and to write fiction, perhaps synonymously.

## Censorship: Making Use of Silences

Using multiple voices and alternating fictional/autobiographical narratives within the diary, Woolf performs through contradiction, refusing specific and gendered designations of identity. Yet the continual presence of both real and hypothetical audiences prompts her to write with a protective caution that sometimes results in self-censorship. Whether the gaps and blanks in Woolf's self-narrative are unconscious responses to cultural taboos or conscious erasures to avoid scrutiny and manipulation, these absences alone say much about the subordinate place of woman in early-twentieth-century British culture. In 1939 she writes in her diary, "All books now seem to me surrounded by a circle of invisible censors" (1984, 229). Woolf articulately positions herself within her culture; what she writes and what she censors become "an aesthetics of inhibition" (Lee 1997, 516).

Worried about inscribing aberrant, rebellious selves within her diary, she encodes, leaves absences, explains aberrations at length, and ignores or hurries through unconventional selves. Woolf's novels, all in some ways autobiographical, provide a forum for Woolf's exploration of the painful areas of her life. Calling Woolf's fictions "the strip of pavement over the abyss of self," Shari Benstock argues that unlike fiction, the memoir threatened Woolf too directly, forcing "Virginia Woolf to look into the abyss directly—something she could not do" (1988, 29). Indeed, Woolf avoids looking "into the abyss" in her diaries, too. In writing few memoirs, she avoids looking directly at the self on the page. In her diaries, too, she turns painful self-awareness to fiction and protects visions of herself. Woolf understands the value of creating and exploring versions of reality in fiction and knows, too, the value of diary silence, its resonance and its echoes.

Woolf uses the drama of the interval, that tension in the unarticulated. Thus, between the scenes and portraits that make up the diary, Woolf gives presence to what is not said: long conspicuous blanks after illness followed by her expressed desire to take the diary "up again"; a few days of writing missed and subsequent apologies; self-conscious elisions she mentions obliquely: "What a gap!" (1978, 125). Woolf's interest in resonant silences appears as she uses her diary to plan what years later becomes *Between the Acts*. In this entry, atypical in style and content from other entries, Woolf acknowledges the presence of absence[7] in women's writing of the world and themselves. She writes in February 1927:

Why not invent a new kind of play—//
as for/instance
Woman thinks: . . .
He does.
Organ Plays.
She writes.

They say:
She sings:
Night speaks:
They miss
I think it must be something in this line . . . Away
from facts: free; yet concentrated . . .
But today is. (1980, 128)

Here Woolf postulates the gaps in narrative. In placing these lines in the genre of drama, she acknowledges the subversion of audience expectation. The unfinished lines foreground silences that "say." Woolf acknowledges the not-saying, yet says much in the emptiness that follows each line, the blanks depicting intention and audience response to imaginative space. She creates silence to imply without words the nature of the unspoken reality of what "Woman thinks." Gaps in the narrative protect Woolf from criticism and appropriation by others and provide traces of personality functioning subtly to shape her identity. As she herself notes on the practice of silence, "[S]easons of silence, & brooding, & making up much more than one can use, are fertilizing" (1980, 317).

Just as Woolf uses deflections, fictions, and silences to elude an audience eager to capture an immutable and authentic Virginia, we, as a later audience, are anxious to discover all that Woolf left said and unsaid about her experience. Her treatment of three topics particularly illustrates alternative unsaying and saying in diary text as opposed to fictional text: her sexuality, her madness, her feminist politics. Each of these subjects, obviously important to Woolf, can best be "read" by juxtaposing her diaries with her other texts, finding gaps in her diary narrative, and locating the clues she leaves in fictional narratives. At odds with watchful others in her diary audience, she deflects the self to fictional characters to have her say.

## More Absences: Sexual/Textual Reserve

If diaries were truly private, Woolf's reserve about sexual matters in her diary might seem surprising. As an object of curiosity she had good reason to be cautious; many rumors circulated through Bloomsbury about Woolf's history as molested, frigid, and lesbian. Wary of Leonard's access to the diaries and the misogynist literary coterie's interest in them, she senses she would deliver herself to the control of others if she were honest and open about her sexual responses. No wonder she wrote the diary with reticence. Her sister Vanessa, certainly, openly joked about Virginia's "coldness" and "crushes." Angry explorations in a diary about youthful abuse by a half-brother—now a member of the publishing establishment, George Duckworth—would open her more than him to scathing criticism. Seen as a sexual curiosity and under scrutiny by Leonard and Bloomsbury, Virginia better served herself by glossing over events and feelings. She could not entirely forget the past and was fearful of present and future sexual expectations.

Outright admissions of frigidity or lesbianism would mark her an exile of sorts in licentious yet censorious Bloomsbury. We cannot make the assumption, then, that Woolf's textual reticence indicates a lack of sexual response; rather, the sensuality of her language combined with a narrative caution suggests that Woolf chooses to close her diary to sexual explanation. Never written in graphic sexual detail and often elliptical, Woolf's diaries nevertheless reveal a sexual Virginia, especially in regard to relationships with women she loves. The diaries display sensual language and subtle erotics. By relegating stories with sexual themes to other autobiographical and fictional texts, she could choose the time and place of their "coming out."

Woolf writes quite explicitly in "22 Hyde Park Gate" of her half-brother's sexually molesting her but says next to nothing in her diary. No doubt this ongoing shame and dread confuses and mars her later sexual relationships with men, but Woolf herself avoids self-analysis. Even in the memoir, where she notes the circumstances and her "resenting, disliking it" (1976, 69), she analyzes the circumstances objectively, searching for a word "for so dumb and mixed a feeling," wondering whether the experience seemed "to show a feeling about certain parts of the body; how they must not be touched . . . must be instinctive" (ibid.). But within the memoir's structure she undercuts its importance to her, calling it a "simple incident" (ibid.). In *Moments of Being*, her tale of sexual molestation comes at the end of a story of George's affectionate and misguided attempts to help his sisters into society. Then quite abruptly she ruptures the amusing narrative by recalling the abuse, closing with "Yes, the old ladies of Kensington and Belgravia never knew that George Duckworth was not only father and mother, brother and sister to those poor Stephen girls; he was their lover also" (1976, 154). This sentence covertly contains anger and loathing, but only in this one instance does she admit its lasting influence.

Indeed, her comments about George in her diary are studiously neutral and rare. In her one mention of him in volume II, she refers to her "Memoir on George." She responds to her essay as a writer, saying, "You should pretend to write about real people & make it all up—I was dashed of course. (& oh dear what nonsense—for if George is my climax I'm a mere scribbler)" (1978, 121). This bland deprecation of her work and by implication George's sexual act elides any strong feelings of sexual rage or confusion. In fact, she seems to imply a fictionality in the memoir itself, giving her room for denial of events.

Her admission that George's actions indeed influenced her sexual response comes several years later in an entry in May 1926: "The heat has come, bringing with it the inexplicably disagreeable memories of parties, & George Duckworth; a fear haunts me even now, as I drive past Park Lane on top of a bus . . . I become out of love with everything" (1980, 87). In this entry Woolf obliquely refers to the dampening effect of earlier events on her ability to "love"; she carefully covers sexual anger while noting the sad effect of "parties, & George Duckworth" and is silent elsewhere in the diary. Perhaps conflicts of shame, rage, and affection for George's familial place in her life cloud her perception of self for too long, but she does not use the diary to clarify.

Others blamed George Duckworth for the frigidity they saw in Virginia. Woolf herself neither sees herself as frigid nor lays blame on her past. She prefers keeping her own council about this matter that so titillated Bloomsbury. Woolf's nephew, Quentin Bell, accepts an interpretation of Virginia's frigidity as truth and tells us that "Vanessa, Leonard, and, I think, Virginia herself were inclined to blame George Duckworth" (1972, II 6). Bell speaks with authority on the subject of his aunt's coldness, recalling, perhaps through the filter of his own youthfulness, the many family discussions about this lack of sexual warmth in her and reminding us, too, of the interest of others in Woolf's sexuality.[8] Following their honeymoon and Leonard's subsequent disappointment in their marital union, rumors circulated through Bloomsbury about her frigidity. These whispers make Woolf particularly reticent. She notes that Clive's criticism of her work, for example, "is founded upon the theory that I cant feel sex: have the purple light cut off" (1980, 275). She responds to his criticism of her writing but ignores altogether his "theory."

Leonard's conversations with Vanessa, which she shares with others, and his obviously autobiographical novel, *The Wise Virgins,* all speak of a frigidity that Virginia Woolf never denies or affirms. The truth to be uncovered fell victim to women's self-censorship even when under attack: "The truth lies buried in what women did not say, in the fiction of female frigidity to which Virginia herself submitted. . ." (L. Gordon 1984, 152). Yet Virginia, from the first regulated by a disappointed Leonard and under the gaze of a public avid for detail, has everything to lose by a sexual discourse, even in her diary.

Certainly Virginia writes only a few references to the marriage bed, always embedding them in the language of a sentimentalizing love: "so completely entire, I mean L. and I" (1982, 130). One ambiguous diary entry in 1917 implies that the Woolfs were not necessarily celibate: "Illusions wouldn't come back. However, they returned about 8:30, in front of the fire, & were going merrily till bedtime when some antics ended the day" (1977, 73). Though reserved about sexual/married life, she delightfully depicts others' sexual exploits. She alludes to Vanessa's sexual exuberance in a wonderfully ambiguous reference to her sister: "Nessa, astride her fine Arab, life I mean, takes further upheavals all in the days work" (1980, 239). She notes in June 1933 that Clive (Vanessa's husband) is "lyrical about lovers" (1982, 109) and questions "Why the bees should swarm around [Adrian]," describing "the quivering shifting bee bag [as] the most sexual and sensual symbol" and writing that "the bees shoot whizz, like arrows of desire: fierce, sexual" (ibid.). About her life with Leonard she says, "Back from a good week end at Rodmell—a week end of not talking, sinking at once into deep safe book reading" (ibid.). Woolf seems alive with desire and certainly knows the feeling but does not connect her sexuality to her fond relationship with Leonard.

Strong cultural codes against women's articulating details of sexual relationships may influence Woolf's reserve; with Leonard's availing himself of the diaries, however, she may feel a reluctance beyond mere cultural conditioning. She exercises discursive sexual responses in veiled references and oblique responses. She says in April 1931, "If I dared I would investigate my own sensations with regard to [Leonard], but out of laziness, humility, pride, I don't know what reticence—refrain" (1982, 18). The "reticence" may be shyness or perhaps the risks that exposure can bring, the risks of "subjection to regulation and control" (Martin on Foucault 1988, 80).

Fearing others' control and caring deeply about their opinions, Woolf may prefer the myth of her coldness to the truth of what even she may perceive as an aberrant lesbian sexuality that both excites and frightens her. The language of the diary clearly displays Woolf's sexual preference for women. When she writes, for example, "Night speaks" . . . / "They Miss . . ." (1980, 128) in her entry foregrounding silent response, she obliquely implicates the unnamed man and woman in inherent heterosexual dysfunction. Using images of sexual ambivalence, Woolf writes in a later entry of the "writhing sausages, looking indecent, like black snakes amorously intertwined," then remembers a dream when Bunny "took me in his arms—pale phantom of old love" (1982, 144). The phallic imagery of the snakes somehow reminds her of the lifeless "phantom" of heterosexual love. It takes a reader to give it that meaning—Woolf merely intimates. In another entry she censures a lively physicality in a homosexual relationship. She deprecates Dady's sensuality, mocking his sexual beauty and Raymond's feelings for him.[9] She says: "& one must agree, I think, that all exhibitions of s—— feeling have something silly, mawkish, about them, though why I can't say" (1980, 266). She implies that sexuality is for others, a word not to be written in the text of the self, a word never spelled out but named "s——." But the word she wants to write is "sapphistry."[10]

As Woolf gains confidence as a writer and as a woman, she writes more confidently in the diary, using "the looser language of secret truthfulness" (Lee 1997, 485), evincing a kind of vitality that draws upon physical experience. This language disrupts the consciously conceived neutrality of her sexual self. In 1923, at the age of forty, she defines women as "pleasure givers . . ." (1980, 234), writes to her "new apparition Vita," and, perhaps because of her past and present sexual feelings, writes "Love is the devil. No character can stand up against it" (1980, 224). In 1924 she insists: "And if we didn't live venturously, plucking the wild goat by the beard, & trembling over precipices, we should never be depressed . . . but already should be faded, fatalistic & aged" (1978, 308). She reports that Vita Sackville-West, her friend and probable lover, has been "implored" by others to resist "the serpent destroyer, V.W. I half like, half mind this" (II 324). In later diaries she mentions "kissing" Helen "on the lips"; her "friendship with Vita . . . over . . . as ripe fruit falls"; Ethel Smyth's adoration of her: "I get . . . two letters daily. I daresay the old fires of Sapphism are blazing for the last time." While many of these references merely allude to Virginia Woolf's sexuality, their explicit sexual language elaborates: "Vita . . . always giving me great pleasure to watch, & recalling some image of a ship breasting a sea, nobly, magnificently, with all sails spread, & the gold sunlight on them" (1980, 146). Often elliptical, a sexual Virginia appears, especially in regard to relationships with women she loves. "Her 'little language unknown to men' suggested sexual skill as well as verbal skill" (J. Marcus 1987, 144).

Woolf reluctantly voices her sexual skill and desire in evasions and near-erasure of sexual history as she tries to conform to heterosexual marriage. Even though Leonard appears to tolerate her "friendships" with women, "by the autumn of 1926 he was finding Vita an irritation, and perhaps a threat" (Lee 1997, 497), prompting Vita to secrete love letters to Virginia in ones Leonard could read. In 1930 Virginia writes only that she "quarreled with L. (about Ethel Smyth) . . ." (1980, 298). Virginia may "plume and preen" in letters (Letters II 489) but not in the diary, replete with "drier, more reserved accounts" (Lee 1997, 480). As Adrienne Rich says, "Women's love for women has been represented almost entirely through silence and lies . . . heterosexuality has forced the lesbian to dissemble . . ." (1979, 190). Woolf's dissembling takes the form of glossing over her desire but using passionate, sensual, almost sexual language to describe the women she loves. She says, "A woman is in some ways so much better than a man—more natural, juicy, unfettered" (1980, 199). Her qualifying "in some ways" soothes the masculine ego of the diary's audience.

Indeed, Woolf's caution in sexual matters is well founded. Her sexuality makes her the public victim of sexual ridicule. A Bloomsbury noted for "buggery" (Woolf's word) strangely sees Woolf's lesbian leanings as amusing, monstrous, and indicative of her coldness. Quentin Bell notes, "To many she must have appeared as an angular, remote, odd, perhaps rather intimidating figure a fragile middle-aged poetess, a sexless Sappho . . ." (1972 II 185). Certainly Wyndham Lewis creates the character "Rhoda Hyman" as an austere and sexually cold aesthete who resembles Virginia in *The Roaring Queen* (1973). Virulently attacking Woolf, Lewis charges that her lack of traditional feminine desire emasculates men.

Woolf's respect for Leonard and her insecurity about her sexual role forbad a self-portrayal as emasculator and Leonard as emasculated. If "male impotence and female potency" ('Gilbert and Gubar 1988, 36) characterized modernism—a theme obviously obsessing Lewis—Woolf declines any hint in her diary.[11] Still, the language within all of Woolf's books, the diaries included, relays a sexual, subtle, and dynamic tension. A Woolf alive to an erotic creativity subtly rehearses the sexual subtexts of her novels.

## Deflecting Sexual Exploration to Fiction

Woolf chooses fiction to depict more openly her views of sexual relationships, their imbalances of power, their terrifying unsettling nature. She views fiction as "disconnected from its author" (Gordon 1984, 98), freeing her to write what she censors in her diary. Her first novel, *The Voyage Out*, gives voice to the innocence of youth. Rachel's almost passive "voyage" into the lush tropics of experience brings consequences of love and sexual ambivalence. Here Woolf creates a heroine concealing as much as she reveals under an oppressive weight of masculine dominance. The tragedy in the novel is Rachel's inability to confront memory and identity. This theme of woman's fear in openly confronting the erotic self spans the length of Woolf's career. Written more than twenty-five years after *The Voyage Out*, Woolf's last fictional endeavor still explores that part of reality that women fear to speak of candidly. Significantly, the repressions and silences of *Between the Acts* are intentional, not accidental.

In this novel Woolf directs readers to read "between" the lines, the acts. Instructing them to find what she leaves unsaid, she points us to a way of reading her diaries. In her novel/play, many characters maintain silences to conceal unconventional thinking that can be "acted out" neither in the play nor in the audience. Woolf's strategies of depicting and imaging the silences in *Between the Acts* foreground the importance of the unsaid.

Isa can be understood as thematically representing the repressed Woolf of the diaries. Isa's knowledge is sexual; she thinks the newspaper story of a girl gang-raped by soldiers is "real" (Woolf 1969, 20) and struggles with sexual desire and antipathy the entire day. Her unconventional passions and her feeling that sex is too often associated with violence render her unable to articulate her own history or to make herself heard in her household. Woolf writes *Between the Acts* to encompass the whole, including the scripted and spontaneous, the tragic and comic, the historical memory and present critique.

Significantly, the not-said becomes as important as the said. Both Miss Latrobe's and Isa's dramas characterize Woolf's use of silence and space to simultaneously say and not say. This process of composing and refusing allows Virginia Woolf to write, like Isa, traces of thoughts not fully articulated. *Between the Acts* not only recognizes the silence that speaks itself in and around the actions and dialogue, but also tragically reiterates the savage anger and impotence of the tongueless nightingale who cannot speak and is forced to swallow her own rage.[12] Thus Woolf's fiction reminds us that the unsaid is not merely a rhetorical technique inviting the creativity of the reader, nor is the unsaid an intentional void allowing Woolf to hide her problems. Rather, the silences "between" the acts of speech function to articulate both the love and anger that cannot be spoken in the context of English culture. Unsanctioned love must remain unspoken. And just as the raped nightingale cannot speak of the sexual crime that has rendered her both raped and tongueless, Virginia Woolf's diary silence on personal matters of sexuality reminds us as well of patriarchal strictures on women speaking the sexual and of Woolf's own sexual reticence and trauma.[13]

The discrepancy between her diary renderings of sexual interest and her fictional explorations into the nature of female sexuality has perhaps enhanced reader interest in Woolf as an expansive sexual woman. We have only to read *Orlando* to see Woolf's refusal to narrow sexual possibility. Her fictional fantasy subverts conventions that confine an individual to one century, or one gender, or one country. The bisexual, captivating Orlando defies sexual category and control, and both Orlando and Woolf seduce readers with astonishing sexual playfulness. By pushing *Orlando* to the limits of novel conventions, Woolf breaks through sexual conventions without inviting the reproach of others.

In contrast, Woolf's diary discourse offers only shaded references to sexual history and preference; she avoids the direct hits of others who wish to judge. As a reader of others' diaries, she may guess that readers, openly or not, often hope for sexual revelation. Indeed, so reticent about revealing her own sexual relationships and so imaginative fictionally about the nature of passion, she has become a central figure in reader configurations of woman's sexuality.

## Repression and Deflection: Woolf's Madness

Even though we recognize that cultural codes of sexual repression influence Woolf's depiction of her sexuality, we may find it surprising that repressive codes also extend to her writing explicitly of the mental instability that plagued her on and off from adolescence. Yet the cultural equation of sexuality and insanity induces similar repressions. In *The Female Malady* Elaine Showalter writes of the "moral management of women" who at the first sign of madness find imposed on them the "ladylike values of silence, decorum, taste, service, piety, and gratitude" (1987, 79). Given the cultural pressure to conform to "ladylike values" and Leonard's very real and understandable obsession with the state of her sanity, Woolf chooses fictional and public articulations about madness rather than private revelations in a diary that will almost certainly result in others' seeking to control and manage her. The diary's immediacy makes control inevitable. Since Virginia was "such a liar about her own health that one doesn't know what to believe" ( VS-W to CB in Bell 1972, 117), Leonard might expect to find the diary key in signaling a forthcoming crisis. Woolf's diary is not the primary text articulating the symptoms, the responses, or the horror of mental illness, however. She represses even this agony in the diary, deflecting her explorations to manageable, fictional ones.

Woolf's madness is a cyclical trauma she grapples with from 1904 until the end of her life. As she writes to her friend Violet Dickinson after months of her first "rest cure," imposed on her by her doctor, George Savage, "I have never spent such a wretched 8 months in my life, and that tyrannical and as I think, shortsighted Savage wants another two. . . . Really a doctor is worse than a husband" (Wolf 1975, 147–48). Ironically, she writes this without having yet experienced the double enemy of doctors (Dr. Savage and four other male, mental specialists Leonard consults) and husband. When she marries, she must worry about Leonard's vigilance and "tyranny" as well as her doctors'.

Leonard's control of Virginia intensifies in proportion to her bouts of madness. From 1913 on he keeps a daily, detailed, meticulous diary of Virginia's health, encoding her mental health in "Tamil and Sinhalese" (Lee 1997, 174). His control extends to what Virginia must eat, how many visitors she sees, how much rest she needs, and when she should exercise. He even weighs her regularly and records her weight in his diary. When he feels Virginia exhibits signs of instability, he moves quickly to consult with doctors to consign her to the "enforced passivity" of the rest cure she so hated (Showalter 1987, 181).

Understandably, Virginia avoids saying much in her diary that might promote Leonard's avid interest. Although she writes fairly often of physical ailments, with occasional references to "headache" or "depression," she is quick to mention her recovery, most often in the same entry. In August 1921, for example, she catalogues at some length a two-month stretch of illness: "wearisome headache, jumping pulse, aching back, frets, fidgets, lying awake, sleeping drought, sedatives, digitalis," and so on. She abruptly says, "Let me make a vow that this shall never, never, happen again" (II 125).

The only long gaps in the journal occur during Virginia's bouts of mania and deep depression, periods of diary exclusion and personal agony in her life. In the publications of the full diaries, her editor, Anne Oliver Bell, notifies the reader of these "spells" by italicized, editorial insertions within the diary text. Even Bell sometimes veils the symptoms of madness with euphemistic references to illness, headache, and flu. Woolf herself limits references to her "queer, difficult nervous system" (1980, 39) to passages written in reflection, when her illness is over: "Once or twice I have felt that odd whirr of wings in the head which comes when I am ill . . . it shuts itself up. It becomes chrysalis" (1980, 286–87), affecting her "personality, her behavior, her writing and her politics" (Lee 1997, 172).

Leonard reports that nearly all of their arguments concerned her illness (1964, 81). Understandably, Virginia tries to hide her sickness from him for as long as possible. This effort keeps her from explicit diary entries about her manic-depressive illness. In 1925, for instance, she says, "[A]h, but how quickly I sink; what violet shadows there are between the high lights, & one, perhaps, as unreasonable as another. But this properly belongs to a story" (1980, 10). This cautious reference to her madness that she dare not explicate in diary writing echoes a longer lament for "expressions" "unheard" and therefore unsaid. In June 1923 she longs to be more social, less cared for, but faces Leonard's "old rigid obstacle—my health" (1978, 250):

> But now I'm tied, imprisoned, inhibited . . . I'm letting my pen fling
> itself on paper like a leopard starved for blood—& I must wash and
> dress—so do not, in years to come, look too harshly upon this first
> outcry, the expression of many yet unheard. (ibid.)

Possibly she chooses the starving leopard image because "leopard" is only
one letter away from "Leonard," the force who too often silences her pen.
Certainly she sees the leopard as power and the hunger her own. By denying herself the power of the leopard/Leonard masculine/sexual/assertive,
she allows her silence, and Leonard, to dominate. The guilt of writing her
desire that would "sacrifice his [Leonard's] peace of mind" clearly stops
her leopard-pen in years to come (ibid.). Although this diary entry shows
strong feelings, such articulations are rare, reminding the reader of
Woolf's reluctance to articulate emotions that must seem painfully close
to the manic rage of her illness. In order to give Leonard "peace of mind"
and to protect herself from becoming even more "tied" than she already
is, she does not often write onto her diary pages what she feels is aberrant.

Before her most serious and most manic illness in 1915, for example,
she says nothing of symptoms and glosses over catalysts to present herself
as a supportive wife. She erases entirely what was clearly a blow to her self-
esteem and a betrayal of her most private sexual insecurities. Immediately
after she read Leonard's indictment of her frigidity in *The Wise Virgins,* her
health declined steadily, culminating in her most serious breakdown
(Gordon 1984). Virginia became "incoherent, excited and violent" and
"took against Leonard" (A. Bell 1977, 39). Virginia's diary entry following her reading of *The Wise Virgins* reads:

> My opinion is that it's a remarkable book; very bad in parts; first rate
> in others. A writer's book, I think, because only a writer perhaps can
> see why the good parts are so very good, & why the bad parts aren't
> very bad. . . . I was made very happy by reading this; I like the poet-
> ic side of L. (1977, 32)

This entry shows either a thorough repression of her feelings or a conscious
pretense. Even Anne Bell admits Leonard's book contains "unsympathetic
portraits" of the Woolfs, and if Virginia recognized those "portraits," her
diary entry is wrenching. The chapter titled "Katharine's Opinion of Her
Sister" fictionally describes Vanessa's advice to Leonard after the Woolf's
lukewarm honeymoon. Both Vanessa and the fictional Katharine console the
distraught husband about Virginia/Camilla's frigidity (L. Woolf 1914, 149;
A. Bell 1977, 6). Vanessa "deprecated the resemblance of the characters in

this novel" to those Leonard knew (A. Bell 1977, 9). Virginia herself must have known she figured prominently in his conception of Camilla, must have felt painfully accused, but she says nothing of his frigid "virgin" so conveniently close to her name of "Virgin"ia. After two more entries, her diary stops as her mania begins.

Virginia ceases diary writing altogether for nearly two years, in part because Leonard and the doctors forbad and then rationed it. Also, she may have broken off her diary ritual for so long because of her fear of revealing herself to Leonard or because the effort to hide herself behind the words was too grotesque. Indeed, when at Leonard's urging she begins her diary again in 1917, her first entries are stilted. An entry in August typically sounds cramped: "Went into Lees . . . saw Cinema; bought several things. Met K.M.—her train very late. Bought 1 doz. Lily roots & some red leaved plants wh. have been put in the big bed" (1977, 43). The reversion to outings, to mentions of others without commentary removes Woolf from the center of her text. With Leonard waiting to hospitalize her at the instant of mental change, she refuses to expose herself. With madness acting so powerfully to change her life and her perceptions, Woolf finds articulation for it in other texts. Her other writings are offered to the public and not considered private; in fiction she feels less vulnerable to personal attack and control.

## Deflection of Madness to Fiction

In an interesting deflection of self into character, Virginia Woolf gives to Septimus Smith in *Mrs. Dalloway* (1925) the madness and melancholy that she only later articulates sketchily in her diary and in "On Being Ill." Unlike her veiled references to madness in her diary and unlike her effort to equate madness and creativity in her later essay, through Septimus Woolf bitterly rages and explores the causes and cures of madness. By creating a male character who "was a case of complete breakdown—complete nervous and physical breakdown" (ibid., 144), Woolf evades the condescending and pitying gaze of British intellectuals brought up knowing that "all mental illness in women was ascribed to their sexuality" (J. Marcus 1987, 101). Through Septimus Smith's voice, Woolf changes the cultural configurations of madness, shifting the blame from the self to cultural causes such as war, society's "little shindy of schoolboys with gunpowder" (1925, 145). Woolf writes of Smith's courage through his wife's discourse but undermines cultural notions of military bravery by Smith's statement that "he has committed an appalling crime and been condemned to death by human nature" (ibid.). Woolf constructs Smith to announce an antiwar stature and a damning antipatriarchy argument while she dismantles the notion that feminine weakness and sexuality cause madness.[14]

With an adept technical maneuver, Woolf equates Smith's "fall" to her own, alternating the narratives of Smith and his wife: Smith rages and suffers while his wife offers a more objective and sympathetic analysis. He speaks Woolf's ravings; Rezia analyzes rationally. Rezia Smith's analysis of Sir William Bradshaw's "treatments" condemns his "worshipping proportion," which made "England prosper, secluded her lunatics, forbade childbirth, penalised despair, made it possible for the unfit to propagate their views" (150). Woolf thus condemns current psychiatric practices through a rational character. In contrast, through Septimus Smith's consciousness, Woolf portrays the horror of madness and is sympathetic to his plight, despairing of her own: "As for the visions, the faces, the voices of the dead, where were they? . . . The brute with the red nostrils was snuffing into every secret place" (222–26). Smith's inability to rid himself of the monstrous hints at Woolf's own imaginings. By using alternating voices of rationality and irrationality, Woolf writes the story of madness, what she calls in her diary "the silent realms" (1982, 171). Fiction frees Woolf to break through that silence to posit an androgynous illness that does not damn the mad.

Woolf's fluctuating care and silence about her illness in her diary and the carefully drawn fictional representations expose the dynamics of marriage and madness, as well as the diary writer's simultaneous hiding and showing in a supposedly private context. In 1939 she writes, "Happily I'm interested in depression; & make myself play a game of assembling the fractured pieces" (1984, 215). Her "game" tries to control the mental fragility that ultimately brings her death. The autobiographical voices and the fictional ones combine to render a more complete subjectivity. Neither can be privileged.

## Repression to Expression: Feminist Politics

As she ages, Woolf becomes accustomed to her audience, both real and potential, becoming increasingly willing to take on the issue of women's rights and place in a patriarchy. Even in the diary Woolf depicts an ever-widening political vision, one that indicts English politics and institutions. As with the subjects of sexuality and madness, Woolf finds greater freedom for expression in texts outside the diary, particularly *Three Guineas*. As a writer in the public domain, Woolf takes risks politically; as a woman in the private realm, she more cautiously examines the volatile subject of man/woman relationships.

Those who seek an ardent feminist in Woolf's diaries may be disappointed, especially in the early ones. Woolf's range forbids a single reading of her attitude toward men and women and their relationships. Employing a strategy of deflection, Woolf plays no polemic politics in the diary. Only by tracing her views through the years of her diary can we locate her fluctuating interest in what as early as 1916 she calls "feminist politics." In that year she writes to Margaret Llewelyn-Davies, "I become steadily more feminist, owing to *The Times,* which I read at breakfast & wonder how this preposterous masculine fiction keeps going a day longer without some vigorous young woman pulling us together" (J. Marcus 1987, 73). At this stage of her life, Woolf does not feel she is the woman to do it. Still uneasy about Leonard's feelings for her, perhaps still unsure of her critical reputation, until the early 1930s Woolf chooses topics of writing, relationships, and cloaked fictions in the diary, not politically loaded feminist issues.

Woolf's responses to individual relationships disrupt any reader's attempt to affirm a gendered political constituency for Woolf. We may impose a feminist reading on her early diaries, but only later does Woolf read herself as feminist. In 1917, for example, she addresses the problem of man/woman relationships but only as they apply to friends. In writing of Dora Carrington and Ralph Partridge's marriage, she says: "[He] wants more control than I should care to give—control I mean of the body & the mind & time & thoughts of his loved. There's the danger and her risk" (1978, 119). Her criticism of Ralph might apply equally to a criticism of Leonard, but Woolf fails to make the equation, choosing instead to sympathize with the "woman," rather than give herself away. And Woolf's sympathy does not always extend to women. Her acid tongue and devastating wit find women of all classes as objects of her derision, especially in the early diaries. She, for example, cruelly assesses "women's faces in the streets! As senseless as playing cards; with tongues like adders" (1977, 149). Again, she may have identified these women with herself, but she does not admit the similarity.

As readers we might look at these two entries as representative. Her feminist sympathy for Dora may be her own identification with and sympathy for herself. Her anger with women in the streets points to an internalized anger at the subordinate situation of the "senseless" faces of the women, the same one she has with relation to Leonard. She turns her anger at controlling men inwardly on Dora, the women, and herself, projecting her fury onto women both like and unlike herself in station and intelligence, possibly sharing their passivity and submerged rage. Other women, therefore, act as safe targets for her self-loathing. In later diaries, however, Woolf finds the will and motivation to direct her anger virulently toward men, who may have been the targets all along. She certainly knows her male audiences may read them but at this later date confronts that audience more directly, even in diary text.

She writes one such direct confrontation in February 1934. After reading J. E. Neal's unflattering portrait of Queen Elizabeth, she says sharply: "a fig for impartial and learned historians! All men are liars" (1982, 201). Entries this angry are rare, but in the later years she even takes on Leonard occasionally, although with characteristic mildness: "L. is very hard on people; . . His desire, I suppose, to dominate. Love of power. And then he writes against it . . . it doesnt matter, to me . . . & yet I hate people noticing it" (1982, 326). Almost always describing his treatment of her in a studied neutrality, a rather suspicious objectivity, she more often chooses to direct overt feminist jabs to others less close to home: Neal, or Ralph, or Clive. Not until *Three Guineas* does she make overt distinctions between men and patriarchal structures in her critique. In July 1927, for example, she says, "Love, love, love—Clive, Clive, Clive—that's the tune of it, thrummed with rather callous persistency; a thick finger and thumb. Now love I dare say nothing against; but it is a feeble passion" (1980, 149). Why she "dare not" speak against love can only be guessed, but in relation to Clive she does just that.

In an entry written the year before her death she goes beyond the personal to indict the businessmen's "male detached lives" . . . this cool man's world: so weather tight: . . . sealed up; self sufficient; admirable; caustic; laconic; objective . . . not a chink through which one can see art, or books" (1984, 241). Aiming her disdain at unintellectual men, her commentary echoes criticisms she has made of Leonard or Clive. Woolf's diary musings more closely parallel her public indictments against men at the end of her life, testifying to Woolf's intense engagement with her art and her feminism. Her cultural interactions and observations change as she and her culture change. Her self-sufficiency and success prompt new relationships with her audience leading to more open exchanges, particularly on the political level.

*Three Guineas* seems to have freed Woolf to write more openly in her diary of her disenchantment with prevailing, gender-coded political structures. Even though Woolf does not often write of her grievances against institutionalized relations between men and women in her diary, a reference to an essay she plans to write ("On Being Despised" [1982, 271]) points to her plan for *Three Guineas* and uncovers her motivation in writing a book that "will need some courage" (1982, 354) because of its feminist political agenda.[15] *Three Guineas* speaks strongly of an intellectual, impersonal, yet committed view of the need to equalize women's power and to restructure the masculine world in order to recognize the worth of daughters as well as sons. In giving "daughters" worth, she gives it to herself as well. As Anne Bell says, "In *Three Guineas* she said what she wished to say and, oddly enough, did not for once deeply mind what others said of it" (1984, viii).

Always mindful of audience, Woolf confronts her public directly in *Three Guineas*. Having had her say in public, she becomes more directly feminist in face-to-face confrontations with others and in her diary. When Morgan (E. M. Forster) offers to propose Woolf's name to the London Library Committee, she refuses, saying, "Rather to my pleasure I answered No. I don't want to be a sop—a face saver . . . years ago in the L.L. He sniffed about women on Cttee. One of these days I'll refuse I said silently. And now I have" (1984 337). Years later Forster tells interviewer Wilfred Stone, "I was surprised to read that remark about her being furious with me in front of the London Library. I was only trying to be amusing" (Stone 1997, 58). Thus, publishing *Three Guineas* makes public the beliefs Woolf had long held and empowers her to greet her critics with greater confidence and directness.

## Audience: The Force of the Internal and External

Caring deeply about what others think and finally shrugging off her very real fear of others' criticism with *Three Guineas,* Woolf becomes aware of a disparaging, internalized audience—a highly critical and mean-spirited self. An audience to be reckoned with, this responsive "I" haunts her. In one entry she says, "Parsimony may be the end of this book. Also shame at my own verbosity . . . Who am I ashamed of? Myself reading them" (1984, 352). Her own perfectionist critical practices perform on her works as well as others. Until she finds the means to throw off the criticism of others, she cannot see that self-rebuke causes her fear of audience. Separating her self-assessment from assessment by others permits her to praise herself, rare indeed. In one instance the split between the reader in Woolf and the writer works to raise her esteem: "I hand my compliment to that terribly depressed woman, myself, whose head ached so often: who was so entirely convinced a failure; for in spite of everything I think she brought it off, & is to be congratulated" (1984, 39). What Woolf "brought off" was writing under the specter of many audiences: a critical audience; a loving but controlling domestic audience, Leonard; and an internalized, highly critical audience of her own intellect.

Given such fear of exposure, a husband who feels he must watch and control, and a public literary "set" avid for a look at Mrs. Woolf, why does she write a diary when other avenues of expression are open to her? The answer lies not only in a writer's habit of expression but also in her own passion to find a multiple conception of her reality and to shape a new vision. She acknowledges the diary's rewards in saying, "Melancholy diminishes as I write. Why then don't I write it down oftener? Well one's vanity forbids. I want to appear a success even to myself" (1978, 72). This therapeutic reliance on the diary to record and reshape her perceptions keeps her writing long after Leonard Woolf's promotion of it relaxes, long after her reputation spreads from her more public writings. Under the constraints that her audiences unintentionally put on the writer, Woolf sees her diary as a place of discovery and negotiation, keeping the valuable, dispersing the troublesome. She says, "Many many deep thoughts have visited me. And fled. The pen puts salt on their tails; they see the shadow and fly" (1984, 342). She articulates both external and internal experiences particularly in the last few years of her life, when she contemplates the multiplicity of being with increasing interest, working toward "synthesis of my being . . . nothing makes a whole unless I am writing" (1982, 161). When she sees herself slipping into insanity, however, her diary entries cover over the horror of her mind's images and workings. During a "peculiar & . . . unpleasant" time for her in 1937 she muses: "The exposed moments are terrifying" (1984, 63). How much more terrifying for her are those few months in 1941 when disabling voices haunt her, signaling the return of an unendurable melancholia. To protect herself, she retreats from self-articulation and exposure.

When the madness returns, so does her caution and her care in hiding it in the diary. She endeavors to control and limit what she perceives, to silence the unacceptable. She seeks to protect both herself and Leonard from the horror that begins weeks before her death on March 28, 1941. She had begun her diary in January as usual, lining her margins, setting up "a diary as a book which she intended to fill, and it underscores a life stopped short" (Podnieks 2000, 106). She makes no mention of her increasing anxiety, admitting her fear only in a letter to Vanessa five days before her suicide. The diary conceals the intensity of her malady in desperately optimistic entries of resolve. Unable to expose herself to her own shame or to Leonard's control, she consciously crafts inconsequential details to override the "black shivers" (1984, 266). She writes a diary of will: "Measure, order, precision are now my gods" (1984, 343). An internal audience judges fiercely, prompting her to promise herself and her husband to keep an "order" she can't possibly maintain. Her dread of exposure comes from her own fears and her knowledge that Leonard and a myriad of doctors would take charge on discovering the depth of her malaise.

In the last entries of her diary Woolf alternates accounts of increasing frankness with those that evince a purposeful withdrawal from inward scrutiny. This oscillation, more than any overt commentary, signals the rupture within Woolf as well as in the text. She must have felt the illness coming on for months. She remarks in September 1940, "As I told Ethel Smyth, one must drop a safety curtain over ones private scene" (1984, 323). In other entries she watches her mental state, even graphs her anxiety, but does it clinically. When she turns her gaze outward, she records rather nasty observations about others but does not tie her observations to her melancholy mind. Woolf develops an enhanced watchfulness that has an edge, a fear, and cruelty. In February 1941 she writes a long rambling entry, stridently and vulgarly descriptive: "powdering & painting, these common little tarts, while I sat, behind a thin door, p——ing as quietly as I could" (1984, 357). She then depicts the "fat, smart" women who eat cakes, and uncharacteristically Woolf asks, "Where does the money come to feed these fat white slugs?" (1984, 357) Her disgust extends to those of her class: "We pay the penalty for our rung in society by internal boredom" (1984, 357). As with entries written early in her marriage, when she teeters on the edge of madness, Woolf writes bitterly, with an impersonal virulence and an earthy yet aesthetic loathing for all persons.

How much Leonard knew of the change in his wife is difficult to determine. Certainly her lashing out was indicative. Hindsight makes her madness obvious. But cannily, she carefully retreats to show more control: "Women sitting on seats. A pretty hat in a teashop—how fashion revives the eye! . . . No: I intend no introspection. I mark Henry James's sentence: Observe perpetually . . . Observe my own despondency . . . Oh dear yes, I shall conquer this mood" (1984, 358). She does not conquer. Four days before she kills herself she writes not of madness or longing for death, but rather determination to "observe perpetually." In her last entry she remarks: "L. is doing the rhododendrons . . ." (Woolf's ellipsis) (1984, 359).

Instead of turning inward, Woolf attempts to step back and observe the beauty of the world and the rituals of domestic life that previously sustained her; Leonard's efforts to prune, snip, and shape that beauty perhaps remind her unconsciously of his care and control. She deflects her gaze from her deteriorating condition and reassures Leonard who—noting her frail mental condition—may have been reading her journal. This last entry surely points to a desperate attempt to fix her attention on an external world. Even war, it seems, appears more immediately orderly than her mind.

## Audience: Catalyst and Trespasser

During the last year of her life, depressed, she says, "It struck me that one curious feeling is, that the writing 'I', has vanished. No audience. No echo. That's part of one's death" (1984, 293). The "echo" of audience had great importance to Woolf as a writer. Such an audience can curtail full disclosure, however, and ultimately reconstruct a writer's intent. Woolf wrote her diary as an "odd mix-up of public and private" (1984, 110), knowing its potential incitements and dangers.

To illustrate the distortion an audience renders on any text, even one generically conceived as personal—the diary—we need only look at an incident that occurred after Virginia Woolf's death. Quentin Bell recalls an evening when Leonard read aloud from his dead wife's diary to an audience of friends. Bell "suspects" that Leonard had "come on a passage where she makes a bit too free with the frailties and absurdities of someone here present" and questions him. Leonard remarks, "that's not why I broke off. I shall skip the next few pages because there's not a word of truth in them" (Q. Bell 1977, xiv). That Leonard and friends would judge Virginia's diaries, and by extension Virginia herself, and decide on her version of truth as lies speaks to Virginia's perspicuity concerning her external audience. A patronizing and judgmental masculine audience turns her diary into a retrospective sham. That Bell, agreeing that Virginia does not write what he calls the "truth," would mention this on the first page of his introduction to her diaries seems unconscionable; he calls into question Woolf's perceptions before he presents them and completely disregards her own recognition that truth, identity, and perception are continually in process, in negotiation.

Woolf, fearing such trespass on the body of her work, wrote her diary as "autobiography in public" (1984, 141), using textual wiles to face her audience, to have her say: "[T]he fears are entirely outbalanced (this is honest) by the immense relief & peace I have gained, & enjoy this moment: . . . The pack may howl, but it shall never catch me" (1984, 141).

## Chapter 2

# Katherine Mansfield:

*"'Damning little notebook[s]'*
*tell their own story"*[1]

A s woman, writer, myth, liar, creator, and actress, Katherine Mansfield positions multiple identities throughout her texts, both fictional and autobiographical. Simultaneously she exposes herself and misleads the reader who looks for the woman behind the story and within the language. Mansfield writes notebooks that manifest her complexity as a woman caught between her conservative New Zealander's background and her progressive/oppressive life in Europe. Her life spent in a state of self-imposed exile, Mansfield feared remaining outside a mainstream she often despised, fighting to enter an established literary coterie she shocked. Elusive, she fades and disappears, then reappears boldly in robes of bright, and possibly false, colors.

Her biographers Antony Alpers, Claire Tomalin, Gillian Boddy, and Jeffrey Meyers all speak about her ambivalently. At once critical and admiring, they find her protean personality exciting and frustrating. Mansfield refuses definition, resists all her life the roles and labels others made for her. She alternately creates and collapses her own versions of self: "Katherine was a liar . . . , a bold and elaborate inventor of false versions . . . ; and if she was the heroine of her own life story, lies became not lies but fiction, a perfectly respectable thing" (Tomalin 1988, 57). In 1903, at age fifteen, Mansfield begins what we now call her *Journal* or her diary. Earlier *Notebooks* contain only childhood stories. She continues writing the personal reflections until her death in 1923. She writes "for" herself, to define herself, but also as a means of communicating versions of selves to others in order to guide their understanding of her. The volumes of her fifty-three notebooks express all the versions of her life, both imaginative and factual, all designed to expose and hide the actress seeking to please the audience. Aware that audiences sneer as often as they applaud, Mansfield enacts alternate versions of a self awaiting the fall but hoping for better: "And God looked upon the fly fallen into the jug of milk and saw that it was good" (1925, 153).

Despite Mansfield's unsavory personal reputation, her short-story collections, especially *Bliss* and *The Garden Party,* exhibit a strong literary talent. A satirical and sentimental writer in both her notebooks and stories, she creates insightful figures whose social and personal conflicts shift as quickly as her world does. Mansfield writes both her fictions and her journals to examine what it is to live in a world that frightens and judges, that takes more than it gives.

Leaving New Zealand voluntarily at age nineteen, Mansfield rushed into the different, equally uncomfortable worlds of Great Britain and continental Europe. Her move from New Zealand, necessary if she was to write and to grow, threw her into worlds where she did not fit. Diary entries of 1909 and 1911 show her pain: "[E]very gate and every door/Is locked 'gainst me alone" (47). In 1917, six years after leaving New Zealand, she discovered her lingering illness was tuberculosis, removing her even further from mainstream social and literary practices but not from her desire to fit in, to be part of something.

In the journal form of autobiography, writers assign meanings daily, and only years later do definitive life patterns emerge. Mansfield's *Journal* opens up interpretive questions about her life and the lives of women everywhere, rather than answering them conclusively and so dispelling them. Her life, her philosophies, her dreams, and her realities defy fixed roles, static ideas. In quoting poet John Keats, she defines her philosophy: "Better be 'imprudent moveable than prudent fixtures'" (127). Mansfield, living for years under the specter of death, extolled movement to avoid stagnation. But her movement and "imprudence" confronted her eagerness to please, putting in motion a life of seeking and evading. Mansfield's diary tells her story, but in her desire to convince her husband and the world of her worth she creates a public-redeeming text.

Readers who believe diaries are secret, confidential—full of outpourings of desire and longing or scandalous sexual revelations—may find Mansfield's journals disappointing. In writing her diaries she often creates more conventional selves than her history can contain. In both her fiction and her more personal notebooks, Mansfield writes stories that fluctuate in meaning, simultaneously conforming to and subverting from within the masculine ethos of modernist Europe. In writing so-called private text, she, as many women centuries before, finds herself "inevitably caught in mimicking male definitions of themselves" (Nussbaum 1988, 154) or, more likely, caught in acting out male definitions of woman.

Mansfield, who "assumed some 20 different names during her lifetime" (Boddy 1993, 101), proliferates identities in each version of her journal.[2]

Thus readers find it nearly impossible to locate any unified self or absolute truth. Unlike Woolf, Mansfield didn't even try to present unified versions of the self for her husband. In April 1920 she addresses the problem of truth and subjectivity in an essay section of the *Journal* titled *The Flowering of the Self*: "True to oneself! which self? Which of my many— well really, that's what it looks like [it's] coming to—hundreds of selves? For what with complexes and repressions and reactions and vibrations and reflections, there are moments when I feel I am nothing but the small clerk of some hotel without a proprietor . . ." (1954, 205). Mansfield acknowledges with acuity her complexity and multiplicity. Her lack of center makes it impossible to be "true" to a self so fractured, sometimes bringing her emotional despair. She nevertheless writes of these proliferating selves in the awareness of the larger psychological and literary movement in Freudian/Modernist England.

## *The Journal of Katherine Mansfield:* Chaotic Choices

The conflicting and paradoxical nature of Mansfield's state of exile unmistakably surfaces in her personal papers. *The Journal of Katherine Mansfield,* edited by her husband, John Middleton Murry, first appeared four years after her death, with a fuller version released in 1954. In 2002, Margaret Scott published her complete edition, *Katherine Mansfield Notebooks.*[3] The *Notebooks* include every entry from the earlier *Journal,* the adolescent diary of 1907 called *The Urewera Notebook,* previously edited by Ian Gordon, and additional notes on paper fragments, quotes from other writers, unsent letters, and the manuscript versions of unfinished stories, outlines, poems, shopping lists, and budgets—over seven hundred pages of papers only recently transcribed, organized, and collated in full.

Mansfield would begin a new diary in the front of a blank book, the entries would dwindle after a couple months, and finally she would write backward or upside down elsewhere in this book or another old or new book a few months later. In handwriting so difficult to read that even Murry struggled with it, Mansfield wrote in many notebooks and diaries concurrently, sometimes pinning pages together later for order. Her journal-writing method illustrates her conflicting need for order and her impulse for something new. Because of the huge number of fictional entries and fragments in the newer edition, I most often refer to the earlier, less complete but more manageable *Journal.* I also include new entries from the *Notebooks* to better reflect the mass of personal papers that tell us much about Mansfield, using the terms *diary, journal,* and *notebook* interchangeably. The fictions, evasions, and bold statements make up Mansfield's personal papers. They all record her impulse to live, to embrace the facts, and to invent new fictions of her life. These personal notebook/journal/diary entries show her experiments in fiction and self-expression mixed haphazardly.

## *Journal* Publication: Letting the Husband Decide

Mansfield's decisions to publish journal entries vary with her mood: Bursts of self-esteem empower her to confront her culture by making public all she writes; bursts of self-loathing lash out to vandalize or silence any self that might confirm her own inadequacy. "One thing I am determined upon. And that is *to leave no sign.* There was a time—it is not so long ago—when I should have written *all* that has happened . . . I keep silence as Mother kept silence" (1954, 254). Equating her own silence with her mother's, Mansfield alludes to women's place as outside articulation, a designation she resents, especially when it restrained her saying/staying power. Inhabiting the periphery of culture and despising her place, Mansfield nevertheless wills her papers to the traditional wielder of control and power over women: her husband. She writes to Murry before her death: "Please destroy all letters you do not wish to keep & all papers. You know my love of tidiness. Have a clean sweep Bogey, and leave all fair—will you?" (Murry in Boddy 1993, 102*).*

Bequeathing all her manuscripts to her chief critic, Murry, may have been an act designed to relinquish her construction of selves to his destruction of them. She instructs him to "publish as little as possible and tear up and burn as much as possible" (Boddy 1993, 99), clearly departing from her wish in 1916 "to keep a kind of minute book, to be published some day (Mansfield 2002 2,33). Her fatigue, her illness, and her sense of resignation heighten her awareness of the very real critical and often abusive response to women's writing. And as she reflects, "Looking back, I imagine I was always writing. Twaddle it was, too" (Mansfield 2002 2, 337). No longer energetic or spiteful, she relishes the erasure of designations that could disturb the more spiritualized self she felt she had become. After years of depicting her various selves as effaced and struggling, near her death she notes her desire for a wholeness she knew to be spurious, but one she idealistically hoped love could bring: "Being made 'whole.' Yes . . . By love serve ye one another" (1954, 259). The contradictions in her papers refute any reality of wholeness, except in this deathbed theory controlled by religious language.

These idealistic theoretical statements certainly contrast with earlier notebooks whose sensuality repeats itself in her description of both nature and woman: "Before me . . . a weird passionate abandon of birds—their strange cries—the fanciful shapes of the supple jacks—Then the advent of Bella—her charm in the dusk—the very dusk incarnaternate . . ." (I. Gordon 1978, 51). Murry's edition includes few references to the adolescent diaries where this kind of sensuality surfaces, and he omits later fictions where Mansfield also relegates her eroticism. Sensitive to Bloomsbury's disapproval, particularly with regard to Katherine, Murry edits his wife's *Journal* to focus on her talent and her intelligence, not her sensuality.

However, after reading all the published *Journals* and *Notebooks,* I suggest that Mansfield censors herself more rigidly in writing her diaries than Murry does in editing them for publication. Murry merely trims and tightens and tidies, smoothing over Mansfield's rougher edges in the *Journal* while she occasionally rips the fabric of convention in the notebook versions. Since Murry had never been able to subdue Mansfield for long in their marriage, her pretense to the contrary, his editorial art could have aided him in creating a new, more acceptable wife. "[Murry] was to spend . . . eleven years being baffled by her, and still longer trying to shape her image into something he could cope with" (Tomalin 1988, 95). But this is only partially the case.

Although Murry's editorial posture undoubtedly influences his final version of Mansfield's *Journal,* subsequent versions and her manuscripts verify his integrity. Scott says of Murry, "I was struck by how much of the material Murry had left unused. . . . How much he had misread, trimmed, punctuated and generally tidied up" (2002, xiv), but she also acknowledges that, in light of the difficulties of publishing the journals earlier, "He struggled on with the deciphering and whatever he did manage to read he published, without defensive explanations . . . almost his only suppressions were names of people still alive at the time of publication . . . he commands a respect and an admiration that no amount of disapproval of his editorial methods can diminish" (ibid.).

The Scott *Notebooks* show a Mansfield who is more aware of her difference, a New Zealander in exile, a woman forever aware of her audience's judgment. This complete version tells more fully a woman's stories and also what can be told—given the pressure of gendered codes and the real presence of audience: father/husband/censor/public. Evident in all the versions of her *Journal/Notebooks* is Mansfield's "sense that exploration, with all its dangers, is preferable to inertia—indeed, necessary, if life is to be experienced to the full . . ." (Hankin 1983, 127). But even as

Mansfield envisions herself as larger than life, enacting roles and disguises, writing her own lines, she constructs restrained versions of self, choosing her facts, creating fictions in which to hide. With audiences in mind—at least much of the time—her own retraction and caution frame the entries. Her response to William Shakespeare's *Hamlet* sums up her vision of what it is to be the subject of a written text:

> To act . . . to see ourselves in the part—to make a larger gesture than
> would be ours in life—to declaim, to pronounce, to even exaggerate.
> To persuade ourselves? Or others? (1954, 275)

## Audience: Presence and Pressure

The cool onlooker haunts Mansfield throughout her life, whether he is her father, her brother, her husband, Bloomsbury, or God. This presence of audience complicates Mansfield's exploring and defining in journals. Readily inviting lovers (and later her husband) to view the contents of her diary and writing to an internalized audience sometimes conceived as her late brother, Mansfield also imagines a potential public readership for these diary notebooks as well. While the journal functions as a forum for independence and a rewriting of self or selves, it acts simultaneously as a site of control by a higher authority who will be its reader and a site of interest for future audiences only sensed as yet. The instant popularity of the 1927 and the 1954 editions of the *Journal* and the 2002 version depend on audiences avid for a peek at a woman who tantalized and mystified the British intellectual world.

Lytton Strachey, appalled by the limited subject in Katherine Mansfield's *Journal,* says, "I see Murry lets out that it was written for publication—which no doubt explains a great deal. But why that foul-mouthed, virulent, brazen-faced broomstick of a creature should have got herself up as a pad of rose-scented cotton wool is beyond me" (Boddy 1993, 101). Others, such as A. R. D. Fairburn, were scandalized by its supposed fullness: "[Mansfield was] a woman whom Mr. Middleton Murray [*sic*] has already done his best to compromise in the minds of the reading public by cramming her incontinently down their throats on every possible occasion. . . . I had no business to be reading certain passages. They gave me the feeling that I had burst in upon a lady in her boudoir at an awkward moment" (McEldowney 1985, 112). The prurience and perversity of this criticism clearly indicate reasons that Mansfield herself, and Murry in her stead, cautiously exposed her notes as "private" text. Looking for a fixed identity or reality, readers of diaries often neglect to consider the play of identities within the swirling language of textual exploration, refusing one truth, one unity.

A diary writer, then, is not merely the object of self-scrutiny but concurrently the object of another's view, another's expectation. If these writers, like Mansfield, want desperately to please the men in their lives, they use strategies of deflection to write selves that satisfy their own momentary sense of self, yet also please their "watcher," the Other.

Recording a dream in 1919, Mansfield writes: "The watcher appeared. He stood always in profile, his felt hat turned up at the side . . . 'Hi, Missy', he shouted to me. 'Why don't you give us a bit of a show out there?'" In the dream Mansfield takes off her clothes and a wave sweeps her away as she yells, "Help! Help!" (1954, 176). The ambiguous smile of the watcher coming closer ends her dream. Mansfield's diary deflects the gaze of such "watchers" to save herself from the nightmare of naked exposure, even while the writing itself saves her from being overwhelmed by a masculine culture that dominates even her dreams.

## An Imagined and Benign Masculine Audience: Brother

A pervasive male culture both entrances and repels Mansfield. She cannot set herself apart from her fascination with "the patriarchal lineage," a pattern of "Father—Boss—God—Fate" that dominates the "fly," her consistent metaphor for those with "bad luck, and ill health" (O'Sullivan 1994, 19). Yet she also cannot assuage her need for and attraction to male approval. In the early, unsettling years of her relationship with Murry, Katherine renews her relationship with her brother, Leslie Beauchamp. In October 1915, soon after their reunion, Leslie was killed during a grenade-training exercise. That year marks a lessening of Murry's influence on Mansfield, as she had confided in Leslie, replacing a lover's intimacy with a brother's. The news of Leslie's death leaves her in "a state of shattered dependence on Murry" (Tomalin 1988, 140), although Murry soon leaves her in France to recover from her shock and illness.

Her diary during this time records an imaginary dialogue between brother and sister that shows a poignant grief and a longing for death. The dead Leslie clearly becomes the audience of an entire section of the journal. She says, "Dearest heart, I know you are there, and I live with you, and I will write for you. . . . I give Jack my 'surplus' love, but to you I hold and to you I give my deepest love" (1954, 86). In writing to Leslie, Mansfield is able to write of her own identity at a time when her dependence on Murry threatened to overwhelm her. Because Mansfield always feels the need for masculine attachment and approval, she collapses her own identity with her brother's, effacing her sense of self by writing of the two of them together. She says she needs to "Lose myself, lose myself to find you, dearest" (1954, 98) and promises to find Leslie in the book she will write and send to New Zealand.

Not until 1920, when she publishes the story collection *Bliss,* does Leslie figure predominately in Mansfield's fiction; the 1922 collection, *The Garden Party,* further fulfills Mansfield's promise to "find" him in her fictional work. In both collections a brother's presence consoles the female protagonist. In "The Garden Party," for example, young Laurie consoles his sister Laura after her visit to a family mourning the death of a son: "She stopped, she looked at her brother. 'Isn't life,' she stammered, 'isn't life——' But what life was she couldn't explain. No matter. He quite understood" (1922, 61).

The Laura/Laurie synonymity and the mutuality of understanding point to Mansfield's appraisal of her brother as part of herself. Certainly in her privileging his place as audience of her *Journal* and subject of her work, she acknowledges his importance as part of the self. In "The Wind Blows" she writes of a brother and sister as one flesh: "Their heads bent, their legs just touching, they stride like one eager person through the town . . ." (*Garden Party and Other Stories* 1922, 42). Writing to Leslie in her *Journal,* Mansfield addresses the self–audience simultaneously. Seeing herself isolated and different from others, Mansfield constructs her self-perspective in relation to others, sensing an audience that looks and judges. As a woman, as a New Zealander, she too often lacks her own image of self. With her dead brother as audience, Mansfield values herself more; he becomes part of her, empowering her: "Dear brother, as I jot these notes, I am speaking to you. To whom did I always write when I kept those huge complaining diaries? Was it to myself? . . . Each time I take up my pen *you* are with me" (1954, 96). His clear presence in 1916 indicates Mansfield's desire to textually represent her brother's likeness. And even though Leslie as audience does not kindle the careful and manipulative discourse that the presence of Murry/husband does, Mansfield's discomfort with her feminine persona surfaces as she equates a masculine formulation with her own: "Perhaps 'the new man' will not live. Perhaps I am not yet risen" (97).

Later, in spring 1916, Mansfield shifts her diary topics from grieving remembrance to intellectual engagements. She emphasizes masculine achievement in comparison with her own, writing of Dostoevsky and Shakespeare until a meeting with her sister Chaddie sparks new memories and stories that she practices in the journal. In reviewing her meeting with Chaddie she addresses an audience who is clearly not Leslie. She apologizes

for not writing much that day and addresses someone who may be Murry
or may be future readers: "Only you see, fool who is reading this, I went out
awfully early" (1954, 113). From this point in the diary she resumes her
self-narratives, practicing stories and reflections that do not always address
her childhood directly. Clearly she has once again changed her self-conception. Her audience shifts to a more public and perhaps less sympathetic one.

## Higher Stakes: Husband as Audience

While Mansfield's journal acts as a forum for independence and a rewriting of selves, it functions simultaneously as a site of control by a "helpful"
but higher authority who will be its reader. The audience of most of her
adult diary is John Middleton Murry, her lover and later husband, whom
she calls "Jack" or "Bogey." They often write in each other's notebooks,
and she sends Murry sections of her journal when away as if to share the
"real" with him and so convince him of her sincerity and worth. She says
in 1922, "I wrote this for myself. I shall now risk sending it to Bogey. He
may do with it what he likes" (2002 2, 187). On another occasion she
writes, "[T]hese pages from my journal. Don't let them distress you"
(ibid., 285).

Murry, this "real reader," was a literary power in his own right. By far
the better known of the two, Murry commands a presence throughout the
journal, and his power competes with Mansfield's own. This subordinating of wife to husband seems all the more strange given Mansfield's success as a writer, her travel, and her antics. But Mansfield, in the journal at
least, sees herself as a traditional wife. And traditionally "the female has a
more passive role; she is subordinated to a landscape which has its own
hopes for her, or her view is limited by the man to man's own viewing"
(Caws 1980, 27). Mansfield's attraction to "man's own viewing" leads her
to write a journal written for a man's "look." Although Mansfield wants
"the power to control her own life without being held in any web of convention" (Tomalin 1988, 45), she also wants to appear feminine, passive,
brilliant, and pure—qualities men admire.

Except for early years troubled by uncertainty about the permanence of
their relationship and by the death of her brother, Mansfield writes with
her husband in mind, often addressing him both directly and indirectly
in the diary itself, most often with an eye toward currying his favor and
proving herself in his eyes. She says in February 1921, "It is only by making myself worthy of Jack that I shall be worthy of what I mean our relationship to be. He that faileth in little things shall not succeed in great
things" (1954, 240). In November of the same year she acknowledges,

"These days I have been awfully rebellious. . . . I want things that Jack can so easily do without, that aren't natural to him. I long for them" (1954, 271). Although this last entry only mildly criticizes, she writes of her separation from Jack's values and of her fear that she lacks what he does not deem important, irrespective of her desire.

Thus Mansfield in her *Journal* alternately conforms to and resists both her husband and her culture's construction of her as woman. In one poignant entry she voices her ambivalence about her role of wife as society sees it: "I don't particularly want to live with him. I'd like to if it could be managed—but *no sacrifices, please.* As to learning—as to being a 'little lovely darling'—it's not conceivable. I want to *work* . . . (1954, 184). In her journal entry she reminds him of her writer's persona, explaining her lack of convention. In an entry that Murry calls "An unposted letter," she chastises an audience, probably Murry, "Your letters sounded insincere to me; I did not believe them. . . . You see—to me—life and work are two things indivisible. . . . I think other people have given you a wrong idea of me, perhaps" (1954, 237). A few months later she writes as a traditional romantic heroine: "But I can say as truly as a girl in love: 'He is all the world to me'" (1954, 252). Mansfield's narrative oscillates between traditional sycophantic conceptions of the feminine and warring aspects of herself that refuse containment by social constructions. With Murry listening, she voices contradictions within herself but nevertheless constructs herself discursively to win his approval and to maintain her self-esteem.

In her short story "Marriage à la Mode" she writes from William's point of view about Isabel, a wife who wishes to conform to a role of monogamous attention to her husband. Isabel says, "God forbid, my darling, that I should be a drag on your happiness," a refrain from within the journal pages. But the story ends with Isabel's failure to write to William though she knows she should: "Of course she would stay here and write. . . . No, it was too difficult. . . . And, laughing in the new way, she ran down the stairs" (*Garden Party and Other Stories* 1922, 167). Mansfield's fictional refusal to write to her husband, to explain herself, and to open herself to his scrutiny evinces her own ambivalence about her marriage and her writing for Murry's eyes. Although the reader's sympathy in this story is with William, the tragedy of conflicting roles and audiences is Mansfield's. "She reveled in change, disguise, mystery, and mimicry" (Tomalin 1988, 89). She uses all of these techniques to both invite and deflect the male gaze: first her father's, later her brother's, then her lovers' and husband's. Mansfield's conflict comes, as Peter Brooks points out, because narratives "need to be heard . . . desire to become the story of the listener as much as the teller" (1987, 55). In Mansfield's diary narratives she clearly invites the audience to read her shifting and evasive narrative performances, willingly suffering their judgment for the sake of the performance.

## The Internal Audience: Self-Fictions, Self-Censorship

Mansfield's indistinct fusion of her life stories from her fictions in her diaries imbues the *Journal* with an aesthetic, artistic quality that many diary narratives lack. Yet this same quality makes the separation of lived experience and imagined experience difficult—if not impossible. She writes most often in first person, yet she also frequently writes in third person to record events of her life as well as stories in progress. One entry, for example, simply says, "But at last she was conscious that a choice had to be made, that before dawn, these shadows would appear less real, making way for something different" (1954, 125).

The "she" represents perhaps a fictional character, though Mansfield does not hint that it does. She observes and she invents, subverting certainties: "'Don't you think it would be marvelous,' she said, 'to have just one person in one's life to whom one could tell everything? She leant forward, put down her cup . . .'" (1954, 175). Whether this entry shows Mansfield's longing for intimacy, begins a story, or records a vignette—we cannot know. Whatever its intention, loneliness prevails. The "she" of Mansfield's diaries cannot be assigned to fictional characters only; clearly Mansfield achieves distance and deflects exposure by referring to herself as "she," too. Searching for a knowledge of self, Katherine Mansfield as woman expertly uses language to both answer and deflect questions, to be both "she" and "I," to build "textual universes that are charged with imagination" (Duyfhuizen 1986, 178). She writes to fictionalize as well as to build her life through language.

Reconciling the oppositions of personal perception, of "I" and "she" can be excruciatingly painful. In Mansfield's story "Miss Brill," two onlookers view Miss Brill as a nonentity and an object for ridicule, "a stupid old thing" and "a silly old mug" (*Garden Party and Other Stories* 1920, 188) in grievous contrast to Miss Brill's fictions about herself. But despite the distance between self-perceptions and the perception of others, Mansfield also acknowledges, through Miss Brill's pain, the need to gain self-worth by others' validation. The character Beryl in "The Prelude" looks in the mirror at her own beauty but knows her perception cannot alleviate her restlessness: "She leaned her arms along and looked at her pale shadow in it. How beautiful she looked, but there was nobody to see, nobody" (*Bliss and Other Stories* 1920, 42). Later Beryl despairs at the lack of someone to see her and give substance to her fantasy of herself: "Oh, God, there she was, back again playing the same old game. False—false as ever. . . . I'm always acting a part. I'm never my real self for a moment" (*Bliss and Other Stories* 1920, 68). For Beryl and for her creator, reality cannot be discerned in the absence of a viewer. The oscillation between fact and fancy, between perceptions of self and perceptions by others exemplifies her changing identities and feelings, her apprehension of truth and lies. Mansfield says, "After supper I must start my *Journal* and keep it day by day. But *can* I be honest? If I lie, it's no use" (1954, 240). Trying to untangle the stories of Mansfield's life as told by her biographers from the tales she spins in her *Journal* can be as frustrating as discovering the "real" self of Miss Brill or Beryl.

More often, Mansfield creates a fiction of her life to articulate an acceptable self. In a rather typical entry where Mansfield worries about her idleness, she says: "But it all goes deeper. Yes, you are right. . . . I have not felt pure in heart, not humble, not good . . ." (1954, 270). But behind the façade other selves emerge. While Mansfield's "she" longs for someone to tell "everything" even in her journal, Mansfield never tells "everything" or indeed "anything" that admits of Lady Ottoline's or Dorothy Brett's or Virginia Woolf's critical perception of her. Ottoline describes her: "She is brilliant, witty in describing people and is certainly not kind or charitable" (Boddy 1988, 56). She knows their disdain.

Mansfield's awareness of the distance between her idealized self-perceptions and the perceptions of her acquaintances and biographers surfaces in her fictions and in her journal as well. She knows the writer and the audience may be at odds, but she still desperately needs validation. In an entry in 1920 she writes, "She began to weep and could not stop. What was he made of—to talk of them giving each other up? . . . Never say again you have imagination—never say you have the capacity to love and that you know pity. You have said things to me that have wounded me for ever. I must go on . . ." (1954, 199). The fluctuation of pronouns "she" to "I" and "he" to "you" illustrates the blurring of her public and private writing, her fictions and her realities. She writes in relation to Murry, and directly to him, confusing her personal voice with her fictional ones, the better to hide, better to answer Murry's condemnations.

## A Wider Audience: Relationships

Mansfield's intense desire to please, displayed in sites of disclosure and censorship, creates a narrative tension in her journal. Destructive relationships with others make her cynical and effacing but at the same time adamant about her need for independence and equality. She says in 1915, "But I am so made that as *soon* as I am with anyone, I begin to give consideration to their opinions and their desire . . ." (1954, 81); a few months later, in writing of the people who became characters in her stories, she says, "Granted that these people exist and all the differences, complexities and resolutions are true to them—why should *I* write about them? They are not near me" (1954, 93). Her constant shifting of allegiances and her fearful interplay with acquaintances leaves her sense of identity diffuse and fragmented. Her own cautious persona, lacking the richness of her personality, addresses a critical audience both real and imagined. "She once told Ottoline that she sometimes did not know when she was acting, and when she was living her own life, adding, 'Have I any real self left?'" (Alpers 1980, 244). This difficulty in separating the self-fictions and dramas from her ideological identities seen by others pronounces itself in the diary.

Mansfield's occasional ill temper writes itself into the diary text, but her vitriol, promiscuous behavior, and unconventionality are remarkably lacking. The *Journal,* for example, shows no references to the "kissing" scene at a 1914 Garsington Christmas party where Mansfield and Mark Gertler,[4] as part of a play, erotically and openly shocked Bloomsbury by antics that Gertler describes as making "violent love" (Boddy 1988, 42). The literate, sensible, if somewhat emotional presence Mansfield centers in her journal hardly seems the same woman whose charade with Gertler made her notorious for her wild and wanton ways. Virginia Woolf, in the early years of their relationship, writes to Vanessa that Mansfield seemed "to have gone every sort of hog since she was 17, which is interesting" (Woolf, quoted in Alpers 1980, 248). Clearly, Mansfield writes a persona into her private text that varies widely from the public's perception of her.

At odds with Bloomsbury's eroticized version of her, Mansfield creates a rather romantic fantasy of self for her diary. She certainly knows that Bloomsbury gossips about her and sees her in a less flattering light than she does herself. In a cryptic entry that seems to refer to a child she conceived but aborted or miscarried, she says, "If one wasn't so afraid—why should I be? this isn't going to be read by Bloomsbury *et Cie*—I'd say we had a child—a love child, and it's dead" (1954, 187). She provides only vague references to the "we," the "child," the time, and all of the background circumstances. She notes that "Bloomsbury" will not read this entry, yet she writes in the shadow of their readership.

As her fame spreads and her relationships with literary men increase, Mansfield becomes aware of herself as a woman who, like her fictional Beryl, is "laughing in the new way." She becomes aware, too, that she has come under the scrutiny of not only a husband but a masculine and literary public also. Ironically, others' textual representations of Mansfield added to the public's interest in her work. Because of her increasing fame and notoriety, she becomes aware that her *Journal* will be of public interest—even after her death. When Virginia Woolf, for example, asks to see her *Journal*, Mansfield promises to send it to her, though she never kept that promise (Blodgett 1988, 57).

Certainly Woolf's interest reminds Mansfield of her place, precarious though it is, in literary London. Indeed, her tentative plans to publish her journal may have been a ploy to defend herself from the gossipy innuendos and the rumors spread about her in the tightly knit literary community. She is clearly wary of the British writing establishment, who read and judged her writing. Mansfield writes to Dorothy Brett upon the publication of *Prelude:* "And won't the 'Intellectuals' just hate it. They'll think it's a New Primer for Infant Readers. Let 'em" (KM to DB, May 12, 1918). Mansfield's assessment of how the literati would receive her work is not far off the mark. Most critics acknowledged her writing talent and creativity, but her relentlessly iconoclastic and perhaps feminine viewpoint confounded them. The *English Review,* for example, criticizes her work as "cruel, passionless and cynical," while others complained of her "narrow and somewhat superficial themes" (Morrow 1993, 73). Mansfield's critics ambivalently responded to her person and her work: "Of course, it is all girlishly overdramatic in the Katherine Mansfield way, but that is no reflection on its sincerity. After all, it was done, and done splendidly" (O'Connor 1993, 177).

Though they couldn't quite dismiss her stories, her personal indiscretions incensed Mansfield's contemporaries. She outraged men. Her rebellious nature and affront to convention provided male authors a characterization to abuse fictionally, even though some regarded her affectionately, as is certainly the case with D. H. Lawrence and A. R. Orage. Fictional and well-documented nonfictional critiques of Mansfield appeared in the literary circle's virulent prose: D. H. Lawrence's characterization of Katherine as Gudrun in *Women in Love;*[5] A. R. Orage's fictional depiction in a series of stories dubbed "Tales for Men Only"; and Aldous Huxley's satirization after her death in *Those Barren Leaves.* They vilify her, ignoring (textually at least) the more passive, feminine Mansfield. Other fictional characterizations and her own fiction and personal letters document relationships and affairs entirely left out of her journal; her diaries certainly do not adequately inscribe her complexity. Murry's own insider status may have made her leery of writing anything that, if passed on to others through him, might increase her exile within that literary circle. She wanted the mask of respectability, particularly in her *Journal.*

From early childhood, "appearances were very important" (Tomalin 1988, 10) to Mansfield, yet she persists in following her own course even when it makes her a pariah. While courting Lady Ottoline's favor, for example, she began a flirtation (possibly an affair though he denied it) with Lady Ottoline's lover, Bertrand Russell. Dorothy Brett, possibly courting Murry, began "mischief making" between Katherine and Lady Ottoline. Brett brought Katherine's so-called treachery to the attention of Lady Ottoline, who accuses her. "'To Hell with the Blooms Berries,' said Mansfield" (A. Smith 1999, 34), responding with more bravado than she feels at this rift. In the published *Journal* no entries at all refer to October 1916, when these antics supposedly took place; the only entry in November discusses "window cleaners" and "death." Her refusal to address her betrayal of Ottoline is no surprise. She leaves out many of her dealings with other people, focusing on Murry, herself, and occasionally Ida Baker, her close companion, whom she calls "L.M." Mansfield may omit these dealings to protect the passive and proper image of herself that she prefers as the subject of her diary. Mansfield's letters, hundreds of them to friends such as Lady Ottoline, Violet and Sidney Schiff, S. S. Kotelianski, Lytton Strachey, John Galsworthy, and Mark Gertler better document her relationships and their importance. She refers to them infrequently in the *Journal.*

She rarely privately reflects or gives opinions about people as we might expect. Her relationship with Frieda and D. H. Lawrence is an exception, as she uses the diary to write in detail of their exploits. The two couples alternately lived together, admired, fought, and finally ignored each other. An entry on January 10, 1915, says: "Windy and dark. In the morning, Frieda suddenly. She had had a row with Lawrence. She tired me to death . . ." (1954, 67). She chooses a letter to Beatrice Campbell, not the diary, as the site for a statement about Lawrence in response to what she saw as his obsessions: "I shall never see sex in the running brooks, sex in stones & sex in everything. The number of things that are really phallic, from fountain pen fillers onwards!" (Boddy 1988, 54). Only rarely does she acknowledge sex in the *Journal.* Her letter shows the wit, sexuality, and mocking tone that Mansfield uses to write to others; the journal most often records sentimental, glossed-over feelings.

A notable erasure in her journal text is the lack of any response to Virginia Woolf. Mansfield's letters to Woolf depict respect and affection: "We have got the same job, Virginia & it is really very curious & thrilling that we should both . . . be after so very nearly the same thing . . ." (A. Smith 1999, 35). Not one reference to Woolf exists in Mansfield's diaries and notebooks, though Virginia Woolf made several references to

Mansfield in her own diaries. She may fear Woolf or merely curry her favor. She writes Murry that "the Woolves . . . are smelly" (ibid., 36), perhaps having heard something of Woolf's early response to her: "[S]he stinks like a civet cat that had taken to street walking" (Woolf 1977, 58). Woolf later makes clear her growing respect and affection for Mansfield. But Mansfield never writes of herself either as positively or as negatively as Woolf does.

Mansfield often writes of herself as rather ethereal, above the lascivious, worldly people who surround her. In December 1920 she says, "I should like this to be accepted as my confession. . . . Everything in life that we really accept undergoes a change. So suffering must become Love. . . . I must pass from personal love which has failed me to a greater love. I must give to the whole of life what I gave to him [Murry]" (*Journal* 228). Woolf's nasty "civet cat" distorts Mansfield's own designation of her sexual presence; according to Mansfield, she is merely taken in by "personal love." In an earlier letter to Woolf she merely refutes her reputation: "[D]on't let THEM ever persuade you that I spend any of my precious time swapping hats or committing adultery—I'm far too arrogant & proud" (A. Smith 1999, 35). Perhaps the split in perception says much about each woman's method of seeing. To Mansfield, "love" and "cat" are both parts of a necessarily fragmented, submerged identity.

For the most part, Mansfield encloses the world of her diary tightly, refusing to acknowledge her successes or failures with others, refusing to compare herself to other writers. Possibly she is simply jealous of others who have more standing than she. Unlike Woolf's diary, Mansfield's journal is largely free of speculation about the reception of her work and says little about the other writers—except Murry—with whom she competes. Feeling a keen sense of rivalry with almost every person she meets and with every writer she knows, she reserves the adulation she gives to writers for Oscar Wilde, William Shakespeare, John Keats, and other dead masters. She only reluctantly writes about her relationships, especially literary rivals, showing her unease in forming friendships and competing in what she perceives as a masculine, misogynist, literary society.

Mansfield uses Chekhov to speak for her when she quotes his *Excellent People:* "'An Author's vanity is vindictive, implacable, incapable of forgiveness'" (*Journal* 126). Even though she may be indirectly referring to her own vanity, she most clearly wants to rebuke the vanity in other authors, fearing as she does their deprecation. But the allusion is oblique. By writing "out" the literary establishment in her *Journal,* she writes "in" her own vision of herself as woman and writer.

## Choosing an Audience:
## Journal Omissions, Fictional Permissions

Mansfield fills diary notebooks with drafts of fiction, layering the large gaps of the personal with imaginative stories. A void of personal narratives censors the most chaotic episodes. In fiction, conventions of untruth and fantasy protect her; in a diary, a genre conventionally regarded as a site for self-exposure and self-examination, Mansfield senses she would be open to scathing and vicious censure were it to be read. Her 1909 notebooks exemplify her silence during deep crisis.[6] Pregnancy, lover's neglect, broken marriage, the death of an illegitimate infant child, and subsequent affairs made Mansfield vulnerable to criticism, and her self-image must have undergone a battering. She did not confide in her diary.

The sad saga and increasing diary omissions begin in late 1908, when Mansfield falls in love with musician Garnet Trowell. Garnet's father, Thomas, had been her cello teacher in New Zealand, moving to England the year before Mansfield did. When she finds herself without lodging, the Trowells invite her to live with them, but when Thomas discovers she has become pregnant, he blames Katherine and throws her out of the house. Garnet's weakness and betrayal and his family's censure at the time of her pregnancy comes in her "first adult year in Europe" (Meyers 2002, 36), "at the most vulnerable moment of her life, when her parents were 12,000 miles away" (2002, 43–44). Feeling attacked, alone, and vulnerable as 1909 began, she feels no better when her mother arrives in May to hustle off the twenty-year-old Katherine to a German convent to await a late-summer birth. Katherine leaves as soon as she can in favor of a "conveniently obscure spa" (49).

She writes next to nothing in her personal papers of her abandonment, the first signs of tuberculosis, a short-term husband—George Bowden, whom she leaves the morning after the wedding—her exile in Germany, and the late-pregnancy stillbirth of Garnet's child, followed by two short-term lovers—an Australian journalist "S.V." and Polish critic Floryan Sobieniowski. She keeps silent about circumstances and relationships but briefly alludes to painful emotions.[7] On Good Friday 1909 she compares herself to Christ and his crucifixion: "I *thirst* too—I hang upon the Cross. Let me be crucified—so that I may cry 'It is finished'" (1954, 39). After a short poem she acknowledges her painful silence: "I cannot say it now. Maybe I shall be able to, much later" (ibid.). A short time later she fantasizes a maternal scene, wondering about the time "when I shall sit and read aloud to my little son" (40–41).

She resumes writing only the impersonal until late June. Then, heavy with a child, she writes, "[T]he pain makes me shiver and feel dizzy. To be alone, and to feel a terrible confusion in your body which affects you mentally . . ." (1954, 41). Before that summer's miscarriage, she writes of the anguish of her circumstances and her determination to raise her child: "[S]ome day when I am asked: 'Mother, where was I born?' and I answer: 'In Bavaria, dear,' I shall feel again, I think, this coldness—physical, mental—heart coldness, hand coldness, soul coldness" (42). Mansfield gives readers condensed glimpses of an agonized, idealized, and histrionic Katherine. Other Katherines were not under scrutiny in 1909 or written in records she later "destroyed" (Tomalin 1988, 69). Mansfield's response to her life in 1909 is "guesswork" (Alpers 1980, 92), though over several years she attempts to fictionalize this episode, writing a plan for the unfinished story, "Maata." Mansfield details the betrayal and anguish of the time but romanticizes a male character's grief and heartbreak, not the woman's (*Notebooks* 2 2002, 254).

Textual evasion even in the masses of papers that comprise her notebooks illustrates one method of self-narrative. Another method of self-production through fictional personae may be more telling during these years. The women at the center of many stories in *In a German Pension* (1911) manifest a deeply rooted fear of sexuality and the inevitable consequences for a woman—the bearing of a child. Mansfield writes of women both seduced and debased by man's sexual aggressiveness; also, during this period she writes of birth as rather horrifying and tragic. In "Frau Fisher," the young woman narrator protests, "'I like empty beds,'" only to be chastised by the Frau, "'That cannot be true because it is not natural,'" to which the narrator replies, compounding her "unnatural" nature, "But I consider child-bearing the most ignominious of all professions" (Mansfield 1911, 31). In "At Lehmann's" a "Young Man" entices Sabina into sexual play: "The room seemed to swim around Sabina. Suddenly, from the room above, a frightful, tearing shriek. . . . In the silence the thin wailing of a baby. 'Achk!' shrieked Sabina, running from the room" (60). In "A Birthday" a young Andreas views a father's insensitive waiting for the birth of a son: "She waited a moment, expectantly, rolling her eyes, then in full loathing of mankind went back into the kitchen and vowed herself to sterility" (71). In all the *German Pension* stories the protagonist becomes aware of a brutish sexuality and the consequent terror of childbearing. The erasure of diary entries in the *Journal* concerning woman's sexual fear and maternal abhorrence points to Mansfield's fear of rebuke, whether her own or others, and her preference for relegating to fiction what most troubles her. She notes in a much later entry in February 1922, "I am a *sham*. I am also an egoist of the deepest dye—such a one that it was very difficult to confess to it in case this book should be found" (1954, 294).

This fear of confession and exposure doubtless plagued her at a time in her life when she was so vulnerable to negative judgments. Her ill health may have reminded her of the early death of diarist Marie Bashkirtseff, whose mother published her diary after her death. Bashkirtseff's diary "made an indelible impression on Katherine" (Tomalin 1988, 42). Knowing that publication of a confessional diary, even posthumously, would open her to vilifying criticism and social ostracism encourages her self-censorship. The price of revelation is too high for Mansfield. She chooses to censor her so-called private papers and to write more open rebellions into stories read as products of the imagination rather than as depictions of actual experience. Such deflection to fiction serves Mansfield particularly well when she confronts the issues of sexual politics.

Mansfield's hostility to man's sexual use of woman and her fear of motherhood does not last long after the distress of 1909. Although always ambivalent about both man's and woman's manipulation of sexual power, she is too interested in sexual intrigue to relegate her desire to strict sexual conventions. Her last two stories in *In A German Pension* point to a changing perception of women's sexuality. In "The Swing of the Pendulum" the protagonist, probably a prostitute, hungers "for the nearness of someone . . . who knew nothing at all about her—and made no demands—but just lived" (105); in "A Blaze" the protagonist acknowledges both her desire and her ambivalence: "I can't help seeking admiration any more than a cat can help going to people to be stroked. . . . I like men to adore me—to flatter me—even to make love to me—but I would never give myself to any man" (116).

The intensity of her sexual desire, ambivalence, and rebellion is missing from the diary text, but if her fiction is any indicator, Mansfield maintains an unconventional sexuality that haunts her throughout her life. Her post-1909 willingness to feign acquiescence to repressive sexual mores, at least as written in her *Journal,* points to a growing sensitivity to others' criticism, especially Murry's, whose presence in her life dominated from 1912 until her death. Mansfield's biographers record her disastrous early marriage, many probable lovers, almost certain gonorrhea, and maybe an abortion. Letters, interviews, and particularly Mansfield's fiction give credence to her sexual rebellion. Yet even the new complete version of her *Notebooks* lacks journal entries to support a reading of Mansfield as in any way licentious. In the "mass" of her *Notebooks* Mansfield minimizes her sexuality and its consequences. In one instance she writes, "I should like to have a secret code to put on 'record' what I feel today . . . the lifted curtain . . . the hand at the fire with the ring & stretched fingers . . . no, its [*sic*] snowing . . . the telegram to say he's not . . . just the words arrive. But if I say more I'll give myself away. B.O.C." (*Notebooks* 2 2002, 218).

Mansfield's fictional women, however, characterize an erotic wholeness that her diary pages lack. Beryl's sexual compulsion and fear in "At the Bay," Bertha's ardent longings in "Bliss," and Hennie's body flowering from "its dark bud" (Mansfield 1922, 139) in "The Young Girl" all expose a woman's sensual, sexual desire and love of intrigue that Mansfield only hints at in her adult private writings. In "At the Bay," Beryl fantasizes: "Her arms were round his neck; he held her. . . . She wants a lover. . . . Let us make our fire . . ." (1922, 52). The desire for power and for sex rests in Hennie, too, as her cheeks "crimsoned, her eyes grew dark. . . . 'L—let me, please,' she stammered, in a warm, eager voice. 'I like it. I love waiting! . . . I'm always waiting—in all kinds of places . . ." (1922, 51). Beryl and Hennie long for men, objects of female desire, representing idealized versions of Mansfield's sexual imagination.

Mansfield creates a more complex portrait of feminine sexuality in the bisexual longings of Bertha in "Bliss": "And the two women stood side by side looking at the slender flowering tree. . . . Both, as it were, caught in that circle of unearthly light, understanding each other perfectly . . . wondering what they were to do in this one [world] with all this blissful treasure that burned in their bosoms and dropped, in silver flowers, from their hair and their hands" (131). Miss Fulton and Bertha's husband both subsequently betray Bertha, speaking to Mansfield's fearful apprehension of the consequences of such desire. Mansfield writes short stories and poems within her notebooks and diaries that imagine the pleasure and the erotic fullness of a woman's sexual desire, as well as the pain that often attends it.

Excluding or encoding references to her sexuality in her personal notebooks is not so surprising when we consider the shame her earlier escapades brought her. Ironically, adolescent women often write openly about sexual matters. Troubled by strict social condemnation for sexual escapades, they seem as yet untroubled by the pain a society—intent on punishing sex as a primal sin—can wield. In 1907, for example, Mansfield rhetorically addresses Oscar Wilde: "O Oscar! Am I peculiarly susceptible to sexual impulse?" (*Notebooks 1* 2002, 101). These early entries—prepregnancy, pre–Murry Mansfield—are most open about her sexuality, often attributing the entries to "A.W." (A Woman), presumably herself: "'Nature makes such fools of us! What is the use of liking anyone if the washerwoman can do exactly the same thing?'" (Journal 1954, 11). Her spoiled, adolescent persona speaks with disdain of lower-class women partly because she fears that sexual longing is aligned with low station and partly because she fears that such desire will reduce her own status as woman. Awareness of class and what behaviors are expected in each class shapes the diary writer's text, and sexuality has often been the forbidden text of the middle class. Mansfield, sensing the cultural taboos surrounding sexual pleasure, writes as "A.W." with an adolescent openness she later loses.

In her ironic A.W. entries she distances herself from her own intense, perhaps foolish, sexual liaisons. Yet she, in the self-absorbed, thickly detailed style of Marie Bashkirtseff, dramatizes her emotional entanglements, using language that elevates the erotic, admitting that "My mind is like a Russian novel" (*Urewera* Notebook 1978, 13). Only in these early adolescent journals does Mansfield openly admit to her bisexuality. Recently published in the *Notebooks,* those passages seem torrid examples of adolescent sexual fantasy and revelation. Recovering fact from fancy in such description is problematic: "We lay down together, still silently, she every now and then pressing me to her, kissing me, my head on her breasts, her hands round my body, stroking me, lovingly—warming me . . ." (*Notebooks* 1 2002, 101). She clearly writes in her adolescent notebooks of her early bisexual affair with a Maori girl named Maata, though she calls it "unclean." These entries are more candid and exploratory than those written later when her conception of herself as wife and writer forbid sexual explication. Although Mansfield's diary entries repress her "sexual anarchy" (Tomalin 1988, 118), she also disrupts and undermines the conventional feminine ethos of passivity she so often constructs.

Her diary entries imply that Mansfield's physical passions are fleeting, unrealized, fantasized, and uninteresting; this is simply not the whole truth. Although she often complains about her marriage to Murry and her sufferings at the hands of others, her complaints are not specifically sexual, and idealized love is her answer to everything: "Mysterious fitness of our relationship! And all those things which he does impose on my mind please me so deeply that they feel *natural* to me. It is all part of this feeling that he and I, different beyond the idea of difference, are yet an *organic* whole" (Journal 1954, 232). When Mansfield moves beyond a lyrical explanation of love and acknowledges physical passions, she fictionalizes and deflects personal engagement by using the third-person pronoun. In one such entry titled "The Blow," a fictional man comes "like a blow on her heart—for . . . 'This—,' tightly, quickly, he caught her up into his arms" (Journal 1954, 153). This diary entry may have been a practice version for the story "The Wind Blows," where Matilda's music lesson with Mr. Bullen excites her sexual awareness. Later in her own room she thinks, "The wind, the wind. It's frightening to be here in her room by herself. The bed, the mirror . . . it's the bed that is frightening. There it lies, sound asleep . . ." (*Bliss* 1920, 141). Although the journal entry and the story share the imagery of wind as desire, the similarity ends there. Perhaps "The Wind Blows" prepares another fiction Mansfield never wrote, or perhaps it is personal text, coded for a diary.

Reality and fantasy as well as fiction and autobiography collapse when Mansfield relegates tales of sexual encounter to fictional stories written within her notebooks. This method tempts readers to suspend judgment, to deflect criticism. This impulse to cover the personal joins the writer's project to fictionalize and fantasize in stories: "For women, borders—of ego, genre, discipline, geography—are made to be crossed" (Diane P. Freedman in Podnieks 2000, 68). Fictions within the diary allow Mansfield to blur the parameters of fiction and autobiography, disguising a sexuality at odds with convention. Trapped by her own course and the judgment of others, Mansfield deflects in fiction and role playing. When she cannot speak of the low and carnivalesque, she creates characters who do, allowing her the freedom to speak her desire while remaining hidden from readers' condemnation.

Sensing that Murry cannot acknowledge the complexity of his wife's sexuality, she evades. Without access to the complete *Notebooks,* with their sexualized poems and fictions, Alpers somewhat erroneously calls "her only explicit statement anywhere on the subject of sexual relations" (1980, 316) the letter Mansfield writes to Murry about her cousin Elizabeth's lack of sexual desire: "I sometimes wonder whether the act of surrender is not the greatest of all—the highest. It 'needs' real humility and at the same time an absolute belief in one's own essential freedom . . . it is *pure risk.* That is true for me as a human being and as a writer" (KM to JMM, November 7, 1920). Equating sexuality to freedom and to writing, Mansfield still represses expression of it in her *Journal.* Her unwillingness to "risk" sexual articulation points to the self-censor that prevents overt articulation of the forbidden. It also points to her awareness of Murry as audience.

Mansfield's journal writing often favors the "imaginary" because her fictional fragments provide the raw material for her work, what she most prizes and most candidly shares for examination and judgment by Murry, a hardly impartial audience. Mansfield pretends to willingly submit to Murry's dominance, forcing her to censor the pen that writes a sexual presence. When the writer is a woman/wife/artist and the reader is a male/husband/critic, his judgment is a crucial consideration. In one outpouring of anger during a separation, Mansfield writes more spontaneously and emotionally than is her usual method. But even in the outpouring she despairs: "If one wasn't so afraid—why should I be—these [diary entries] aren't going to be read by Bloomsbury *et Cie* . . ." (*Notebooks* 2 2002, 182).

As the specter of an audience—particularly Murry—appears, Mansfield hesitates and wavers in diary fragments. Such entries deflate Mansfield's surface positions. She sometimes prefaces a criticism of Murry with a statement of her loyalty, perhaps to disarm him, perhaps to take away her statement's sting: "There is the inexplicable fact that I love my typical English husband. I do lament that he is not warm, ardent, eager, full of quick response, careless, spendthrift of himself, vividly alive, *high-spirited*. But it makes no difference to my love. But the lack of these qualities in his country I HATE—" (Journal 1954, 158–59). If the list of complaints were not so long, so revealing of Mansfield's disgust with Murry's values, we could rely on the love she posits for him. Surely the hate she deflects to England she directs to Murry as well. As this entry shows, Mansfield's restructuring of selves and attitudes in her journal does not altogether mask rage and rebellion. It undermines her fantasies of idyllic love and marriage. In using such strategies, she protects the sensitive, creative, conventional woman that she longs to be. Her diary pages record her efforts to appease a man who wants more than she can give: "It's like his Why is lunch late? As though I had but to wave my hand and the banquet descended. But doesn't that prove how happy he would have been with a real WIFE!" (Journal 1954, 148).

As Brett said of Mansfield, "Her great delight was a game she played of being someone else. . . . She would act the part completely until she even got herself mixed up as to who and what she was" (Boddy 1988, 62). Role-playing in her diary deflects the reader's gaze, allowing pretenses and covers. She recreates selves to inhabit conventional centers. She writes both to love Murry and undermine him, to question convention and bend to conventional restrictions: "I thought of Jack . . . within reach—within call. I remembered there was a time when this thought was a distraction. . . . It took away from my power to work. . . . I, as it were, made him my short story" (Journal 1954, 233). Professing her love, she also notes the effect an attention-demanding man has on a woman writer; the man instead of the art becomes the center of the project, heresy to Mansfield.

At nineteen Mansfield writes on the "bogey" of socially inscribed love: "It is the hopelessly insipid doctrine that love is the only thing in the world taught, hammered into women, from generation to generation . . ." (37). The mature Mansfield also calls love's expectation a "bogey," the name she reserved for Murry in their life together. She obviously recognizes the enemy as "Bogey," whether Murry or love, even as she acknowledges its enticing entanglements.

Mansfield foregrounds her dependence on the conventional and romanticized forms of love in her personal journal narratives and relegates her critique to the vast number of fictional fragments and narratives within her notebooks. Not surprisingly, her published fiction thematically depicts romantic love as exploiting women. Interestingly, her fiction often blames "love," not the men women love, for unhappiness. Her creation of Linda in "Prelude," a woman whom marriage and children did not serve, allows Mansfield space to portray her mother fictionally and permits expression of her own doubts about culture's expectation of women. In thinking of her husband, Linda critiques the uneasy balance of affection and power that traditional marriage promotes: "For she was really quite fond of him; . . . If only he wouldn't jump at her so. He was too strong for her. There were times when . . . she just had not screamed at the top of her voice: 'You are killing me. . . . I have had three great lumps of children already . . .'" (*Bliss and Other Stories* 1920, 62). Mansfield herself echoes Linda's despair when she says in her *Journal,* "I am become— Mother. I don't care a *rap* for people. I shall always love Jack and be his wife but I couldn't get back to that anguish—joy . . ." (1954, 184). Mansfield's marriage to Murry disappoints her, yet she makes childish and peevish complaints and rebuttals of his criticism in the notebooks. Only her fiction powerfully expresses her ideological critique.

## Shifting Audience: Shifting Text

The 1914 notebooks destabilize Mansfield's conventional-wife persona as she records her passion for Francis Carco and what Murry calls their "stupid and deeply-disappointing" affair (quoted in Meyers 2002, 111). In several entries she writes of longing for their intimacy and sexual engagement. In August, dissatisfied with Murry, she desires another lover to "nurse me, love me, hold me, comfort me" (Journal 1954, 61). These entries so boldly express the need for another man that they are startling in Mansfield's journal; she habitually reconstructs all reference to sexual desire in oblique but romanticized entries focused on Murry.[8] But the 1914 entries record her obsession with Carco's letters and finally her excitement in traveling to France to be with him. She even writes overtly of lovemaking: "And F. quite naked, making up the fire with the tiny brass poker—so natural, so beautiful—and then he was gone (Journal 1954, 75) . . . the act of love seemed somehow quite incidental, we talked so much . . ." (78), playing down her sexual response, emphasizing intimacy. She thus simultaneously confronts and conforms to traditional moral and ethical teachings that urge women to nurture men but repress sexual desire.

Mansfield wants to please both herself and others by her virtue but is sexually promiscuous. Her biographer Meyers, however, believes that she was faithful to Murry after her affair with Carco ended in 1915. She longs to escape the confines of a life too alien and too dull, longs to do "the other thing with moderate care" since "Jack is not really interested" (*Notebooks* 1 2002, 287). Even though Mansfield dreams of another lover and certainly risks much in her flirtations and brief affairs with other men, the idealized lover did not materialize for Katherine, as he or she seldom does, at least never for long. But the articulation of the fantasy, the specifics of her longings for Carco, and at least one rather overt expression of bisexual desire point to Mansfield's refusal, at least in 1914, to be subordinated to a dominant male ethic that represses sexual choice in women.

An overt reference to her ongoing friendship with Ida Baker, or L.M., as she calls her, a mostly present companion to Mansfield, similarly disrupts the idealized-wife presentation of herself, illustrating a further subversion of traditional sexual strictures. In a section titled "Toothache Sunday" in March 1914, Mansfield writes of L.M.: "And as I tucked her up, she was so touching— . . . that it was easy to stoop to kiss her, not as I usually do, one little half-kiss, but quick loving kisses such as one delights to give a tired child. 'Oh!' she sighed, 'I have dreamed of this' . . . I could not kiss her lips. Ah, how I long to talk about it sometimes . . .'" (Journal 1954, 53–54). L.M.'s sexual longings and Mansfield's tenderness and simultaneous revulsion are rarely addressed in the diaries, though Mansfield sometimes refers to L.M. as "wife." Mansfield's journal entries often mention her need to have L.M. work for her or do favors for her, her sense of the inevitability of L.M.'s presence. Her journal illustrates a pattern of criticism, not the attachment that she displays in her letters to L.M.[9] Given Murry and L.M.'s coolness toward each other, Mansfield probably uses the fluctuating narratives of letter and journal to conceal her mixed loyalties. Murry, after all, read her journal. "Her . . . merciless playing off of Ida Baker against Murry was surely an aspect of her deep-rooted propensity to bisexuality" (Hankin 1983, 38). Murry's jealousy dictates that Mansfield must gloss over such feelings. On January 1, 1919, Mansfield writes: "J. was very chagrined because I thought of [L.M.], and not only of him. That rather spoiled his New Year. We ought to have clasped . . ." (Journal 1954, 154). Mansfield's regard for Murry's feelings prevent articulation of her own.

Constrained by cultural codes, Mansfield for the most part hides her sexual ambivalence in her notebooks though her practice fictions certainly play with sexual themes, occasionally even bisexual themes. In 1920 two fragments equate the kissing of a woman with "kissing a church candle" and kissing "nuns who have prayed all night in cold churches" (Journal 1954, 202, 220). Both fictions begin "I kissed her" and end with the other woman's disparaging the speaker, once directly, once by calling on the "Father." The first entry Mansfield calls "Wickedness," the next "The Kiss," and both seem to equate loving a woman to both the spiritual and the wicked. She ends her second attempt at writing this vignette by saying, "(But still I haven't said what I wanted to say)" (221). Mansfield makes these ambiguous fictions impossible to locate in terms of sexual or spiritual philosophy, though their ambiguity may be her failure to say what she wishes.

Women-identified writers, lesbians, and by extension bisexuals, "although silenced . . . [are] not altogether voiceless, for according to the logic of Foucault's repressive hypothesis, what is prohibited returns in new and resignifying forms, shaping and recontextualizing the manifest content of the text" (Loftus 1977, 36). Mansfield, caught up in the compulsory heterosexuality of western culture, still occasionally taunts Murry with her bisexuality. At a time when she wavers between leaving him and staying with him, she writes from Paris: "[T]here arrived 'du monde' including a very lovely young woman, married & *curious*—blonde—passionate. We danced together" (Boddy 1988, 45). She quickly retracts this affront to his masculinity by writing him the next day of her intense longing for the conventional life of "a chinese nurse with green trousers and two babies who rush at me and clasp my knees" (ibid., 46). Mansfield's need to both provoke and please Murry promotes her vacillations, moving her from scenes of transgression to scenes of surrender.

Mansfield's adolescent diaries and her *Notebooks* of 1914 and early 1915 exhibit her boldest depiction of her sexual nonconformity. During these years Murry was not the audience of her journal, and her feeling of reckless sexuality left her rather unconcerned about future readers. Although they often separated for various reasons, they never did sever their marriage. After May 1915 Mansfield's entries say little either of her sexual nature or of any liaisons that follow. Murry once again becomes her audience. "But Jack & My work they are all I think of" (*Notebooks* 2 2002, 125). Though she reflects on the past and their relationship is marred by separation, she sees Jack as the center of her emotional life, or so her diary implies.

## Resisting Her Audience: Foregrounding Change

One strategy Mansfield uses to configure the contradictions within her identity is emphasis on change. The diaries foreground fluctuations of method, of feeling, of mood, of place, of health. By constantly shifting the papers and notebooks, the subject matter, and the emotional temper of the diary, she not only explores reality rather prosaically in the modernist traditions of refraction and distortion but also resists containment by any audience anxious to accuse and control. By switching narratives she refuses appropriation by Jack or by the English.

Her exile from man, woman, culture, God—partly self-willed, partly beyond her control—assists her in resisting containment. Mansfield's ill health and restlessness dictated that she move from place to place in search of warmth, stability, health, and doctors. Banishment protects her from others, but she consequently mourns the loss. Textually, too, she fragments versions of herself, allowing glimpses, then drawing away from exposure. Such fluctuating narrative postures are typical of diaries written over time and are particularly striking in Mansfield's notebooks: "I can never be Jack's lover again" (Journal 1954, 86) shifts to "Jack is my first thought" (129). The shifting advances and retreats typify Mansfield's dealing with others and her confrontations with cultural pressure. Mansfield's widely divergent responses to her audiences may be her attempts to manipulate the feelings of others as well as to resist their values.

To simultaneously appease and defy, Mansfield "conceals" much of her interaction with others but breaks the silence at times to let her anger and jealousy speak. She scathingly criticizes Murry's relationship with Dorothy Brett, for example. She uses her diary to complain to him of his neglect and to beg for his loyalty: "J. let fall this morning the fact that he *had* considered taking rooms in D.'s house this winter. . . . Was their relationship friendship? Oh no! He kissed her. . . . Who could count on such a man! I am simply *disgusted* to my very soul" (Journal 1954, 208). Playing the betrayed wife rather than acknowledging the adulterer in herself, she fears others' appropriation. She notes, for example, "M is too jealous. He is like a hawk over his possessions" (150). Therefore, Mansfield tells tales of self as she wishes her audience to read them. And because of her uneasy relationship to others as well as to her own sense of self, the tone of the journal changes in response to mood swings ranging from despairing to euphoric.[10]

The emotional Mansfield nearly always gives way to the intellectual woman capable of writing fiction that "dramatizes the interconnection between the desire to escape from reality and the desire to change it" (New 1999, 110). Sometimes a feminist sensibility more apparent in her fiction slips through her obsessions with love, Jack, illness, and art. Mansfield struggles with the roles of man and woman and the importance of those roles in creating the larger culture. Within the diary text, part of a poem called the "butterfly" depicts the precarious nature between the masculine and feminine, the fragile and the aggressive:

But just at that moment
a dirty-looking dog,
its mean tail
between its legs,
came loping down the lane
It just glanced aside
at the butterfly—did not bite
Just gave a feeble snap
and ran further.
But she was dead. (Journal 1954, 152)

The vulnerability of woman meets the "mean tail between" the legs of man, though her "it" seems to render the dog genderless, giving the poem a neutral stance. Mansfield's underlying themes of terror and alienation in a man's world politicizes the poem. In letters she verifies her explorations of gender, showing a wit and sharpness not so evident in the diary entries. In 1919 her white-and-black cat "Charles Chaplin" had kittens. She writes Woolf about the surprising turn of events: "He would only lie still when I stroked his belly and (I) said: 'It's all right, old chap. It's bound to happen to a man sooner or later'" (Meyers 2002, 183). Mocking gendered constructions, she enjoys the theoretical stripping of male power in humorous emasculations—but only in letters, poems, and fictions—evidence enough in any case.

## Her Last Audience: Invitation to Laughter and Grief

Mansfield often breaks the tension between the personae within the notebooks and her audience with humor, thereby undercutting the intensity of another's judgment. She invites us to laugh with her most often at the tragic—and serious—progress of her illness. In her entries she uses discursive techniques designed to distance the inevitable. In 1921 a series of diary notes (marked by crosses and checks to designate future publication) seems to mock the approaching death she fears: "The red geraniums have bought the garden over my head and taken possession" is followed by "J. digs the garden as though he were exhuming a hated body or making a hole for a loved one"; a bit later "Dark Bogey is a little inclined to jump into the milk jug to rescue the fly," then finally "the champagne was no good at all . . . there was something positively malicious in the way the little bubbles hurled themselves to the rim, danced, broke . . . they seemed to be jeering at her" (*Notebooks* 2 2002, 158–64). More pointedly, a response to one of her many doctors ridicules the medical establishment that sought to control and cure her: "Saw the fool of a doctor to-day. Diddle-dum-dum-dee! Cod is the only word! Bad-in-age! Flat-ter-ie! Gal-an-ter-ie! Frogs!" (Journal 1954, 198). Her cynical humor jeers at the doctor and her own hatred.

A limerick written in July 1919 records her fear and skepticism:

"Tedious Brief Adventure of K.M."

A Doctor who came from Jamaica
Said: This time I'll mend her
or break her
I'll plug her with serum;
And if she can't bear 'em
I'll call in the next undertaker. (Journal 1954, 178)

Whether to cheer herself or Murry or subsequent audiences, these entries invite laugher and speculation: How does she feel? What is real? Who speaks? In another entry she intimates that her flippant speaker might be "'Mr. Despondency's daughter, Muchafraid [who] went through the water singing'" (Journal 1954, 166). Mansfield's attempt to make light of her illness and Murry's response to it cannot disguise her resentment and fear of death. Her humor, her satires, ditties, and reports on happy days speak to a pervasive yet often undermined optimism. They articulate an intense desire to live and an underlying dread. Mansfield, trying to alleviate the couple's horror at the progress of her illness, uses humor to invite shared laughter, not disaster.

Bravely facing death while trying to outwit its cruelty, Mansfield nevertheless finds the illness and her loss of future nearly unendurable. These lines surface throughout the last notebooks—rare but poignant: "The worst of it is I have again lost hope. I don't & can't believe this will change. I have got off the raft again and am swept here and there by the sea" ((*Notebooks* 2 2002, 326). Sometimes she creates sentimental metaphors to describe death's shadow: "The flower petals fold. They are by the sun/Forgotten. In a shadowy wood they grow/Where the dark trees keep up a to-and-fro/Shadowy waving. Who will watch them shine/When I have dreamed my dream?" (Journal 1954, 188). Mansfield encourages a shared fantasy: "Ah, darling mine," inviting Murry to join her in sardonic laughter and to dream with her as "petals fold" (ibid.). Mansfield's gentleness may have been an effort to counter her own fear and Murry's response. In another entry she angrily throws back his words:

"*[H]is* nerves, *he* wasn't made of whipcord or steel, the fruit was bitter for *him*" (Notebooks 2 2002, 179). The journal makes clear that despite both their efforts, Mansfield's dying is "difficult," as Mansfield suffers for years, moves from place to place, arranges both their travel arrangements, and tries to maintain a marriage in the face of personal tragedy.

The most moving parts of her notebooks are those entries in the last two years, so obviously written to gain Murry's admiration and to revivify their flagging spirits. "*Important.* When we begin to take our failures non-seriously, it means we are ceasing to be afraid of them. It is of immense importance to learn to *laugh at ourselves.*" Written three months before her death, Mansfield next asks quite seriously, "What remains of all those years together? . . . Who gave up and why?" (Journal 1954, 331). Feeling she should laugh, she despairs, torn between helping her "reader" get through her death and facing it honestly herself.

Trying to work out life's mystery and her own reaction to the death that stalks her, she sends her diary entries to Murry: "And when I say 'I fear'—don't let it disturb you, dearest heart" (Journal 1954, 334). The sheer number of references to illness and death belie both her flippant, disregarding dismissals and her transcending idealizations. As early as 1915 she posits a "fiery energy . . . to bear suffering" (Journal 1954, 70). When her brother Leslie dies, Mansfield mocks any fear of death, remarking: "[N]ot only am I not afraid of death—I welcome the idea of death" (Journal 1954, 86). But from 1918, when she finds the "bright red blood" from her lungs, she speaks of an intense longing to live: "How unbearable it would be to die—leave 'scraps', 'bits' . . . nothing real finished" (Journal 1954, 129). Positioning herself as writer with much to keep her busy, Mansfield staves off death for a while at least. A fiction within the diary pages speaks to her heightened sense of vulnerability. When a friend reaches out to the ill Eve, inquiring about her health, Eve "waves her away. 'Don't be too nice to me!' . . . There were tears in her eyes, her lips were trembling. 'I shall make a fool of myself if you do'" (Journal 1954, 308). We never see the weakness of tears in Mansfield's personal entries; her notebooks serve as a site for mental courage, her last hope. The enfeebling emotional character of her illness she most often places in diary fictions and fragments, not in personal entries.

She creates a text that goes on, even in the face of death. A diary is open ended, never finished, never inviting closure. Her diary records, fictionalizes, and reworks her life—becomes a hedge against death. Two months before her death she writes: "My spirit is nearly dead. My spring of life is so starved that it's just not dry. . . . Ah, I feel a little calmer already to be writing. Thank God for writing!" (Journal 1954, 332). Her last entry does not record a reconciliation with death but lists words she wanted translated into Russian so to better communicate at the Gurdjieff Institute, where she spent her last months. As an earlier journal entry states: "[W]e do not feel our own death, and write stories as though we were never going to die" (Journal 1954, 171). What Mansfield once labeled her "vile little diary" (Journal 1954, 63) provides the writer with a new story of selves that will never be finished. She cannot record her own death.

## Chapter 3

# Violet Hunt:

*Mythmaking in*
*"Her Book of Impressions"*

O nce upon a time a woman of much wit, talent, and considerable fame lived in England among a literary circle who considered her the "center" of their intellectual society. The literary greats of the late-Victorian, early-Edwardian period gathered at her home, South Lodge, in Campden Hill Road, Kensington, to talk, drink, argue, edit books, and be charmed by their hostess, Violet Hunt. Though her current biographers Joan Hardwick and Barbara Belford place Hunt at the center of the circle because of her force and talent, for nearly a century others saw her as important because of her connections to famous ancestors and the men whom she dazzled. A younger and lesser of the literary "lights," Douglas Goldring, in his *South Lodge: Reminiscences of Violet Hunt, Ford Madox Ford and the English Review Circle,* for example, begins his autobiography/biography with a flourish of name dropping, recalling Hunt as the hostess who entertained literary London: Joseph Conrad, Henry James, Cunninghame Graham, Robert Browning, Oscar Wilde, and most influentially, Ford Madox Ford (1943). Ancestral connections of Hunt and Ford likewise overshadowed Hunt's achievements, if not Ford's: Mrs. Alfred Hunt, Violet's mother; Dr. Francis Hueffer, Ford's father; Ford Madox Brown, Ford's grandfather; Matthew Arnold, Violet's family friend; Canon Greenwell, Violet's godfather and a famous archaeologist; Christina Rossetti, famous poet and Ford's aunt; and other pre-Raphaelite poets and painters of Hunt's and Ford's parents' generation. Enchantment seems to surround Violet Hunt.

In noting the influential and famous, however, we should not give short shrift to Hunt herself. In writing about Hunt, past writers emphasized the "senile decay" (Wallis diaries in Belford 1990, 276) that characterized Hunt's old age, or Ford's fame and her connection to him. Lost are her own remarkable achievements. "For though Violet had qualities Ford lacked—qualities which she managed to infuse into one of his best novels, *The Good Soldier*—he was the greater figure of the two, and she was aware of it" (Goldring 1943, xii). Hunt's most recent displacement occurs in the 1983 publication of 'her 1917 diary. Editors Robert Secor and Marie Secor titled it *The Return of the Good Soldier: Ford Madox Ford and Violet Hunt's 1917 Diary;* Hunt again is subsumed by Ford. The diary is "his" only insofar as he occupies a place in the "content" of the diary. In getting the diary published the Secors depended on Ford's fame rather than on Hunt's life and talent.

The recent Hunt biographies do better. Joan Hardwick's 1990 *Immodest Violet* looks closely at this woman with the "colourful and dynamic past" (xv), making excellent use of Hunt's fiction to intuit and explain the woman writer. In her 1990 *Violet* Barbara Belford uses newly discovered diaries to examine the woman, "Victorian vixen," and "Edwardian Egeria" (11) more completely than those previously seeking the key to Hunt's character. Yet even Belford—or her publishers—cannot resist the subtitle: : *The Story of the Irrepressible Violet Hunt and Her Circle of Lovers and Friends—Ford Madox Ford, H. G. Wells, Somerset Maugham, and Henry James..* Hunt, the hostess and mistress, enchants, overtaking her literary achievements. In many respects she herself shaped this legacy.[1]

Hunt tells her own story chiefly in relation to Ford's supremacy; her tale becomes a story of the Beast who overwhelms a willing Beauty. In *The Desirable Alien at Home in Germany,* a public travel diary written in 1911 and published in 1913, and the far more personal diaries written throughout her life, Hunt explicitly plays out her confrontations with the mythic and the real of her life with Ford Madox Ford. The *1917 Diary* provides an interesting private counterpoint to *The Desirable Alien,* cowritten with Ford and meant for immediate publication. Her *1917 Diary* was hers alone, not cowritten, yet it too focuses on Ford or his absence. These two diary narratives and the quasi-autobiographical *Zeppelin Nights* that Hunt also coauthored with Ford illustrate the way his presence and later absence as editor and audience influence Hunt. Her shaping of the texts performs the shape of the self.

## Shadowed by Ford: Living and Writing "Their" Mythology

Hunt had obviously won Ford's respect for her literary abilities when he suggested she write her travel diary/memoir, *The Desirable Alien at Home in Germany.* But Ford being Ford, he then appropriated it, adding chapters and notes, finally publishing it under both their names.[2] Her obvious adoration of him and her willingness to forward his career at the expense of her own made Hunt a more-than-Muse that Ford used to further his own reputation.

Hunt's achievement at the time she met Ford was nearly equal to his own: "She was well launched in literary England, not only as a contributor to such journals as *Black & White, Chapman's Magazine, The Venture,* and the *English Review,* but as a novelist of some merit and popularity, notably her 1908 publication of *White Rose of Weary Leaf* (Secor and Secor 1983, 14). In her lifetime Hunt wrote seventeen novels, collaborated with her mother, Margaret Hunt, on another, coauthored two more works with Ford, wrote a collection of short stories, a memoir of her life with Ford, and a biography of Elizabeth Sidall called *The Wife of Rossetti.* She made her living by writing, and the best literary journals reviewed her: the *London News, London Review,* and *The Athenaeum* (Belford 1990, 102). *The Literary World* acclaimed her as "one of the smartest dialogue writers of the day" (Goldring 1943, 5–6), and even Henry James told her she was a writer of "confirmed genius" (Belford 1990, 164). Flushed with admiration in the early days of their relationship, Ford tells Hunt "they will make a 'goodly couple,' beside whom such literary lights as Shaw and Galsworthy will appear but 'slow-witted fools'" (Secor and Secor 1983, 15). Certainly in the early days of their relationship Hunt saw herself as an author equal to Ford.

As their uncertain relationship progressed and she permitted his Edwardian masculinity to dominate her adapted Victorian femininity, she craved a position of "wife." Hunt's take-charge willfulness and ironic concern for social acceptance confronted Ford's waffling nature and his "German instinct for games" (Belford 1990, 154). Caught in the destructive crossfire of restrictive ideology and sexual individuality, Hunt felt trapped. Marriage would, she thought, release her. Her role as conventional wife/nurturer was doomed.

Responding to her obsession to possess and be possessed by Ford, Hunt writes texts both fictional and personal, public and private, shaping Ford into a hero/husband and herself into a supplicant/wife. In turning their lives into narrative, Hunt duplicates bourgeois social formations in the diaries and *Zeppelin Nights.* She thus participates textually in constructing her own illusions and cultural myths. The tensions within these texts point to Hunt's knowledge—conscious or unconscious—of their precarious nature, but she is caught. Thus she writes from within social and class paradigms, though often subversively. When Ford turns to Stella Bowen and others for his nurture, Hunt puts into play the personae of the wronged woman and the abusive cad in her *1917 Diary* and autobiography, *I Have This to Say* (1926). Ultimately the early myths Hunt creates about their "marriage," his "genius," and her "romance" undermine her as surely as Ford's own manipulations and betrayals.

Certainly all her autobiographical depictions and narratives alienated her from literary London, an audience less concerned with truth than propriety. Ironically, Ford's fictional renderings of their life together received accolades, then as now. "[Ford] depicted and transformed his relations with Hunt in . . . novels not because he shared her need to defend her conduct against criticism by the outside world, but because he was an artist who needed to reconstruct reality in ways that allowed him to accept it and himself" (Secor and Secor 1983, 28). Hunt's own artistic reconstructions are seen differently. The woman whose vitality and unconventionality inspired Henry James to call her the "Purple Patch" and the "Improper Person of Babylon" (Secor 1986, 32) simply undermined the ethos of feminine literary restraint, then and now.

Early rebellions and refusals to conform to sexual restrictions make her involvement with the married Ford unsurprising. Her scripting their future in romantic and conventional terms is even more so. Known for her conversational brilliance and "nasty wit" (Belford 1990, 13), even before Ford, Hunt's flamboyance and personality explicitly confronted conformist constructions of femininity: "Popular rumour credited her with being very French and fast, a fashionable and faintly vicious blue-stocking" who in her girlhood was called by friends "'the immodest Violet'" (Goldring 1943, 42–43). In order to modify these contradictory depictions to win Ford's hand in marriage, Hunt invented a new persona for herself, one Ford could dominate. This persona masquerades in the costumes of respectability and conformity, making an uncomfortable and fictional space for Hunt. Although Ford appropriated much of the textual Violet Hunt and consumed her emotional interest until her death, a more vital Hunt still manages to maintain a subtext of rebellion and refusal that threatens the continuing masculine assumptions about her work and her life.

## Ford as Subject and Audience: The Context of The Desirable Alien and the 1917 Diary

Although Violet Hunt kept diaries from 1882 in which she first recorded Oscar Wilde's now legendary proposal of marriage to her in 1879, none of them except the *1917 Diary* and *The Desirable Alien* have been published, perhaps because Hunt wrote these two diary texts during the years of her involvement with Ford.

Ford entered Violet's adult life in 1907. She was forty-five, eleven years older than the dapper Ford. Through a series of social visits and literary collaborations surrounding *The English Review* they became intimate, Ford telling her by May 1909 that "he was in love with her" (Secor and

Secor 1983, 13). The liaison was vastly complicated; Ford was already married to Elsie Martindale Hueffer,[3] the mother of two of his daughters. Elsie was ill and indisposed to entertain any of his literary friends; Ford was miserable and "most susceptible when he was unhappy" (Mizener 1971, 177). Goldring saw Elsie as "a fanatical Catholic—not of the gay, tolerant, 'merrie' England type, but more on the lines of 'bloody Mary'" (1943, 22); recent biographers more generously depict Elsie as "fretful and unhappy," somewhat tolerant, even of Ford's adulteries. Nevertheless, the "marriage was under great strain" (Hardwick 1990, 39). He was miserable and set out upon a pattern he was to repeat with various women: "Ford seemed able to stay in love for five years, and drag the relationship on for a further five, and no more" (Kavanagh 1996, 54).

He wanted Hunt as his "wife," but Elsie refused to give him an English divorce and demanded that he pay support for her and the children, something that Ford did only by the monetary largess of Hunt, at that time a wealthy woman. For the rest of his life Ford took a "wife" many times (four he lived with, several others with whom he had affairs). On the "wife's" income, he lived with each for many years, only to leave her for another when he became restless. Only Elsie legally married him under British law. For a time Hunt, as his mistress, happily pretended friendship.

Hunt's "life crashed" (Belford 1990, 168) when Elsie "caught" Hunt and Ford as they left the train together after a trip to France. Though Hunt swears they were "chaperoned to the hilt, or the nines!" (Hunt 1926, 84), she acknowledges her desire to marry, to gain a respectable place in London society: "One had to take . . . all the care in the world to prevent one's flopping, feminine, vulnerable character from getting smirched. . . . Marriage? At that moment, standing bewildered, worried, and frightened, I would have taken cover—married anyone!" (ibid., 86). Although their relationship became a scandal, Ford convinced her that their marriage was merely a matter of time, of law, of citizenship. Perhaps foolishly, Hunt felt hopeful. Early-twentieth-century women's fiction exhorts women to give everything up to love: "If love is true and pure, it will 'endureth all things . . . [and] never faileth.' If it does fail, it isn't true love. . . . These stories all encourage idealistic faith in the power of 'true love'" (Searles and Mickish 1984, 270–71). In 1912, frustrated and furious with English law that kept him married to Elsie and financially bereft, Ford fled to Germany in the hope of procuring German citizenship and a German divorce. Ford, then Hueffer, had many kin in Germany and was told that a year of residency would win him a German divorce. Hunt, eager and in "love," willingly pretended to be Ford's lawful wife even before the questionable German/French ceremony took place, if it ever did.

Ford told *The Daily Mirror* that he "had married Hunt in Germany," explaining that he "was able to take advantage of German law because he was heir to large Prussian estates" (Secor and Secor 1983, 18). Elsie threatened to sue the paper and a retraction was printed. But real scandal erupted furiously in 1913, when *The Throne* pictured "Mrs. Alfred Hunt, joint authoress with her daughter, Miss Violet Hunt (Mrs. Ford Madox Hueffer) . . . of a forthcoming novel, . . . 'The Governess'" (in Belford 1990, 29). Elsie sued. *The Throne* refused to retract the name of Mrs. Ford Madox Hueffer in relation to Hunt. This suit "would bring to a costly and humiliating conclusion Hunt's and Ford's pretensions that they were legitimately married" (Cheng 1989, 535).

The marriage's validity was of overwhelming importance to Hunt. Her family withheld funds and visits from her niece Rosamund because of Aunt Violet's "giddy and godless life" (Secor and Secor 1983, 17). Her longing for marriage went much deeper, however. The codified representations of love and marriage of the early twentieth century legitimated only women who were married; the unmarried woman held stigmatized roles of spinster/waste or fallen-woman/threat. Hunt, "fallen" after several love affairs with married men, craved love and respectability. An unsympathetic Goldring writes: "*Married!* That was the dream of Violet's life, to be able, at last, to parade a husband" (1943, 81).

Hunt's *Desirable Alien* records their mythical marriage, her self-division as wife/writer, and the couple's desperate ploy to escape English law yet retain the trappings of civility and moral repute (1913). But when confronted by a vicious Elsie, public exposure in English courts, and an increasing anti-German sentiment as politics began to change, Ford and Hunt came back to England, turning their backs on Germany. "In all probability, in a fit of exasperation, Ford exclaimed: 'Hang it all. What does it matter? Let's go home and say we've been married'" (Goldring 1943, 97). When the *Throne* debacle exposed them, Ford let the issue of their "marriage" die; Hunt fought bitterly but was no match for the system, especially given the lack of any authenticating papers. Rather than join her in the fight for their "marriage," Ford lost interest in the law and its dictates and simply lived with Hunt until boredom and The Great War brought him his escape.

Her life had changed, her dreams had shattered. "The story was so tangled and the uproar so intense that no one ever found out what really happened . . ." (King 1995, 91). Hunt always insisted she and Ford had married, though she says in *I Have This to Say,* "to vouchsafe the whole truth at this juncture would, I am told, land me in prison for three months without the option of a fine" (1926, v). Her close friend Rebecca West contended that Hunt and Ford were married in France, but Hunt would only finally say she thought she "was in law—his wife. I have been rudely taught since that it was not so—that I never did become a legal wife" (ibid., vi). For Ford as for his fictional heroes "the distinction between marriage and adultery, wife and mistress vanishes and we discover yet again the anguished confrontation between a weak hero, unequal to the demands of the woman he loves, and a frustrated wife/mistress whose frustration brings her to act as a soul-destroying fury" (Webb 1977–1978, 592). Even though the "hero" is devastated, the pattern savagely shatters a "wife/mistress." She must live with the social reverberations of airing her complaints, what society considers taunting exhibitionism.[4]

This turn of events ultimately brought Hunt to the year 1917, a year in which she wrote a diary vastly different in style, content, and tone from the 1912 *Alien* diary. But as different as these two "life-texts" are, Hunt wrote both exposing the ambivalent role of a woman who supports, yet subverts, prevailing western cultural mythologies. And an audience was on her mind.

## Victorian Conventions: The Travel Diary

*The Desirable Alien,* ignored by all but a few scholars, has been called an "impressionistic book about Germany" (J. Miller 1990, 211), an "extravagant panegyric to Germany and German life" (Cheng 1989, 535), and "a very satisfactory book about a country" (Ford, 1913a, vii). Hunt refers to it only once in her memoir, noting that in the couple's "escape" from Germany in 1913 she had a copy with her: "My new book—all about Germany!" (ibid., 249). But *The Desirable Alien* is not exclusively a documentary text about a foreign country; Hunt wrote it in the fashion of Victorian travel diaries, making it a text of exploration: of a foreign land, of a Victorian honeymoon of sorts, of the self.

Victorian women's travel diaries "help them visualize themselves and their place in the world differently" (Huff 1988, 119); when it records a honeymoon, it records the couple's "transformation that was both highly visible and deeply private" (Michie 2001, 230). The travel diary's public nature shapes the experience as well as the text. Because diaries do not depend on narrow and predictable generic conventions, as the writer and audiences change so do the forms, the emphases, and the narratives. To many English women, England stood for "restraint" and their travels stood for "freedom" (Huff 1988, 123–24); for Hunt, writing as mistress/wife, this is particularly true. Hunt clearly followed the conventions of Victorian women's travel diaries, deciding for the most part on personalized narrative rather than rigidly impersonal conventions. *The Desirable Alien* is a circulating discourse, moving in and out of subjective diary modes to objective documentary rhetoric, placing Ford variously as audience, cowriter, and amender.

Hunt records an idyllic trek in a land giving her an anti-biographical new chance for love and a new persona as a married woman. Only in antiautobiographical subtexts does she present and cover over personal experiences and struggles—hence, a "book all about Germany." She envisions a vast audience: her "husband," whom she wished to charm and win forever, and the German and British public as well. She entertains her audiences with much wit and zest, recording images, responding to events, reflecting on what it means to be a woman living "abroad." Necessarily, Hunt, a woman of much candor, must write for herself as well: "For I am . . . a non-sifter of evidence, hasty, liking to scorch through to my end, and within, egregiously, incredibly sincere" (1926, 8). *The Desirable Alien* taxed Hunt's sincerity, caught in the whirlwind of quasi-marriage, English gossip, and German law.

Beginning with her "Introduction: How One Becomes an Alien," Hunt throws herself headlong into the project of becoming "German," being a "wife," and supporting Ford's endeavors. From the start she perceives herself as an "alien," traveling throughout the country as a tourist while pretending to a preordained and fated German soul. "My Germanhood was obviously Fate" (1913a, 5). She inhabits no real place in Germany, roving everywhere with Ford, soaking up German character, and writing a travel journal to please others. Her emotional investment in Ford, and thus his project, triggers her eager performance. Presumably at Ford's suggestion, she writes the book as evidence of their sincere love of Germany and civilized marriage. Clearly, Ford and Hunt use the book to seduce German authorities into granting Ford citizenship and a subsequent divorce. "The book, in fact, tries to present an endearing image of Ford and Hunt as a neo-connubial couple, he stolidly lecturing in a bullish Germanic way and she lovingly and domestically trying to please him" (Cheng 1989, 536). But outspoken and rather uninhibited, Hunt resiliently lives housed in the new self-promulgated domestic and passive Hausfrau; she writes both personas in the journal, weaving an entertaining, subtly subversive self-text within the political narrative.

Ford's agenda for the book is purposeful, political, public; certainly he uses the quasi-journal format for his own rhetorical ends. He says in the preface: "So you have here a book of impressions. If I did not like it I should not be writing this introduction; if I had not very much admired the kindly, careless, inaccurate, and brilliantly precise mind of the author, I presume the book would never have been written" (x). Ford's affectionate condescension introduces what he feels is his superior grasp of German history and character, telling readers that Hunt's "first impressions" perhaps "colour[ed]" her information and response (viii). In a sense he excuses her observations as mere journal entries, though he notes that Hunt's impressions "are formed" from childhood teachings by German governesses and "the good Grimm!" (ix). He interjects his masculine difference in assessing culture, describing how educated gentlemen form their views: "But, were I writing a book about Germany, I think that I should see first what Bismarckism, Nietzscheism, and agnosticism of the Jatho type have made of the land of the good Grimm" (ibid.). Thus he gives her views a fairy-tale status that contrasts with his own informed versions. If she errs or offends, naivety is the cause. By reminding readers repeatedly in the preface that this is a book only of Hunt's impressions, especially first impressions, Ford addresses her work to heighten its role as travel narrative, deflecting its propagandist characteristics and interjecting his own agenda: "[T]here is no such thing as Germany as distinct from England . . . people are just people" (xii). He thus places himself as an international humanist that, given his Hueffer name and German kinsmen, allows him to be as German as English, no traitor to either country. To that extent *The Desirable Alien* is indeed a panegyric, a propaganda piece written to gain personal ends, Ford's first—secondarily and romantically, Hunt's.

## *The Desirable Alien:* Ford's Control of Audience

In 1913 Chatto and Windus published *The Desirable Alien: At Home in Germany,* described as "by Violet Hunt with Preface and Two Additional Chapters by Ford Madox Hueffer." Playing to readers in England and Germany, the title describes not two aliens but one, presumably Hunt, Ford the one "at home in Germany." Each chapter focuses on a trip to a German site and responds to it, highlighting the author's surprises about German culture and history. Hunt's engaging titles capture reader interest: "Beer Gardens v. Bear Gardens," "Grand Dukes and Gipsies," "Bones, Babies, and Anabaptists." Others more plainly follow travel book conventions: "Celle," "Trier," or even "Lions and Lace Curtains." Hunt's easily defined chapters promote the text as a traditional travel journal. She organizes by place, rather than date, the twenty-two chapters dividing her year in Germany. Hunt, following diary conventions of her precursors, does not foreground her alien status in both England and Germany. She adopts the woman traveler's discursive tradition of correcting her own "misconceptions and those of others by comparing and contrasting two ways of life" (Huff 1988, 121). Without really betraying the country of her birth, she thus follows Ford's plans for her textual liaison with Germany. He leaves it to Hunt to write charming, domestic observations and entertaining, humorous pieces about their exploits in their new country. Her ironic wit often leads her dangerously close to satire, but Ford's intrusions into the text provide correctives to her "nonsense" (Hunt 1913a, 175 n), enabling him to negotiate textually the duplicity inherent in their project—to be both English and German, unmarried and married.

Ford's two contributions, Chapter VII ("Utopia") and Chapter XVI ("How It Feels to Be Members of Subject Races"), formally explore his politics and personal philosophy. He choreographed the sequence of his chapters to position serious issues of political morality within pages made comic by "a slight, wiry, lanky, ex-Englishwoman" whose "spirit fainted many a time, where a stout, heavily-clad German Frau leads cheerfully" (81). Ford, in his "Utopia," seriously imagines political and cultural perfection, hoping to "exhaust the intellectual and artistic sides of our community" (49), and then acknowledges that "such a town is impossible . . . unthinkable. And yet from this town we are writing" (51).

In "How It Feels to Be Members of Subject Races" Ford analyzes the causes of Prussian domination and reservedly pretends to respect and understand its heroic, dominating culture and warlike stance.[5] Thus, Ford pretends to honor the "superiority" of German institutions over those of the British while philosophically honoring colonial dominance. Lest others suspect his motives, he surrounds this propagandist tract with Hunt's more personal and ironic observations about "the domestic life of nations" (52). It is Hunt who voices their differences in apprehending the culture and history of Germany: "And all the way from Hildesheim, Joseph Leopold and I were thinking, from totally different standpoints, of the great and important town we were about to visit" (220). Hunt's charm mitigates the politically charged agendas of Ford, making them more palatable to both English and German readers.

Less palatable today are Ford's footnotes, his exertions of control over Hunt's text. He corrects her errors of perception, contradicts her observations, and rides roughshod over her book; the lengthy notes seem to intrude upon the text itself. "Ford is an ubiquitous and God-like presence throughout" (Cheng 1989, 536). In the first few chapters Ford writes infrequent and short notes, but by the text's end, when Violet increasingly critiques her impressions of Germany, many of Ford's footnotes are longer than her original narrative. Even though he often softens his intrusions by humor, he obviously prefers his impressions to hers, retelling her narrative from his own point of view or calling into question her version of events. When Hunt, for example, expresses astonishment at signboards bearing the words "Only for Old Ladies," "Verboten to Old Ladies," and "reserved for Cavaliers," Ford remarks in a footnote, "I do not believe that these notice boards ever existed. Our author was probably hypnotized into seeing them by the English belief that such things exist in Germany" (1913a, 268).

Ford's defense of Germany at Hunt's expense furthers his political agenda. And even though he injects ironic humor into the text, in doing so he denies Hunt the authority of her own voice. When, for example, she notes the poor repair of German monuments and the shoddy way the Germans treat their ex-military men, saying "That is the way they save the Government's money in Germany" (262), Ford footnotes his assertion that "It is the way they do it in England, too" (262), adding a full paragraph on governmental systems. His footnotes assert his "superior" censorious place in her journal. His pandering to Germany's political power may have prompted him to gloss her text to undermine her acute observations that readers could have perceived as anti-German. When Hunt says, "All my days in this land are rounded off by a silence—the silence of a German forest" (123), we must consider that her own muffling by Ford must have been equally hard to bear: "I am always afraid of offending Joseph Leopold's Catholic susceptibilities" (107). Though she makes this remark within a humorous context, Hunt often bore the brunt of Ford's "susceptibilities." As "Joseph Leopold," Ford served as both audience and intruder in Hunt's text, soliciting her desire, promoting her narrative, forcing her surrender to his controlling consciousness. His forceful presence leads Hunt to rhetorical moves that affect both the form and the content of the diary text.

Unlike Virginia Woolf's diary or Katherine Mansfield's lifelong journal, Hunt's *Desirable Alien* follows a tradition of short, spontaneous travel diaries often meant for publication. The "union of the universal and the personal" (Kirchhoff 1990, 337) imbues much Victorian autobiography with a heightened sense of responding to public commonalities, the audience visible. Though the performance may be subtle, from its outset *The Desirable Alien* was planned with plural audiences in mind, complicating Hunt's ability to tell her tales. It called upon her powers to structure experience enigmatically to please whom she could without relinquishing her own narrative pleasure.

## The German Audience: Praise and Politics

Hunt gives obvious attention to her German audience, referring to "my readers," in the pro-German context of her first chapter, "How One

Becomes an Alien." She describes to her readers the German vineyards who "are going to induct me into the sacred and mysterious rites of German citizenship" (16) and defines her writing task as "writing a book about Germany" (80). Desirous of convincing German authorities of her own and Ford's sincerity of purpose in becoming German citizens, Hunt writes openly of their pleasure in German citizenship: "In our own principality, so I am told by Joseph Leopold, his name is a name of awe; here he is apt to get casually designated as 'a German Princeling' or 'some Serenity or other'" (4). She adulates certain German institutions and vistas, reveling in their excellence. The Wirtschaftsgarten she calls "reasonable," "utilitarian," and "poetical" (65); "The Kur" is "that great German institution" (89); trains in Germany glide "swiftly and sweetly (106); the wine country is "a great green landscape that lay beneath the sky like a jewel. . . . It was pure religion" (309).

Her hyperbolic praise complies with Ford's purpose of the book, the seduction of German authority. She plays to a rising nationalistic and sentimental vision of Germany; through humor and irony, however, she manages to avoid writing propagandistic essays such as those Ford included. For example, she writes of viewing a parade of "smart officers of My nationality" on her first day as a "German," saying, "but thank God—I am advised to thank God—I need not call myself a Prussian, though, perforce, the Kaiser—a 'sacred' Prussian—has constituted himself my First War Lord" (4). She draws on a tradition of women travelogue writers, focusing on her "odyssey" in Germany, what Mary Wollstonecraft calls "the incidental occurrences, the strange things that may possibly occur on the road" (1967, 9). Hunt's seeming spontaneity deflects the imagined German audience's suspicions about the sycophantic nature of the narrative as she urges German magistrates to note their superior culture through the eyes of a new and rather naive narrator.

Such playing to German audiences depends not only on her adulation of Germany but also on her deprecation of the inferior land, institutions, and people she and Ford left. An Englishman is likely to be a "tricksy, moody genius" (Hunt 1913a, 29) and have "weak gastric juices" (40). She quotes George Meredith's opinion of the dullness in the English caused by "their sports, their fierce feastings, and their oppositions to ideas" (44) and questions whether it is the "restless Celtic elements in the English population . . . that has unsettled it" (69). Long descriptions of German meals often end with allusions to "maimed" (164) British cooking; German architecture is practical and beautiful, English architecture built only "for pretty" (130). She damns England, and by extension she praises Germany: "I am glad to think that the Puritan spirit in England, which vetoes colour, charm, gaiety, and all attempts at beauty . . . cannot prevent the gas-lamp's flare, however dreary" (78). The "colour" and "charm" of Germany needs no such faint and false light, or so Hunt implies. However, in her later memoir she recalls "the colours of everything, since Rotterdam, were not positively distasteful but raw and strident, as they always are in Germany . . . nothing 'pretty-pretty' anywhere" (125). In *Alien* Hunt seeks to ally herself with German readers, reveling in their virtues. 'Her applause for Germany and her critique of England serve Ford's purposes for the book: "impressions" of "my beloved country" (1913a, x).

Whether her German audience believed in her sincerity we cannot know. Hunt and Ford had to flee Germany just as the book was published in England; World War I split Europe into polemical camps, and the force of English patriotism and German guns brought Ford and Hunt home to England in a hurry. It is unlikely that the book would have influenced German lawmakers in ensuring his citizenship and divorce as Ford had hoped. Nothing he had done in over a year in Germany persuaded German authority to honor his petitions. Ford overestimated his own literary importance and that of literature in general on the German authorities. They simply were not the audience he imagined them to be.

## The English Audience: Background Watchers

Ford's imagined audience for the book was unequivocally German, and Ford's influence on Hunt cannot be underestimated; Hunt calls Ford and Germany her "Fate" (5). Ford calls Hunt's presence with him in Germany "blind destiny" (x). But Hunt still regards England a "safe shelter" (15) despite its gossip and its divorce laws; she writes for an English audience as well as a German one. Given all her barbed critiques of British culture, with a wry English wit she still manages to assure English audiences of her thorough English womanhood. She regards the Germans as rather unsubtle and Teutonic, seeing only the obvious. She depends on an English ironic humor to gain her native audience's sympathy.

Hunt depends on her tone and subtle subtexts to entertain a British audience attuned to irony, comfortable with self-satire. As the book won a measure of success in London, careful readers may have been aware of Hunt's uncompromising Englishwoman persona at the heart of the German adventure. In the first chapter she reports her "brooding over all the privileges" she had lost when she applied for German citizenship, not the least of which was freedom to march for women, "for I had chosen to belong to a country where women do not even dream of emancipation" (2); she cuts the critique short and ponders others' applying for alien status looking "by no means downhearted" (3). She ends Chapter I rather regretfully, noting that when she returns to England "I shall be an—I trust—desirable alien" (16), affectionately regarding her native land and already planning a return. In the next chapter she adulates German hospitality but notes the near scandal her "harem skirt" from England caused to German sensibility. She reports the "husband" of the house as "silent . . . probably already [he] saw the police of his native town politely requesting me to desist from giving the natives of H— food for reflection. And so, indeed, it proved" (25). Here Hunt mocks the provincial German prudery and the omnipresent German authorities, while allowing English audiences an insider's status, at least where fashion is concerned.

She seeks to win her English audience through her pervasive use of English literary allusion that shapes the text and provides irony. She begins the book with parodic lines from *Twelfth Night:* "Some persons are, of course, born Germans; some achieve citizenship. . . . Others, again, have the honour thrust upon them" (1). Shakespeare's trickster Maria writes these lines in a forged letter to bedevil and entrap the puritan Malvolio. By beginning *Alien* with comic, ambiguous references to the large yawning gaps between appearance and reality, she calls her own text into question. Like Maria, Hunt twists a text to her own use, mocking her writing, her own love madness, and her audience. Also, she comically draws a comparison between herself and Malvolio, both recipients of a dubious honor "thrust" upon them, in Hunt's case a new citizenship. Her fanciful use of Shakespeare clearly speaks to an English audience familiar with the subtleties of Shakespeare's art. In order to deflect German criticism about her use of English literature throughout and to play to her German audience, she introduces the reader to a German "master of the house" who is thoroughly versed in Shakespeare, though enigmatically she says of his knowledge of other English authors, "To him they were as recondite, as undiscoverable as Shakespeare" (28). Although she seems to be talking of the "master's" knowledge of the private lives of authors as opposed to their works, her phrasing certainly evokes some doubt about this German's deep understanding of English literature.

Hunt's project to charm British audiences by employing shared cultural references and excluding all but the most educated of German audiences must have been conscious. Her book, after all, is written in English, to be published in England. In Chapter V, for example, Hunt's sharp tongue turns on Germany none too subtly, and she uses English allusion both to deepen and obscure her critique. She notes, "No misery shows in Germany. . . . But, on the other hand, no one ever looks very happy in Germany" (52–53). Although Hunt deflects her criticisms by many positive details about German life, from the lack of slums to the "good liquor," she mocks their "collective contentment." She ties to German culture Wordsworth's "senile ideal 'to live without ambition, hope, or aim'" (53–54); she further alludes to Michael of Northgate's medieval text, "Ayenbite of Inwyt"[6] (54), to further promote her insight into the German's' lack of conscience coupled with a plethora of sentimental regret. Hunt finishes her paragraph bitingly by invoking Shakespeare: "Perhaps, individually, Germans dimly realize that they are fulfilling the ideal summed up by Rosencrantz and Guildenstern for the benefit of Hamlet . . . 'happy in that they are not over-happy'" (54). In comparing Germans, even "dimly," to the two nonentities called from Wittenburg to betray Hamlet, Hunt's criticism becomes scathing, but English audiences see this more clearly than German ones.

The most prevalent method Hunt uses to win approval from both German and English audiences is her collapsing of cultural boundaries, her effort to see herself and the world as universal. Her definition of "culture" shows a sophisticated grasp of what modern scholars take for granted: "I consider 'culture', so-called, to be only education-deep, and in no way instinctive" (28). Hunt's work follows Ford's example, but her humanism seems more specific, more grounded in the details of culture than in politics. She compares her enjoyment of Wirtschaftsgarten to her childhood memories of "The Strawberry Gardens near Maiden Castle" (66). In Chapter XVII, "Queens Discrowned," she so blurs the British royal families' histories that the English become German and vice versa. Retelling a court scandal in Germany, Hunt remarks, "George was the mumpish son of the Electress, who might *par impossible* have some day to go over and reign in Great Britain" (224). In the same chapter she equates "depressing" suburbs in Germany with those of "say, Hamilton Terrace or Addison Road" (238). Ford feels obliged to assert Germany's ascendancy in this equation, however, and footnotes her reference saying Hunt was wrong to "confuse . . . disorderly" London suburbs with "carefully planned" German ones. He goes on to say that since Germany gave England "reasonable and utilitarian Rulers," Germany should also consider giving the British "plans" for the "development of modern cities" (239).

In this way Hunt argues for the equality of the two cultures whereas Ford insists on German superiority, despite his earlier preface eradicating the significance of national character. But then Hunt speaks as one "'at home' in the family circles of all three nations" (30), referring to France as well as Germany and Britain, and prefers a less authoritarian insistence on German ascendancy. In becoming a citizen of the world, Hunt shows her willingness to adapt. The Germans might see this as positive, while the English might feel less betrayed. But Hunt's motives in playing to the

English audience, even though she dare not offend the Germans, may have been her practicality. In *I Have This to Say* she writes: "We had both taken London *en grippe,* but in my heart of hearts I knew it *would* be London in the end—at any rate, London for six months of the year" (1926, 162). Though ostensibly writing to further Ford's plans for German citizenship and to please her German readers (not the least of whom was Ford himself), the British Hunt writes also to win the English; she knows that despite Ford's plans, she would remain English.

## The Joseph Leopold Audience: Most Personal

Hunt tells us in her later memoir, "We two—who were to 'rule the world,' in lover's parlance—must do our best to make our own corner of it healthy. I must manage to play up properly to a genius, and, as a hardy motorist once said to me, 'not clutter up the brake!'" (1926, 126). In 1911, for Violet Hunt and Joseph Leopold Hueffer the "corner" was Germany. Joseph Leopold was to write books as "money was to be made" (ibid.), and Hunt was to make life comfortable and fun for his genius. In their years in Germany, Hunt wrote the book *Alien,* making whatever money "was to be made." As it turned out, Ford could not write during this period. He was constantly frustrated by writer's block, caused he said, by all his embroilment in English and German law. To become a German citizen, Ford was required to live in Giessen, which Ford thought provincial and deadening. Never the man to flourish in confinement, Ford preferred to socialize and travel. Though Ford was a prolific writer, Hunt insists that he could write only when "he could shut the door on writs and duns, bores and viragos, refusing to be confronted with any of the problems that beset an author unfortunately doubled with a man" (ibid.).

Of course, the frustrated "genius," as Hunt calls Ford, insists on overseeing Hunt's text to ensure its Germanic precision. That the diary/memoir is Hunt's makes no difference to Ford, who assumes a coauthorship while writing fewer than twenty pages of text. At most, Ford is audience/editor, and editors "must worry about any reputations that the diary might damage" (Blodgett 1988, 45). Ford, of course, was fanatical about his own reputation. As author, Hunt was most worried about saving her reputation by winning him, using her book to flatter and tease him, to love him and win him to marriage. In collusion, she centers her diary on him.

Ubiquitous, "Joseph Leopold" becomes Hunt's created character. She portrays him as writer, genius, and German husband who instructs her in an overbearing but appealing manner. Her pronoun use in *Alien* is as often "we" as "I," and a very specific "we" it is: "We went, Joseph Leopold and I . . ." (1913a, 72). After an early chapter describing her trip to Germany and emphasizing the presence of Joseph Leopold's mother as chaperon, she plays the new bride to his husbandly power, demure and outlandish in turn, learning her husband's culture willingly and imperfectly. In her first description of the German town of H——[7] she remarks on the storks that she has "come so far to see" and notes, "Joseph Leopold said: "They have come out of the wood"" (22). This entry typically tests her perceptions against his, quoting his exact words, including his perceptions in her own phrases. His footnote "Storks never come out of the woods. They never go in them . . ." (22) shows Ford's characteristic response, denying his words, dryly humoring the author for her naivety. Hunt often quotes Ford, as if his exact words give veracity to her account, flattering him by her attention, mocking him gently for his stolid speech. When Joseph Leopold instructs Hunt, for example, on German forests, she questions him about the possibility of wild animals and records his answer: " 'Es kann wohn sein' (It might easily be), says Joseph Leopold" (122). This verbal jousting provides much of the charm of the book, though Ford's genius and Hunt's foolishness is the theme of their game, Hunt granting him his subtle slights.

Ford's footnoting *Alien* tempts Hunt to interject incidents to please him. At the end of an anecdote in which someone mistakes Hunt for Ford's "mother's companion," she says, "Of course, Mütterchen looks ridiculously young" (36), flattering her "mother-in-law" and taking the sting out of the insult to her own age and position. In describing the costume of the Hessen women, she writes of the "vast woollen petticoats, 'kept out,' as we women would say, by bolsters at the hips, of a strong stained-glass-window colour, suggesting the pictures of Ford Madox Brown" (103). Hunt's reference to Ford's grandfather's art as it applies to German settings and scenes shows her politic approach to wooing Ford. As she says later, "All this time I was being told, like Bluebeard's wife, not to go queering any pitches by the exhibition of unfeminine curiosity" (1926, 169). Hunt's need to be herself and to be a perfectly acceptable wife according to conventions of a country about which she knew little necessarily brought about a radical split in her concept of identity, one that manifests itself in her writing in the diary.

## Playing to her Audiences: Splitting the Subject

Hunt's author/persona contradiction stretches the narrative in various directions, disallowing any one subject position. Though Hunt makes the effort to appear together/unified for her audiences' sake, a spirited, mischievous Hunt surfaces to face a self who imagines herself as the German patriot-wife of Ford the patriarch. In attempting to be all that Ford and his newfound compatriots expect, she revivifies a distant German heritage, reminding readers that her mother "had been an old resident in my new country" (37), remembering childhood visits, recalling her French governess, Milly, "a German in disguise . . . a spy" (5). Speaking to Germans of Germany, she embraces a heritage not quite her own. In other passages, however, her voice becomes reflective, more private, and much less consenting: "I had chosen to belong to a country where women do not even dream of emancipation . . ." (2). The tension between the various subjectivities in the narrative, from German Frau to feminist Englishwoman, exposes the fraying seams of a work simultaneously private and public.

In essence, her role of German wife is a masquerade, though she is loath to admit it to herself or her audience. She tells her audience of her obedience to her husband: "He ordered me to go in, use my newly-acquired German, and engage rooms . . ." (163). Later, after telling of wonderful German meals and a visit to a German circus, Hunt says, "And now I must take the bitter taste out of my mouth with a pretty story" (171). How she acquired the "bitter taste" is ambiguous, but clearly as the teller of stories she seeks to make "pretty" what is sometimes unpalatable.

Yet Hunt insists on imbuing her stories with sharp and sometimes antagonistic observations. German character sometimes suffers in consequence. When reporting on German children, for example, Hunt notes the "affluence," the "gorgeous and variegated garments," and the "tumble-down, decrepit appearance of the abodes from which they pour" (186). Fascinated by the "officers" in Germany, Hunt reports on her hate and fear of soldiers, remarking on the "aggressiveness of a Prussian officer" (207), the "horrid jimp-skimp ill-made grey ulsters that the Einjährige wear" (208), and the way "these rude handsome men . . . infest every walk of life" (208). Even though she notes the beauty of "the flamboyant cloak of grey" and remembers that one of them was "polite," her negative perceptions of the German military texture her prose.

Hunt forges on bluntly, critiquing German life and institutions with a seeming disregard for the disapproval of her audiences. Yet Hunt is canny. In one case her criticism is couched in the middle of the chapter "'Drizzlin' and Officers." She begins by extolling the virtues of sewing, edges into her critique, and minimizes her cuts by turning her impressionistic diary into a romance at chapter's end: "During the war scare of 1910 eighty-four thousand men were quartered in Trier. . . . The citizens did not mind that, for daughters went off marvelously . . ." (209). By giv-

ing primacy to marriage over war, Hunt reminds readers that her perceptions emerge from within a feminine perspective; she makes her critique
less dogmatic by that reminder.

Ford tries to rescue her manifest disgust at this highly regarded German
institution by footnoting correctives and treating her perceptions as comic.
He doubts her ability to "penetrate into the psychologies of these gentlemen"
(207), says she would see "precisely the same thing in England" (207), and
corrects her slur on "regimental bands" by recalling his own pleasure at such
displays. Ford's resculpting of an erring Violet Hunt in *Alien* presents yet
another Hunt identity into the narrative. Ford's validation or lack of same
concerning Hunt's identity comes through his frequent notations throughout
the book. His footnotes imply that Hunt is a highly imaginative, too inven-
tive recorder whom Ford must set straight. When Hunt remarks on official
costumes as promoted by the government, Ford remarks in a footnote, "I do
not know what may be our author's authority for making this statement, nor
do I fancy that she knows herself"(125). When Hunt is most critical, Ford
shifts reader attention to the identities that Ford creates for Hunt so that she
does not undermine his purpose for the journal. Ford's image of Hunt is
overlaid on her own, exposing the double nature of her narrative and the
complexity of her writing for multiple audiences.

Hunt's travel narrative thus becomes a text of point and counterpoint,
with Ford allowed the last word. This honeymoon diary trope
"imports . . . a popular cultural rendering of the ideal honeymoon as a
learning experience in which the husband figures as a guide" (Michie
2001, 239). Nevertheless, Hunt's intelligence, vivacity, and sense of fun
emerge even under the heavy weight of Ford's corrections. Though Hunt
never exposes anything of herself or of him that is particularly negative,
she creates characterizations and personae that contradict, shift, and
charm the reader into glossing over the dissonance.

Hunt's persona as a naive storyteller grants her a narrative freedom.
Hunt, an experienced writer of fiction and hardly naive herself, self-con-
sciously crafts the feminine narrator in *Alien* to protect her narrative from
Ford's heavy-handed interference. Her feminization of the chapter on the
German military, for example, may have saved Hunt's "incorrect" perspective from Ford's excision. Ford follows Hunt's critique with his own chapter
called "Subject Races," praising the Prussian ability to "administer . . . to
enrich us" (1913a, 217). He undoubtedly feels a masculine authority is
needed to exert some influence. She follows Ford's rather weighty treatise on
politics and war with "Queens Discrowned," refuting a purely masculine
view of history, emphasizing the historical connections of Germany and
England through their women, their romantic alliances of lovers and hus-

bands, and the economic betrayals of those same men. She traces her own love of history and its connection with the "Now—!" (249) throughout the lengthy chapter, personalizing the historical perspective. Hunt places her nostalgia and homesickness in historical narrative in order to position herself happily beside Ford and his German relatives in the next chapter.

## Hunt's Silences: Keeping Her Audience Interested

In any diary where a very real audience peeks over the shoulder of its writer, that writer may build in silences, using the act of erasure to subvert the power of audience control. When that audience also has the last word, as editor Ford did over Hunt's *Alien,* the writer contrives the silences, choosing which subjects must be ignored completely and which can be inserted cleverly without inviting the censor's notice.

One subject Hunt chooses to put under erasure was her illness, undefined even in her later memoir, *I Have This to Say* (1926). Her illness during "their first year in exile" (145), in "the days I seemed to be bleeding to death" (142), occasioned two separate surgeries, the last more severe than the first. Hunt's symptoms, vague even in her memoir and ignored in her diary, point to what women today still call "female problems," and her last operation probably was a hysterectomy. During this time "Ford was getting domiciled for his naturalism" (145) while Hunt, "weak and tottery from illness" (144), returned to England because "I was British enough to want a British opinion" (147). In this memoir Hunt refers to her illness by remembering Ford "dying just to run across to me to see how I am, which would of course be suicidal to his hopes" (145). Indeed, he escapes German control for a bit and surreptitiously visits Hunt for ten days following her operation. As she says years later of 1911, "I was still ill, worn, carped at, criticized" (172). Writing *Alien* that same year, she excludes references to her illness and surgery though they surely influenced her impressions of Germany and limited her travel.

Decentering herself from the text, Hunt may have considered personal revelations regarding illness not only extraneous but also inappropriate. In one passage she alludes to an illness "contracted in the course of the next few weeks" (1913a, 191). She thus explains her inability to buy and bring back to health a starving dog. The dog's malady, brought on by neglect from his German owners, acts as a metaphor for her own flagging health. In later memoirs she includes reflections on the toll illness took on her work, her travel, and her relationships; her near exclusion in *Alien* verifies her use of that travel diary to visualize Germany in ways that pleased audiences, not to convey a spontaneous rendering of experience.

Her narrative of omission may have resulted from her desire to authorize the marriage fiction within the text. To admit she had problems associated with both middle-aged and sexually licentious bodies destroys the fabricated marriage fantasy subtext that empowers her impressions of life in Germany. Hunt, educated within Victorian literary traditions, strongly equates the strength of the body to that of text. Had her illness conformed to the virginal Victorian heroine's delicacy, perhaps she would have found a place for inclusion of this important personal crisis. Since she opted for a bodily image of the wiry, strong Englishwoman, acknowledging illness would undermine her purpose. Hunt chooses a young bride persona who writes a honeymoon diary, rather than include evidence of a body or marriage beset by conflict. She writes her desire for traditional Victorian womanhood: wife and mother. Neither the feminist nor the wife could admit the frailty that menopause or syphilis might bring.[8]

Her concern for her semi-youthful bride image expresses itself throughout the text. Goldring tells us that Hunt lied about her age, and she certainly does not create a middle-aged, forty-eight-year-old persona in *Alien.* She alludes to herself as "an alien bride" (Hunt 1913a, 26), hopeful for children, blurring her desire to see "the homely cabbage which ushers English babies into the world" (21) with her potential as a mother in Germany. Her age and her illness prevented any possibility of bearing a child in 1911, when most of *Alien* was written. But this reproductive impossibility becomes part of the dream fiction of the text. In her memoir Hunt mentions Ford's wish that "If he had a child it should be Christened in Germany" (1926, 177). Ford surely knew that Hunt was beyond childbearing age and knew her operation must prevent even a miraculous conception. Impossibility meets desire, and Hunt pretends for her own sake as well as Ford's. Early in *Alien,* when Hunt sets up the idyllic marriage plot, she hints at the importance of children in making a home, calling on the myth of the stork to solicit Ford's complicity in feigning the possibility of family. Perhaps the Germans, ignorant of Hunt's age or condition, promoted the idea of a family citizenry. As Joseph Leopold introduces Hunt to their new house, he confesses: "[O]ur house . . . is new—very new—too new. . . . It did not seem as if a nest of storks would find that high pitched roof an easy platform whereon to raise a large family" (1913a, 21). Her youthful, fertile persona simply did not exist except in the imagination.

Hunt's endeavors to consolidate her English birth with her supposed German citizenship encourages the use of a strong, zesty persona at the expense of a sympathetic, but weak identity. "A brilliant skater on ice," Hunt was known for her vitality (Sinclair 1922, 106). Her 1911 frailty would be especially galling when contrasted to the stolid Germans she depicts in *Alien*. She says of German young women, "All the girls were gay, and with good figures, though inclined to be stout . . . rosy cheeks" (1913a, 58). Though she repeatedly talks of the "phthisic" (58), "ethereal" (90), "haggard" (78) Englishwoman, she often chooses an observer's persona who reports. Certainly she never aligns herself with the ailing and infirm. Her English audience depended on her vigor to give the lie to her depictions of English frailty; the German audience expected in her an exemplum of the "noble female creatures" of Germany (103).

Linking disease with age, Hunt avoids reference to a changing body that implies the "loss" of sexuality and reproductivity, those traditional male-held values concerning women. Hunt knew what men liked and knew too their attitude toward illness. Certainly she knew Ford's attitude. Ford "found the excitement of sexual exploration irresistible and the sympathy of an attractive woman necessary to the dramatization of himself as the unjustly suffering man" (Mizener 1971, 177). Certainly he didn't want a fellow sufferer usurping his position. Hunt must have suspected this about Ford's character. In her novel *The House of Many Mirrors,* the ailing Rosamund, dying of a mysterious female complaint, "becomes hopelessly caught," forced to listen to her husband "adumbrating his theories of the illness which he conceived her to be suffering" (1915, 142). "Only really healthy specimens please him" (162).

Since Hunt will not die, as Rosamund does, she chooses to negate the influence of her illness by refusing to give it textual veracity. She remains in *Alien* as a vital and healthy "specimen," her unspoken sexuality intact.

Acknowledging the silences that accompanied her public persona and hence her writing, Hunt writes, "Yes, I know they are puzzling, my great white silences . . . , absurdist lacunas in my narration of the things that impressed me, the things that depressed me as they fell in the course of the flurried years 1908 to 1914" (1926, v). In *Alien* years earlier, Hunt wrote in "lacunae" willingly, in keeping with Ford's wish to "preserve appearances" (Secor and Secor 1983, 20). Ford writes his own passion for privacy into his *No More Parades,* in which he describes Tietjen's regard for restraint in making the private public: "[T]he instinct for privacy—as to his relationships, his passions, or even as to his most unimportant motives—was as strong as the instinct of life itself. He would literally rather be dead than an open book" (1962, 70). Obviously in suggesting to Hunt that she write a book of impressions, Ford encouraged her impressions of Germany and the external world; he wanted to limit her disclosure of their personal affairs.

With the stakes high, Hunt writes the travel diary as citizenship ploy

and honeymoon trip, ever aware of its fictions. Such narratives traditionally served "as a backdrop and sign of the transformative cultural work of
marriage" (Michie 2001, 234). Traveling with Ford first as fiancée and
then "wife," writing a book at his behest, Hunt avoids portraying herself
as one with German women and instead equates herself with the abused
"queens" of German kings, English in a foreign land. This scene, late in
the book, indicates Hunt's fatigue, her ambivalent sexual feeling in her
ambiguous role of not-quite wife or mistress, not-quite German or
English.

Called upon to present the couple as husband and wife blissfully traveling throughout their new country on an extended honeymoon, Hunt
must rely on conventional marital sexual depictions, that is, neutral,
unspoken, assumed. Hunt's avidity for a wifely role enabled her to write
of traditional scenes of marriage. But juxtaposed to these scenes she
couches depictions of nature, fairy tales, and history redolent of her passionate, sexual nature. Hunt, all her life interested in the emotional and
sexual interplay between men and women, acquiesces to Ford's sensibility
in this book she calls her own and turns away from the rather destructive
erotics that underpinned their relationship during the year or so of the
journal.

Ford effectively silences the emotional flamboyance, what Goldring calls
a lack of "emotional reticence" (1943, 42), which normally characterizes
her writing. But as anyone who seeks to repress an integral part of one's self
and literary method, Hunt lets her interest and engagement in sensual and
sexual matters surface intermittently, if only to hint at the "devil's cauldron
that had been preparing succulent horrors for me ever since 1908" (1926,
116). Hunt's relationship to sexuality might be described as "succulent horrors," her desire warring with a kind of tragic inevitability; she needed "to
live always in the boiling middle of things or, to mix metaphors, in a world
of thin ice and broken eggs that will never make an omelette" (ibid., 123).
This "boiling" invites the inevitable punishment reserved for the promiscuous antiheroines of the fairy tale. In *Alien* she used these sexually
charged morality tales to tell and foretell her own story.

Hunt's use of fairy tales circulates evocative, sensual, and sometimes
grotesque images. Highly erotic language retells these stories, imbuing
recollections with a sexual presence that unsettles the glossy exterior of the
"impressions" of Germany. She recalls the "leaping firelight" that accompanied her childhood listening and uses words and images recalling a
primitive sexuality: "Beauty and the Beast" is replaced by "The
Woodcutter's Child," a tale "savage," "unromantic," and "incomplete" (8).
Hunt remembers her governess telling this "horrible, grotesque" tale,

implying a castration at the story's center, causing a "shiver" (ibid.). "[A]fter that night the story was tabooed by our elders . . . it was vulgar" (ibid.). Hunt's continued enjoyment of the savagery of Grimm's tales hints at unresolved sexual anger.

Hunt eroticizes nature in *Alien*, especially the rivers of Germany, suggesting the fluidity of woman's sexual desire, the depth of the darkness that underlies its social signification. Moving through the Valley of Apollyan, the river is ""so big, so black, so simple, so straight in its bed . . ." (14). Masculine seduction and fertility meet the river: "Old, grey, helpless, and forlorn, the banks look under the glare of the truculent virile shafts of gold that are fostering and ripening the vine screens . . ." (ibid.). Through her language Hunt joins masculine and feminine nature: "I go gliding into the country of my adoption, insinuating myself by these peaceful methods of penetration" (15). Written early in her year in Germany, Hunt overestimates her feminine insinuation and peaceful penetration into the masculine Ford and his country, Germany. Her role of wife undermines much of her power while Ford plays the authoritative German husband.

Critics of her day regarded her as a "tragic realist" (Sinclair 1922, 111) and a "psychological realist . . . [an] incorruptible truthteller" (117–18). A more recent review of her work notes that she and her characters "could not retreat from the sexual awareness and self-sufficiency by which [they] lived" (Secor and Secor 1978, 26). But in *Alien*, a book that was to be regarded as her journal of "impressions," she only obliquely explored the sexual and confined her haunting, psychological realism to portraying German character, refusing a depth of characterization in favor of a comic domestic farce for herself and Ford. Given the complexities of the Ford/Hunt "honeymoon," unsurprisingly she leaves Celle "brown, dusty, parchment-like," feeling "chilly and grown old" (1913a, 248).

## Allusion as Disruption: Grimm Germany

As part of the travel narrative convention and as part of her intention to focus on their public life together, Hunt describes scenes from all over Germany. In many she emphasizes the colors, the scenic beauty of the countryside, and the charm of the villages. But she dispels the typically pro-German discourse by literary techniques within the travel journal. Using these strategies subtly, Hunt alludes to a personal engagement with her "mate" and Germany that the surface narrative belies. Using the motifs of light/dark and German fairy tales, for example, Hunt alludes to a darker, frightening Germany that contradicts her more sanguine portrayals. Although she often mentions England shrouded in fog and darkness, she talks too of the light of sun, of the lamp that shines in England despite the repressed overlay of English life. In describing Germany, the bright sun might "glare" on many days, and her many references to the black and rather horrifying forests undermine her brighter depictions. In her chapter "Pax Germanica: Servants, Fairy Tales, and Tailors" she seems to embrace German life while simultaneously exposing a darker side that does not fit Ford's rhetorical agenda. Using her familiarity with "the legends of Grimm," she explores the depth of German forests and their attendant myths of wickedness, treachery, and misery. She tells of one "particular afternoon" when "the sun was not 'shining bright, no gentle breeze was blowing among the trees, and everything did not seem gay and pleasant . . .'" (63).

This "favorite" Grimm beginning is prologue to her own tale, which she compares with the tale of two doomed lovers, Jorinde and Joringel. As she and Joseph Leopold walked through the woods, "We were on the fringe of a much deeper, darker patch of forest . . . and lost even the consoling sight of the red disc of the sun" (63). Hunt's tale ends with the horrible cry of a wild cat, filling her with fear and horror. This story introduces the darkness of German forests, symbolizing the wild and primitive nature of Germany. In "Princes and Prescriptions" she notes the "fierce electric light" (97) of the Kur-Haus but reminds readers that the King "is your Commissioner of Woods and Forests, your head of police, all in one" (102), juxtaposing a harsh civility to an even harsher primeval system. In "Blue Pates and Schoppen" she recalls a walk through a forest where she loses the sun: "It seems at one time utterly gone out and departed this side of the earth; at another gleaming sudden and angry between the dark bars like a woodcutter's fire" (122). Hunt thinks Germany has within it a malevolent force that cannot be contained. The forest embodies this power: "[T]he forest is so big and you are so little" (122). Hunt increasingly sees her place with Ford in Germany as insignificant; she expresses her unhappiness only in subtexts to conserve Germany's, and Ford's, approval.

Hunt's references to myths and legends both soften and deepen her contemporary critique of Germany. In "Celle" she pictures "The little candle of legend that flings its light on a naughty world . . ." (260). Through "the very least tamely light" (ibid.), she obliquely exposes all that the dark forests tend to darken and silence. She mocks the all-male smoking room, commenting that an "adventurous female . . . [may] follow her Orpheus into a milder sort of hell, rank with tobacco fumes" (278). Her long analysis of Browning's "model of all wandering sages and nomadic geniuses . . . , The Pied Piper" (178), gives Hunt the opportunity to explore the German treatment of artists through another's reworking of legend, allowing herself criticism at three removes. She praises artists ("these moral lynch-lawyers") and criticizes those who betray or underpay these "pipers," mocking " 'Hamelin town by famous Hanover city' . . . full of every conceivable form of exploitation of the legend" (181). Because she dare not offend her diary's audience with personal tirades against German practices and her fears for Ford, she shows her disdain for German "exploitation" within a grander analysis of poetry and legend.

Through legend, Hunt imagines the dangers and cruelties of a Germany full of "wonderments, witches and warlocks" (184). Even her enthusiastic portrayal of the wine country includes mention of the "curse" of the "envious sisters Three Eyes and One Eye" (304), which made the region fertile yet fraught with mystic and fearsome power. Hunt's mythic passages disrupt glowing accounts of her newfound country. She evokes worlds of myth and fantasy, worlds that may not exist except in the imagination of the teller. Just as the Pied Piper did, Hunt hopes to "bewitch" the "fat, self-sufficient burgomasters" (178) by her subversive tale.

## Having Her Say: In Fiction

Ford's ambivalence about her roles of wife and mistress along with their precarious marital position made Hunt's experiences in Germany peculiarly akin to the macabre *Tales of the Uneasy,* which she wrote the same year.[9] These tales depict Hunt's "characteristic leaning to the gruesome and uncanny" (Sinclair 1922, 107), particularly in relation to the dynamics of passion between men and women. The "uneasy" bespeaks the twisted, powerful emotions between the man and woman centered in each story. Autobiographical in a psychological sense, the tales indeed expose the sexual tensions and displacements between strong, erotically motivated women and men who are destroyed by these women. Secor and Secor note that "in these ghost stories Violet Hunt often seems most frightened of herself" (1978, 18). Indeed, her heroines seem to be self-portraits of women driven by desire and turned savage by the cold manipulations of men who will not or cannot commit themselves to love or passion. Hunt, in "The Telegram," writes of the flirtatious Alice Damer, "not an outrageous, noisy, ill-bred flirt but what is known as a quiet flirt" (1911, 4). As Alice ages she feels the pressing need to marry, but fears her need will be destructive to herself and the man who "must" be her husband. In "The Operation" Hunt writes of the wife-mistress-genius triangle, noting that Florence "[w]ith fond remorselessness . . . had driven him to drive his wife to divorce him . . . , as if unconscious of the larger issues she was stirring—another woman's happiness, a man's honour, and an actor's art, for

Joe was a genius" (ibid., 41). Mabel, "little Lady Greenwell" in the story
"The Memoir," worries about her husband's penchant for young women,
saying, "He was a born flirt, and he was eight years younger than his wife.
Wives, who were burdened with odious supernumerary years, must, of
course, give their man a little rope" (75). Alice painfully notes that
"women simply 'clawed him' for their parties, and adored him for their
boudoirs" (ibid.). In these stories Hunt assiduously studies the psychological strands of desire, both sexual and emotional, in her characters' entanglements. The contraries of socially inscribed marriage and socially
repressed sexual desire surface in possessiveness, destructive dependencies,
and masculine aggression disguised as passivity.

The plots are commonplace, but the contorted psychologies of the
characters make them indeed *Tales of the Uneasy.* "The Prayer" is her most
chilling story. A character called Alice deprives Edward of his will by the
strength of hers; Edward then turns on her to recapture his own vitality
at her expense: "Where she was pale he was well-coloured; the network of
little filmy wrinkles that, on close inspections, covered her face, had no
parallel on his smooth skin" (21). Alice's consuming love turns back on
her, destroying first their relationship and then her life.

These stories fiercely foreshadow Hunt's obsessive love, Ford's betrayal,
and Hunt's subsequent decline. She had seen and feared his fickleness and
her own passion and knew he would use both against her. The sexual language Hunt uses in her stories tells the reader where the destructive will
resides, and the ferocity of the stories denotes a channeling of frustration
and fear that she dare not insert in *The Desirable Alien.* Hunt relegates the
themes of erotics, betrayals, and sexual politics to her fictional *Tales of the
Uneasy* lest she be deemed undesirable by her audiences in writing of such
issues in autobiographical text. What Hunt feels "uneasy" about inevitably
surfaces in *Alien,* however, denoting the strength of her feelings.

Deflecting criticism and ostracism, she speaks in a comic, resistant, and
disobedient voice seemingly allowing correction by a higher, German, and
masculine authority. By creating a persona who both is and is not Hunt,
rather the mythic wife of Ford, she embarks on a journey more fictional
than she wishes to concede. Hunt thus negotiates the rugged course of
multiple audience expectations. Her many audiences exhort her to tell all,
but their expectations both shape and stifle the telling. To negotiate this
double bind, she mythologizes her German experience, telling her own
story within a text of contradictions, gaps, and uneasy juxtapositions.
When critic Edward Garnett says of Ford that "Facts never worry Joseph
Leopold much!" Hunt responds perhaps to her own project as much as to
Garnett's criticism: "And why should they? [Facts] were made for slaves

not for gipsies; for policemen, not for authors. Truth and fiction are probably all one—part of the cosmos . . ." (1926, 209). Hunt therefore uses
"facts" to create her "cosmos." As these bewitching stories imply, romantic enchantment cannot last forever, nor could the fantasy of the Hueffers.

## Autobiographical "Impressions": Change

Enchantment with Germany could not last long in the years 1911 and
1912. As Hunt puts it, "The promise of the rainbow was not to be fulfilled.
We could not see the blood-red ray in the spectrum, but Germany was all
wrong with us!" (1926, 183). The approaching war, which finally not even
Ford could ignore, and Ford's boredom with the divorce/marriage question
leads them irrevocably back to London. Unwilling, however, to end *Alien*
by articulating doubts about the "flattening" Prussian presence beginning to
haunt Ford and Hunt, she ends ambiguously, motoring back into
"Belgium—for the time . . ." (1913a, 327). She sustains the energy of her
fantasy of Germany and her marriage to Ford even as the book's close intimates a broadening of scope, an "alien" returning to a world more familiar.
In the last paragraph Hunt emphasizes the drinking of the "healths of several nationalities . . . Belgian, English, German, and French—" bringing her
internationalism full circle. To the bitter end she maintained an integrity to
a book whose purpose all but unraveled by the time of publication.

Leaving Germany and returning to London, Hunt found to her despair
that she returned with nothing accomplished: no marriage (at least no
"papers") and no freedom from the law's imposition. Earlier, temporary visits to England had brought them hundreds of invitations to parties to
honor them both. Not this time. Ford's wife Elsie sued *The Throne* for
referring to Hunt as "Mrs. Hueffer," and the English courts investigated
Hunt's false position of "wife" with ruthlessness. Ford faced bankruptcy,
and although he did not mind "so much" his loss of financial security, he
was bored silly with Hunt's obsessive explanations of the "Marriage
Mirage" (Belford 1990, 183): "All this damned me thoroughly with Joseph
Leopold" (1926, 199). But the scandal of *The Throne* and the 1913 publication of *The Desirable Alien* brought them under scandal and scrutiny.

Hunt—angry, obsessive, and afraid—did not thrive. She was shunned
by society, by her old friend Henry James, and by Goneril and Regan
(Hunt's names for her traitorous sisters). Whether literal or figurative, the
honeymoon was over; Hunt had to face the reality of an unmarried life
with a man increasingly absorbed with his writing, his plans, his friends.
Her "zealous public crusade" to legitimate herself as Mrs. Hueffer "alienated" Ford further. Finally, in 1913 Hunt and Ford again toured "the

Rhineland" with friends. She meditated "on the failed fairy tale of living in a castle with her medieval knight. To make herself more miserable, she reread *The Desirable Alien,* with its prodigal portrayal of a nation that no longer existed (Belford 1990, 209). Neither did Hunt's life as Mrs. Hueffer. By 1914 the romance of Ford and Hunt was dying.

Indeed, Hunt's loss of Ford as a sympathetic audience changed her. 'Her *Alien* playfulness changes to increasing acrimony. At his behest, Germany was the subject of "their" *Desirable Alien;* Ford's fame and sense of history were to be the center of their coauthored *Zeppelin Nights.* Their partially autobiographical *Zeppelin Nights* traces the transition in their relationship. Even though *Zeppelin Nights* may deserve no true place in a study of Hunt's diary narratives, its transitional and autobiographical place in her writing with Ford and about Ford make it pertinent. In it, Hunt endeavors to place Ford and their relationship in a fictional and viable literary narrative. The equivocations she writes into that text move tellingly from the hopeful and zesty narrative of *Alien* in 1911. In *Zeppelin* Hunt rather frantically elevates Ford to a central position of knowledge and fame, yet exposes, perhaps unconsciously, the pomposity and cruelty of his personality.

Hunt doubles her narrative role with that of her fictional Candour Viola, creating gaps and slippages in appraising Ford as Serapion. Viola mirrors Hunt's passion and folly in loving him. Hunt views her persona, Mrs. Candour Viola, with a cynicism that springs from her own appraisal of her romantic and ridiculous naivety where (Ford) is concerned: " 'No . . . no . . . no!'" Candour called out. Serapion looked at her with that superior air, that air of masterfulness that made us all wonder how she could do anything but detest the fellow" (1913b, 305). Hunt's parodic voice and Viola's adoration coalesce to provide a frame for Ford's genius and arrogance. Hunt positions him in *Zeppelin Nights* as both subject and audience, with Hunt herself peeking from behind the portrait as a court jester, dancing in attendance and subtly subverting his performance.

Hunt, less willing in 1916 than in 1911 to bury her own wit and genius under Ford's more famous presence, met critical acclaim for her part in writing *Zeppelin.* One reviewer says, "There are flashes of Miss Hunt's genius dispersed throughout the volume, and one is sensible that she has made a heroic attempt to leaven the mass of Mr. Hueffer's dull offensiveness" (Prothero 1916, 293). Certainly Hunt's intent to win back Ford's fading affection by again offering her talents at the altar of his presence was undermined by such reviews. Ford had become less an authority for their shared "impressions" and more an enshrined subject in someone else's narrative. Thus, the double narrative of paternal origins that

Ford empowers in *Alien* becomes in *Zeppelin Nights* a double narrative choreographed by feminine direction. The pleasure of the performance was clearly Hunt's.

Alas, *Zeppelin Nights* is their last performance together. In it Hunt depicts Viola's tears and Serapion's enlistment in the armed forces, which for Ford took place in 1915. The book foreshadows Hunt's heartbreak and Ford's betrayal so painfully written into her *1917 Diary*. As *Zeppelin Nights* ends and the *1917 Diary* begins, Ford begins to openly court other women, embarking on his long, ambivalent process of ridding himself of Violet Hunt. The Ford in *Zeppelin Nights* is the Serapion who embodies art: "'Oh, but tell him he's too valuable,' Candour appealed to all of us. 'Art alone is too valuable'" (306); the Ford in the diary written a year later is "my Frankenstein monster" (Secor and Secor 1983, 58). Yet despite the monstrousness of Ford in his relationship to Hunt, in each of Hunt's overt autobiographical portraits of her relationship with Ford, *Alien, Zeppelin, Diary*, Hunt defines herself solely in relationship to him. His presence as audience, coauthor, and lover in the first two of these three books overshadows her own prosaic reality. In the *Diary*, his absence similarly overshadows her own performance as a person, and she bitterly displays a self-inflicted self-abasement. The effect of the loss of Ford as lover and as audience on her sense of identity and on her life stories becomes glaringly clear in Hunt's *1917 Diary*.

## *1917 Diary*: Without Fantasy, without the "Other" Audience

The *1917 Diary* shows Hunt still laboring under her obsession with Ford. Clearly he is not a coauthor; his centrality of subject remains. They no longer collaborate, and he no longer functions as her audience because of their estrangement. The diary is particularly interesting when compared to the travel diary, *Alien*. The romance, the myth, the fairy-tale prosaic quality, the subtlety and humor of the subversions and disruptions—all are gone, to be replaced by a stark view of reality, a bitter and cynical "psychological realism." After much disappointment, for example, she ponders once again living with Ford, saying, "[I]f I go on with him, it will be a dog's life—(or a bitch's)" (1983, 59). Thus, she replaces her flirtatious recognition of Ford as omniscient audience by abrupt, detailed depictions of her life both with and without him.

The diary, "a monodrama, complete with recalled dialogue and choral commentary" (Secor and Secor 1983, 7), lacks the dialogic quality of man/woman conflicting voices. In *Alien* Hunt seems to speak with Ford, or to him, or against him. But this quality of woman using her feminine

wit and vitality to question and subvert male genius and authority is completely missing in the *1917 Diary*. She no longer organizes by picturesque
impressions but tells a chilling, labored, daily tale of betrayal and suffering. Hunt writes as a woman badly bruised and conflicted about the man
at the center of her experience.

In her obsession with Ford, Hunt includes his name or the initial *F* in
nearly every entry, recording what he does, what others say about him,
and her own deprecation or defense of him. She notes that Eleanor
Jackson tries to disillusion her "about F telling me of all his inclinations
to all my female friends (well favoured) attempted kissings and so on!"
(44). She records Ford's saying "You & Brigit will claw each other &
either she will get me—or you. That's life. Take what you can get" (52).[10]
And although she records many of these entries without commentary,
sometimes her despair is all she writes: "Oh what is the good of my life,
hanging *in ribbons* round a man who does not care for me!" (55).
Occasionally she merely faces facts: "I am not F's mistress. I can't be his
friend. I *won't* be his wife" (70). Her resolve to confront the truth of his
absence never lasts long, although she is brutally honest about her obsession. She writes in November: "But Ford dominates me to such an extent
I *can't* keep up an attitude" (83).

Hunt's diary, "the wretched thing" (73), records entry after entry of a
life consumed by the idea of Ford far more than by Ford himself. Hunt's
own persona surfaces only by inference, by what she says and how she says
it. Her self-reflections center on Ford's responses to her. Readers may feel
sadness and impatience in reading this diary, whose bleak entries detail
Hunt's emptiness and heartbreak. She desperately clings to a man who
plays her for a fool, who has nothing of substance left to give her. When
Hunt met Ford, she had hoped for "a respectability thus far denied her
and, perhaps, a last grand, passionate fling, if not marriage" (Belford
1990, 145). When the passion and the fling and the "marriage"' evapo-
rated, so did her self-worth. Her life seems wasted on a romantic conception of woman's need for man.

Hunt's frankness and self-justification about sex indicate that she either
sees herself as sole audience or wishes for Ford's occasional audience.
Certainly the larger audiences of *Alien* no longer exert any kind of presence; the Ford of 1911 has become the Ford whose guilt is measured by
sexual indifference, infidelity, and boredom. When Hunt speaks of sex she
speaks to herself of her frustration, but she seems also to speak to Ford,
fixing blame on him for her "loveless bed" (77). She writes: "I long to be
able to tell him that I have not love for him enough and not even respect
only an unholy passion that will last till I die" (61). She despairs that "He

has toothache adroitly every night at 10" (63). Given her constant chron-
icling of her frustration due to Ford's nights of refusal, her blunt critique
of him as a lover seems surprising: "The night he permits himself to be
passionate. He was not: only brutal and coarse" (71). Perhaps she addresses this paradox of desire and disappointment when she tells him, and
records the telling, "We must be ineffectual lovers but lovers—or else
part" (72).

As time passes, Hunt records the increasingly bitter fluctuation
between desire and hatred, passion and indifference: "A row at night. F
has gone sick. His face is all scratched—by me" (74). The next day Hunt
records: "The awfullest day . . . mostly together, but dreary. F declares
himself 'impotent'—This is the latest" (ibid.). These stark entries written
with poignancy, but without elaboration, expose Hunt's thwarted sexuality and its relationship to her troubled sense of identity. Without Ford's
wanting her, without his desire, she cannot feel complete. Clearly it is not
Ford's sexual ability that fanned Hunt's desire, but his reluctance and his
cruel strategy of setting himself up as sexual prize to a woman who "can
give Ford what he wants, tho' he can't give me what I want" (83). Hunt
has reason to struggle with her own desire and his. He tells her and she
records: "'If I could have another woman I might desire *you*. I was nice to
you in the Brigit time.'" As Hunt says, "It seemed perverted, but F is so
queer. I took it calm" (80).

Hunt struggles between culturally embedded constructions of the
Victorian and Modern woman. "What did these Edwardian women
want? The vote . . . and personal autonomy, but especially 'sexual freedom'" (Clausen 1996, 15). More tragically, many like Hunt longed for the
middle-class respectability of marriage—hence her malaise. Ford's blatant
"double standard" of sexual relations ruptures Hunt's sense of her freedom
and smashes a sexual liberation that was all the compensation she had.
"What the double standard hurts in women . . . is the animal center of
self-respect" (Dinnerstein 1976, 73). When Hunt fearlessly puts her sexuality in play and then is rejected as woman, wife, mistress—she turns her
rage inward.

Ford's confessions and their combined failures flatten her sense of identity. The diary entries show a sexual malaise with astonishing destructive
capability. Hunt, a woman raised in Victorian England to define herself
in relation to men, seems left with nothing when she can neither arouse
nor reproduce. As she says at the end of the diary that marks the end of
their relationship together, "If he isn't ravenous for me, then there is no
need to try & come together" (Secor and Secor 1983, 85). Throughout
the year Hunt looks for her failures, and Ford's, to find the cause of the

collapse of their relationship. She derides Ford for his lack of sexual passion for her, but clearly she blames herself for Ford's failure. In a bitterly acrimonious and physical argument, Ford tells Hunt, "I'll tell you what I'll do. If I go away & have a quiet time for a couple of months . . . I'll be able to make love to you." As Hunt says, "That was the limit." The following day Hunt records, "I wrote to F saying how deadly ashamed I was. I did not love him enough to preserve my self control when he tormented me" (81). These horrifying looks into the sexual dynamics of a "tormented" woman and a man who accuses her of having " 'a bed room mind'" (54) expose more than the lives of Hunt and Ford. These entries vibrate with the sexual dysfunction too typical in patriarchy.

## No Longer an Audience:
## Ford's Continued Economic, Erotic Manipulation

The conflict between economic and erotic power relations glaringly illumines the text of their lives and the diary itself. Hunt makes no attempt to soften the implications in her "factual" accounts, willingly portraying herself as the fool in order to paint Ford as the cad. Complicating an already complex relationship was Ford's constant need for money. Though Hunt's riches fluctuated wildly in their years together because of her own familial conflicts and the litigation brought about by her relationship with Ford, Hunt always had more money than Ford. From the start of their relationship she gave Ford large amounts to keep his children in private schools and to keep his wife at bay. In *Alien* she never mentions money, and the reader might erroneously assume that Ford's larger fame and husbandly power meant he supported Hunt. Despite what Goldring calls "Ford's magnificently 'un-commercial' attitude and his devotion to the 'great abstractions'" (1943, 24), he needed money to live. In their early years together Hunt gave to Ford without thought, noting only that she refused Ford money for "a pony and trap for the children to go to church in during the holidays" and "the deluge of words that followed, of cruel felicities of speech, apt verbal lunges——*le mot juste* . . . applied to a palpitating shrinking Mentor at home!" (1926, 173). But once Ford enlisted and it became clear that he no longer wanted to love or bed Hunt, the acrimony of a woman wronged both sexually and economically erupted from her diary pages. Hunt records without gloss Ford's financial manipulations.

One Friday in June Hunt writes, "F kissed me. I lent him 18 lbs. for his mess bill . . . (Secor and Secor 1983, 64). In September Hunt tries to figure out how to pay a debt of Ford's that she is not supposed to know about. After paying for a trip of his, "He had no money on him . . . he was kinder than he has been for 5 weeks" (75). Three days later Hunt sends him a "10 lb. cheque to send Phillips. He will be enraged" (ibid.). In recording a quarrel in October, Hunt says, "Then I said bitterly that I had thought he had been different downstairs (at the moment I had promised to—give money). He raged" (81). Hunt's generosity, increasingly scarce, demands payment in real affection, something Ford cannot quite return. The circumstances of their economic relationship clearly outrage Hunt and weaken Ford's ability to loosen their entanglement.

The cultural mandate that gives men superiority so that they might protect and support the weaker sex obviously is not often borne out in Ford's relationships. Ford's sexual anxiety certainly rested in part on his dependence on a woman he no longer desired; Hunt was patron and lover, and he needed one without the other, an impossible feat. Goldring attempts to excuse Ford's obvious and rather heartless monetary expectations from Hunt for the year of their break-up: "We can only guess that he felt that women owed him something and that, on various grounds, including his position as retiring warrior, he was entitled to take what he wanted from them when he could get it" (Goldring, quoted in Secor and Secor 1983, 25). The payment Ford extracted from Hunt for his "love" devastated her; she writes: "What is to become of me? I am *ballottié* by the caprice of one man—I, a genius as he says. Ruined" (61). As for Ford, "He paid as he went along: in caresses" (56).

## Without Ford: Changing Subjectivity, Changing Audiences

Knowing Ford will leave, Hunt tries to halt his progress even as she readies herself, searching for a self on every page. Hunt, fifty-four when Ford leaves her, knows that "age will come" (Secor and Secor 1983, 64), that "people think our alliance has, too, gone the way of all (younger) flesh" (46). A friend tells her that Ford "asked for 'something young'" (76). In all these entries she painfully ignores the "I," underscoring the loss of her identity in losing her youth and desirability. Hunt exposes herself in each entry: when she was "drunk" (63), when she agonizes over her vain attempts to arouse him (75), when she commits her "first infidelity to F" (60).

Hunt writes in her own frailties, her inadequate coping mechanisms in the face of her despair. She mourns the loss of Ford but also the loss of youth, beauty, love, hope—in short, her culturally structured identity. "She was too old to apply the new doctrines [of sexual liberty] to her own heart-aches, too old, also, to eradicate her instinctive respect for the Victorian conventions she had defied" (Goldring 1943, 132). And thus she suffered a terrible sense of self-defilement along with a feminist fury over what man, specifically Ford, could give her: "Love without breadth, depth, or thickness, without dimension. . . . For the object—set up like an ikon to be worshipped, perfunctorily, with genuflections and lip-service, a queen in the game of knights and castles" (1926, 220).

Intelligently aware of both the forces of ideology and her own willfulness, she uses her diary to record the struggle of a changing subjectivity. She knows she must forge an identity independent of Ford, but she deeply fears the loneliness and the loss of life's purpose: "I am better but so lonely" (Secor and Secor 1983, 56). In some way her diary replaces the shared texts she wrote with Ford. In the diary she tries to construct a woman's identity that can live without relation to a man, without marriage, but her prose betrays her loss of faith in this endeavor. She writes of events and conversations, leaving behind the fairy tales, the coy playing to audiences, the comic personas, the willing pretense of deference to masculine authority. Her diary reads as a blunt, naked document. Leaving behind her customary wit, she writes for a purpose other than publication, other than the need to record the circumstances of her life. She writes to explore new possibilities of being, to reify her worth.

For this year Hunt records a drama, a domestic tragedy. But she does not speak in a monotone or as one subject, one fallen heroine. All of the raw and fractured aspects of her subjectivity speak in the diary through abbreviated entries, informed by snatches of dialogue. Her shrewdness conflicts with her willingness to dream and idealize her relationship with Ford; her self-destructive anger conflicts with her feminist impulse to affirm herself as woman; her "dangerous frankness" conflicts with her desire to be accepted by "the upper-middle-class society whose approbation she craved" (Secor and Secor 1983, 9–10). Hunt seeks to understand how her love for Ford turns to fury at his weak betrayal of her. She relies on recording conversations and rendering events without comment to characterize her preference for "a natural ugliness to artificial sentimental beauty" (Sinclair 1922, 118). Of course, Hunt's vision is not that simple. At the heart of the diary is her unstated belief in the sanctity and beauty of love and the rage she feels in finding it all a sham. Her irony betrays her sadness, her sociability underscores her loneliness. Her entries in their entirety comprise not so much a "choral commentary" as a shattered soliloquy.

The *1917 Diary* gains its power precisely because it speaks to Hunt herself, though she despairs that she cannot know who or what that self might be. She confronts her fractured identity as the "other" audience. Hunt's audience may be warring selves, one of which is the culture embedded within her, theatrical and passively judging. Her agonizing self-analysis, one aspect of the self warring with another, parallels her acute consciousness of a culture at war with itself, a culture where men and women viciously destroy each other, a culture where women inevitably play out lives of "rage" and "boredom" because their voices are stifled and dependent on the permission of men to become public.

## Returning to the Public Eye: Hunt as Author

The *1917 Diary* records the life of a woman who fears for her very survival, in her own eyes and in the eyes of others. But survive she did, moving beyond the deflating circumstances of a lost lover. After Ford left her she wrote five more books, all successfully received, all critiquing an aspect of the dominating masculine culture that she experienced so directly and insidiously. She wrote *Their Hearts,* an autobiographical tale of growing up with sisters; more *Tales of the Uneasy;* and *The Last Ditch,* a critique of the impact of the war. Even in 1932, at the age of sixty-nine, she published *The Wife of Rosetti,* a retelling of history showing the power of a man, Rosetti, to exploit a woman artist's nature and ultimately destroy her. As the years passed she became "The brave old dear!" yet Hunt, still talented, still confrontive, certainly did more after Ford than "keep her end up!" (Secor and Secor 1983, 34–35).

*The Flurried Years,* released in England in 1926 and published in the United States as *I Have This to Say,* brought out the scorn of those who nevertheless honored Ford's remaking of their lives in *The Good Soldier* and *No More Parades.* Even though *The Flurried Years* delineates her obsession over her loss of Love (her capital letter) and reputation, Hunt writes with wit and insight, clearly doing more than exposing Ford, really looking for answers to the questions about sexual relationships and culture asked implicitly in her *1917 Diary.* The success of her cultural critique can be measured by the fury of the male critics: Goldring calls the book an "indiscreet, painful and pain-causing volume" written to "release her pent-up emotions and distraught nerves" (1943, 76). Bohum Lynch tells Goldring, who scrupulously retells, "From what I hear of it I imagine V. H. has cleaned up her mind once and for all of *that* topic: but, Lord, what a cat she is. (Most women are, really)" (ibid.). Hunt's critique of man's inhumanity to woman cuts deep.

If these telling novels, biographies, and autobiographies do nothing more, they do record "two subjects that obsessed her: the impact of war on the women left behind and the propensity of men, especially artists, to exploit women" (Secor and Secor 1983, 35). Hunt's autobiographies and diaries expose a culture that can still reduce woman to "cat" and "old dear" and the rage that attends such subordination. Hunt took the raw materials of her life and reformed them into sometimes witty, sometimes scathing penetrations into the darker side of masculine dominance and feminine acquiescence. But these rhetorical depictions cost her.

## Circulating among Audiences: Having Her Say

Hunt's intelligence, wit, and social acumen surface in her writing through the acuity with which she wields words to enchant those who read. Ford called Hunt a genius; Goldring, "a catfish in a decorous aquarium" (1948, 171). To Henry James, "Violet was 'society,' the 'Improper Person of Babylon,' 'the lady about town,' . . . the 'great Devourer'" (Belford 1990, 128).

She aroused others with her awareness, and her ability to articulate that awareness made her both respected and feared. A gifted "plotter" with psychological acumen, an "emotional sensualist," Hunt uses rhetorical maneuverability—learned during her years of collaboration with Ford— to satisfy diverse reading publics and, alas, her coauthor. Ford's validation mattered all too much, and she endeavored to please him by pleasing their readers. She succeeded remarkably for a time.

"Too vivid to be quenched & too unique to be displaced," as James called her, Hunt took years to recover from the loss of Ford's adoring gaze and advising pen. Writing *"Mon métier a disparu,"* she connects the loss of self to a loss of the personae she constructed for him; she felt she could no longer write, could no longer create an adequate version of herself if she "can't somehow write to Ford" (Secor and Secor 1983, 69). The sense of failure to "appear" properly and to gain her audience's lasting affection and validation haunts Hunt's last published diary as she rather bitterly searches for a way to reinscribe herself. In a later memoir she reflects, "[T]here comes, sooner or later, according to the sets and the entries and exits of other actors, one's own supreme moment. One is on. And that entry, being but human, one may so easily muff. That moment, some will say, I did muff" (1926, 3). We can only decry a cultural system of values that encourages women to judge the performances of their lives through the gazes of masculine arbiters.

## Chapter 4

# Doris Lessing's
# *The Golden Notebook:*

## *"An Exposed Position"*

"'Why aren't you honest with me Anna?'. . . he began examining her notebooks, his back set in stubborn opposition to the possibility of her preventing him. . . . Anna sat still, terribly exposed . . ." (Lessing 1973, 272).

When Tommy reads Anna's notebooks and decides that she is "dishonest," that her previous concealment of the notebooks is "arrogant" (274), and that she is "making patterns out of cowardice" (275), Anna feels the presence of "some invisible enemy . . . something evil . . . an almost tangible shape of malice and destruction" (270). When Tommy goes home and immediately attempts suicide, Anna fears her own complicity. Ironically, his exposing of her through his reading of her so-called private text brings about Tommy's blindness, symbolically pointing to his inability to see or understand what she had written and why. His interpretation of Anna's text confirms his narrow view of existence; his vision fails, but he blames her. What Anna has written for herself he judges as her failure, bringing him disappointment and despair. Anna turns her anger at Tommy's intrusion inward on herself, despite his trespass against her and her notebooks. She regards her truth as dangerous and open to misunderstanding, written in notebooks she has not guarded well enough. Knowing that he misconstrued her work only feeds her guilt. In some inexplicable way her life, her notebooks have ruined Tommy. She feels she has failed in her role as writer, woman, surrogate mother, wise advisor. That Tommy debases her by his appropriation of her notebooks, his rigid judgments of her, and his readiness to find her at fault never occurs to Anna.

Doris Lessing's *Golden Notebook,* in both the "Notebook" and the "Free Women" sections, depicts women's fear of exposure in all their discursive practices but particularly in the diary, or "notebooks," as Anna calls them.

A study of Lessing's novel enables us to see clearly through both theme and structure the forceful presence of audience on women who—like Virginia Woolf, Katherine Mansfield, and Violet Hunt, and perhaps Lessing herself—use literary strategies to claim their own stories and rewrite cultural scripts without calumny.[1]

Women such as these try to mediate the relationship between oppression and writing, between personal and cultural. They feel particularly vulnerable to masculine imposition and definition because they are at the mercy of men's judgment, domestically as wives and lovers and professionally as writers. Lessing's autobiographical fiction foregrounds the issue of audience and its influence on a woman writer's production of autobiography. Lessing, through Anna Wulf's narration, strategically circulates autobiography in fiction to stage images of selves that displace the author/autobiographical presence; in this way Lessing/Anna avoids the "insistent, cynical inquisitors and consciences" (Sprague 1987, 68) of the inhibiting characters/readers, usually, but not always, male.[2]

Anna, like Lessing, declines a simple autobiographical or fictional reading of her text. Anna narrates the novel titled *Free Women* and the four notebooks that also make up the text within *The Golden Notebook*. The notebooks house even more fictions, sections of stories that prompted Anna's published *Frontiers of War;* a new novel she is writing in her yellow notebook titled *The Shadow of the Third,* narrated by an autobiographical Ella; tracts and letters by comrades without literary talent; two diary parodies in the black notebook; and hundreds of newspaper clippings.[3] The notebooks and the *Free Women* sections overlap in subject matter, merging and parting, resisting any separation of the fictional Anna from the fictional Ella.

The tricks and false clues within Lessing's novel subvert any narrow reading, including the feminist theme of the dangers of the male audience and presence to women writers, but the colliding fictions and characters mirror the fear and rage that may reside in women writers whose critique of culture make them vulnerable to "disgust, irritation, or voyeuristic curiosity in the reader rather than solidarity and sympathy" (Felski 1989, 116–17).

Lessing's novel occludes authorial presence and complicates any notion of a knowable "I." Deliberately forcing a multiplicity of readings of the text (and by extension herself), Lessing creates a text that itself cannot be located at one center, with one set of characters, one theme, one plot. A Chinese box of texts within texts and thematic mirrors and deflections capture the prismatic quality of diaries, a term Anna rejects in favor of "chaos" (1973, 41). Lessing perforates fictional/autobiographical genre boundaries, challenges perceptions of truth by multiple perspectives, and explores themes and counterthemes to evade authorial containment. Her public challenge illuminates those strategies of multiplying and dispersing readings of self more subtly embedded into the diarists' texts.

Theorizing themselves through fictions as well as more prosaic autobiographical fragments, Lessing, her Anna, and the writers of my own study evade a knowable, seamless presence to better "tell" as well as to avoid being "told."[4] Woolf writes in her diary to tell her existence and to make sense of her life as she perceives it, just as her homonymic double Anna Wulf struggles to make order in the "scramble" and "mess" of her life. But like Woolf, Anna represses parts of her experience—her bout of madness, for example—that threaten her relationships. These she relegates to fiction, allowing herself to write reflectively of "the new dimension . . . away from sanity" (613) in a discursive practice of fictionality, not of privacy. Both Woolf and Wulf illustrate the diary writer's reluctance to speak of cultural taboos and their own aberrant subjectivities.

Both the fictional Anna and the writer Virginia may relegate their more nonconformist perceptions of themselves to story form in response to an audience reading their diaries as private. They may also be responding to their own preference for fiction as a site for imagining their life stories. Anna's perception of herself as a creative writer eclipses her identity as a diary writer, forcing her to ponder, as did Woolf, "why did I not write an account of what had happened, instead of shaping a 'story' . . ." (63). As readers we must be mindful that the fictionalizing of experience for publication and within diaries may be more than an effort to hide behind protective walls; producing fictions may also be a matter of funneling experience creatively for art's sake, to entertain potential readers. Lessing uses the yellow notebook section to extend her notion of the fictionality of experience and foreground the role of the artist/author in writing even diary discourse. Just as Katherine Mansfield writes poems and story fragments within her diary and as Hunt tells of legend and fairy tales within *The Desirable Alien,* Lessing's similar strategies enable us to read more clearly their purpose in writing multiple fictions within the diaries.

Anna's disregard for genre, her fictionalizing what may be autobiographical, parallels the techniques of Mansfield and Hunt in many ways; Anna's manipulation of text casts light on Mansfield's chaotic compilation of many diaries, her inclusive fictions, her desperate appeals to Murry, her inclusion of letters, parodies, and poems. We are made aware, too, of Hunt's strategies of layering with legends and fairy tales her diary/fiction narrative in *Alien.* Lessing creates a novel from a supposed mass of scraps (which may or may not be autobiographical), while she resides outside all of these proliferating texts, subverting author location, preventing the reader from overly defining the writer: This "defect . . . may now seem less serious and more interesting because of the critical doubt surrounding the viability of the unified subject" (Valerie Sanders in Newey and Shaw 1996, 154). The texture of *The Golden Notebook* defeats efforts by readers, both Anna's and Lessing's, to narrow and reduce experience, to contain the feminine within a single narrator or a single reading.[5]

In a strategy designed to overturn limited readings of diaries, Lessing/Anna divests diaries of their traditional status as texts of personal disclosure by a self-reflexive parodying of the diary form. The parodies of diaries appear in the black notebook under the "Money" section; Lessing thus structures Anna's notebooks to mock the economic underpinnings of writing a diary for publication, to mock the reading public avid for glimpses of the so-called "private" lives of others. Anna "amuses" herself by creating a masculine persona who writes an "imaginary journal of the right tone" (Lessing 1973, 434), full of exotic place names, cryptic comments on money and romance, and quasi-philosophical musings: "June 22nd. *Café de Flore.* Time is the River on which the leaves of our thoughts are carried into oblivion. . . . Am writing a porno for Jules called *Loins.* Art is the Mirror of our betrayed ideals" (435). Lest the parody escape the reader, Anna notes that she "concocted another thousand or so words" (436) with a friend. Subsequently they published this pseudodiary. Anna and her collaborator invent next another diary "written by a lady author of early middle-age, who had spent some years in an African colony" (437). This persona could be Lessing, Anna, or no one at all.

The parodies, the collaborator, and the self-reflexive refusal to acknowledge the diary text as personal are all designed by Lessing to question the myth of diary as private. As Lessing invites her readers to see Anna's notebooks as parody, her own *Golden Notebook* becomes a meta-parody that both presents and misrepresents assumptions about private writing, particularly women's writing. Diaries begun as records of the personal sometimes become texts that provide impetus to further fictions, distortions of private thoughts and emotions by their very nature, especially when publishers, friends, lovers, and public readers become part of the diary process. Anna, for example, experiences much frustration in trying to shape her diary according to preconceived notions about what a diary should be. Anna struggles with her blue notebook, the one she has designated as diary: "[T]he blue notebook, which I had expected to be the most truthful of the notebooks, is worse than any of them . . . but this sort of record is . . . false" (468). Lessing manifests through Anna a deep-seated wariness of language's ability to reflect truth and the willingness of the writer to expose herself in imperfect words. Both the author and her character question the possibility of a personal discourse that resides apart from the stories an author creates. For Lessing the private becomes public and the public emerges from the private: "Now I must write personally; but I would not, if I didn't know that nothing we can say about ourselves is personal" (Lessing 1974, 98).

Anna, writing the personal to represent impersonality and vice versa, juxtaposes fictions to her more "factual" notebooks, telling the same stories differently in each but in such a way that truth and fiction seem to inhabit both the fictional and autobiographical texts. We simply cannot locate Lessing's truth or Anna's or any autobiographer's unless we as readers willingly suspend both belief and disbelief, willingly see fiction as autobiography and vice versa, and willingly acknowledge difference and impossibility as all true or all fiction or neither. Our vision must expand to take in multiple readings that break through realist/autobiographical considerations.

The story of Tommy, told in part at the beginning of this chapter, confuses fiction and autobiography even within the fictional frame of Lessing's novel and provides a telling example of an author's refusal to depict for readers an absolute version of their own experience. "Free Women 3" explores Tommy's attempted suicide and resulting blindness beginning with the italicized tag: "Tommy adjusts himself to being blind/while the older people try to help him" (371). The blue notebook, "which tries to be a diary" (474), records a different result of the suicide attempt and indeed tells of a quite different Tommy, who becomes a socialist and marries a "ghastly wife . . . girl'd do beautifully as the wife of a provincial businessman with slightly liberal leanings" (547). The disparity between the tragic Tommy in the "Free Women" section and the disappointingly healthy and shallow Tommy of the diary points to the ambivalence of Anna toward her young accuser. The notebooks register Anna's disappointment in him and what he has become, but Anna's "Free Women" sections underscore Tommy's role as judge, observer, blind seer.

Tommy has become a man much like his father, Richard, a man who threatens Anna with "'I'm going to see that you're exposed'" (509); Lessing cleverly conflates the father and the son in their exposing of Anna, the son in private, the father for public consumption. In the notebook section, then, Tommy is blind only in a metaphoric sense, as is his father. Neither man can "see" Anna's attempts to live ethically. Anna's fictions illumine her fears: for the privacy of her notebooks; of the power of language to both depict and misrepresent. Lessing forces the reader to see Tommy symbolically, autobiographically, fictionally—yet not realistically. In giving up our quest for truth, for the real Tommy, we must also give up our quest for the "real" Lessing. Anna's so-called autobiographical notebooks and the novel provide a "rich shadow to the public Free Women . . . reshaped for public consumption" (Sprague 1987, 80); but we must note, too, that the notebooks are fictions within Lessing's *Golden Notebook.* She protects herself and her women characters with refiguration, which Anna calls "an evasion" (1973, 197). Lessing, in her later autobiography *Walking in the Shade,* says it is impossible "to describe a writer's life, for the real part of it cannot be written down" (1997, 92), impossible to "fully convey the richness, complexity, and mysterious 'truth of the process of writing'" (94).

When a writer distorts private autobiography by turning it into fiction, she may do so because she wants to go beyond a diary discourse too closely allied to the personal. Yet "an evasion" into fiction may also be an attempt to truthfully and reliably represent experience as both of and outside the personal. As Susanna Egan reminds us, autobiography has political context as the writer is responsive to and inclusive of community (1999). Lessing's valuing of the community's consciousness over that of the individual's leads her to use "a whispering complexity of insinuations" (Lessing quoting Henry Green 2001, 62). These deflect attention from the writer herself to broader issues.

This reaching beyond personal experience to say something more can inhibit an artist, even in a notebook, as Lessing illustrates. Anna, fearful about writing anything at all, frequently uses crossouts, brackets, asterisks, doodlings, and newspaper clippings pasted in notebooks in lieu of her own commentary. In infrequent authorial narrative intrusions, Lessing describes Anna's resistance to asserting her own views; after Lessing's bracketed description of a notebook page with a black line through it Anna notes, "I drew that line because I didn't want to write it. As if writing about it sucks me further into danger"[6]: the danger of articulation, the danger of writing what she "feels," and the danger of writing to "name" it (Lessing 1973, 479). In this specific case Anna wants to avoid relating a dream in which she recognizes "a malicious force . . . in that person who was a friend" (ibid.). She simultaneously fears her own unconscious depictions becoming hard text and the "malicious force" of the friend the dream reveals to her. Interestingly, her fear of audience here is her fear of the self as writer/reader and the fear of another's malevolent disapproval. The complicated proliferation of readers prevents her articulation. Somehow if she draws a thick black line through her text, she undermines the power of her words and finds safety. Anna, looking for "the safety of anonymity" that she admits she knows "too well" (486), prides herself on her ability to "name" her emotions in writing but in one of many such maneuvers searches for ways to undo what she has done discursively.

This painful process of editing her own experience illustrates her desire to write something of importance in establishing who she is and what she feels. Much like Mansfield, whose halting entries frustrate her sense of what she wants to say, Anna finds that words "are nothing, or like the secretions of a caterpillar that are forced out in ribbons to harden in the air" (476). Perceiving themselves as writers, Anna and the diarists we have queried endeavor to display their literary capabilities even in diaries to an audience that may be imagined or quite real. Anna, pressured by an inner mistrust of her ability to write "'the truth'" and an external fear of readers who judge not only her writing but her very being, mitigates her writer's anxiety by focusing on others, blurring fact and fiction, erasing and editing, hiding her writing, refusing both wholly private and wholly public discourse.

Anna, anxious to dilute the personal in favor of something larger and stronger, represses the self in all but the short-lived diary in the blue notebook, which she dismisses as "destroying the truth" (341). In all her other writings, even the notebooks that purportedly tell her story, she resists the "sick Anna . . . the I.I.I.I" (628). In writing in the black notebook, for example, Anna tells not her story but Willi's, saying, "But I don't want to write Willi's history" (72), only to return to him to admit her own complicity in his dominating arrogance. She says, "It was from Willi I learned how many women like to be bullied" (98). She implies but denies that she was once one of them. Much later she writes that Max, her ex-husband, was "(Willi in the black notebook)," a man who made her feel overcome with "helplessness" (230). Ironically, her feeling of helplessness "made me write about him before" (ibid.) as Max and now as Willi in the reflective black notebook. She limits a personalized rendering of Max to one short diary entry and a long history in which she changes his name to Willi.

Even as she writes these autobiographical entries within the notebooks, she notes "these words will have no connection with anything that I feel is true" (ibid.). Lessing, through Anna, displays her view that the denials women write sometimes engender panic. They know "something strange happens when one writes about oneself, that is, one's self direct, not one's self projected. The result is cold, pitiless, judging" (571). Having felt the heat of others' responses and reactions to her notebooks, "Anna is torn between individualist and interdependent ideals and an interdependent sharer of selves" (Franko 1995, 266). Diarists' apprehension of their inadequacy as writers extends to the "judging" that the written word engenders.

The complexity of female/male sexual compacts complicates the writer/reader relationship further and may impose additional fears of judgment. Where the "Free Women" section and the yellow notebook cross in *The Golden Notebook,* Anna collapses autobiography and fiction to speak of the real misgivings women have about self-disclosure in both private and public discourse. Anna's and her fictional character Ella's efforts to write while under a sexual spell and under the male gaze presumably critiques the effect of romantic love and the consequent sacrifices that love demands in women.[7] Anna records a double despair through her fictional double, Ella. She cannot write for a time, and when she finally succeeds, she knows she will lose the man she loves. Sexual and discursive impotence commingle to make Ella, and Anna, afraid. Desperately trying to please by subordinating the writer in themselves to the mistress, they lose their ability to articulate honestly what they see as true. Anna writes sporadically, convinced of the failure of her words. Michael has contempt for the notebooks he is forbidden to see and exhorts her to do something real, to write a novel. Anna for a time can write nothing at all, then writes and hides her work. Her fictional character has more success, but it is a success marred by her perception that her novel contains "nothing very startling" (212). Because Paul belittles her project, Ella (like Anna) first hides her novel, then finishes it and publishes it as he begins to withdraw from her. Paul reads it and scorns what he sees as "revolution . . . women against men" (213). He seems desperate to hurt her for her revelations, responding to the novel by telling her "'you'll have ice applied to your ovaries yet'" (214). His deliberate unsexing of her comes from what he perceives as the threat to men her novel represents.

The "end of the affair" (212) comes with the novel's publication. Ella's worst fears are realized. Her exposed self occasions his betrayal, perhaps because he feels her writing betrays his sex: " 'Well, we men might just as well resign from life'" (213), he tells her, and he "resigns" from her life. Ella clearly represents a fictional Anna, who struggles to finish her own novel (about Ella) under the gaze of Michael, who classifies her notebooks as a waste of time and her novel as wasted effort.

Anna's obsession about what Lessing calls "the sex-war" (Introduction, x) prompts her to write ideas for stories exploring this topic that most unsettles her, "The Woman's emotion: resentment against injustice, an impersonal poison" (333). One section of the yellow notebook contains thirteen fictional fragments, all of them explorations from different points of view of men and women in love; nearly all of these thirteen fragments reference Anna's experience, occasionally openly autobiographical. She ends the plot exploration in "*11 A Short Novel" by commenting on Mother Sugar's theories, then writing: "(This sort of comment belongs to the blue notebook. I must keep them separate)" (537). Coming as it does in the middle of "Anna's" fictions, this comment reminds us of Anna's struggle to separate and rigidly control the various aspects of her life. Rigorously relegating to fiction those experiences and feelings too uncomfortable for diaries and notebooks, writers avoid defenseless positionings.

The story fragments themselves sharply critique relationships. Anna's mistrust of men, her depiction of women "starved for love" (531), the power of love to corrode the health and work of women, the widely varying nature of men's and women's needs—all these become subjects of Anna's fictions. Anna consciously creates fictions to critique the very precarious nature of women's relationships with men. She explores this need for deflection, for relegating to public discourse private considerations in "*14 A Short Novel." This fictional fragment outlines the effect on a relationship and on the diaries themselves when a man and woman "married or in a long relationship secretly read each other's diaries" (538). They soon find the same resolution, each keeping two diaries, one "locked up," one "for the other to read" (ibid.). The betrayal each feels when the truly secret diaries are discovered "drives them apart for ever" (ibid.). Lessing, through Anna, explores the danger of the "private diary" in the relations between men and women, then quickly changes fictions and goes on to explore in "*15" the "emotional deadlock" of an American man and an English woman.

Both "*14 A Short Novel" and "*15 A Short Story" record in fictionalized fragments Anna's reading of Saul's diary and the consequence. Desperate to know whether he is sleeping with someone else, she sneaks to his room and reads the diary. After she writes of her discovery she puts "(*14)," referencing the earlier story, drawing closer the fictions in the notebook section and the fiction of the Free Women sections. She finds his diary's chronological order stilted and artificial because it so differs from her own technique of sectioning off by subject matter. But she cannot resist reading it for a glimpse of the man she feels has hidden himself from her. She says, "I sat there on the bed, trying to marry the two images, the man I knew and the man pictured here, who is totally self-pitying, cold, calculating, emotionless" (571). Though she acknowledges that "something strange happens when one writes about oneself" (ibid.), with the lifeless quality of diary prose, she cannot resist reading Saul's view of their life together. Shocked, she observes that "I'm full of a triumphant ugly joy because I've caught him out" (573) and then starts another story "(*15)," her story of "emotional deadlock" (538).

In this section about diary discovery, written in the diary part of her notebooks, Lessing through Anna thrusts before the readers the despair of finding another's private vision so different from one's own. Anna's reading of Saul's diary ironically heightens her anxiety about her own exposed rhetorical nakedness. She hides her notebooks, then searches for his. And because she is a woman, she turns her fury inward when she reads of his betrayal. "The entry, I don't enjoy sleeping with Anna, cut me so deep I couldn't breathe for a few moments" (573). His casual indifference to her and her willingness to snoop in "someone's private papers" (ibid.) shock her. Her discovery undermines her conception of herself because his version of their life together so differs from hers, and she gives his version credence. After days of sneaking up to read the diary she admits it to him, hoping to transfer some of the humiliation of the reader to the writer: "His face . . . showed fear, then rage, then furtive triumph" (580). He defends his version of events and his promiscuity and turns to attack her jealousy and possessiveness with "a vague, spattering boastfulness" (ibid.).

Rather than feeling caught and exposed as she does when her notebooks are scrutinized, Saul feels victory at his superiority, a masculine pride at having taken what he wanted and having been discovered. Later she returns to his diary; "it was lying carelessly exposed" (587), and Anna wonders whether he has meant for her to see the entry that says, " 'Am a prisoner. Am slowly going mad with frustration'" (ibid.). Whether Saul purposely wrote for her discovery or not, the entry "cancelled out" (ibid.) what Anna had perceived as the week of happiness that preceded the entry. Anna's reading of the entry begins her regression into madness, a loss of self that parallels Tommy's reaction when he reads her notebooks. Unlike Saul, who makes use of Anna's curiosity to assert his superiority of vision, Anna becomes consumed with guilt at her notebooks' failure to convince her unauthorized reader, Tommy, of her personal worth and the integrity of her vision. Milt, a potential lover of Anna's in the "Free Woman 5" section, also reads Anna's diaries, although she tells him, "I don't want you to read them" (659). At her insistence he finally stops, relieving them both of the burden of exposing her attempt to "Cage the truth" (660).

Diaries are dangerous documents for the reader and the writer, making them both vulnerable to what lies within. These fictional renderings record the painful loss that can result when readers trespass onto a text that both reader and writer perceive as private. In excruciating detail Lessing images the consequences of careless diary writing, a carelessness avoided by the women writers in this study. Lessing thus overturns the conventional definition of diaries as private reflections of a unified self. She explores intentionality and motivation and depicts the complexity of relationships between writers and readers that proliferate selves as well as readings.

Within the narratives of the various parts of *The Golden Notebook*, Lessing builds an awareness of audience that she ties to the threat of male appropriation, an awareness central to a woman autobiographer. "Since autobiography is a public expression [a woman] speaks before and to 'man.' [She is] attuned to the ways women have been dressed up for public exposure, attuned also to the price women pay for public self-disclosure . . ." (S. Smith 1987, 49). Writing within the structural ambiguity of notebooks and fictions, Lessing mitigates her self-exposure. But she places her women characters in the harsh light of male interest and criticism, exploring the effect on the writer of masculine interest and imposition. The diaries within the text are as exposed as other autobiographical and fictional sections; for Lessing the diary shares with more traditional literary genres the same analytical scrutiny by others.

This visibility prompts many women writers such as the ones who are the subjects of this study to devise rhetorical strategies to protect themselves from the men in their lives whom they wish to please. In the yellow notebook, where Anna writes her novel *The Shadow of the Third*, Ella, Anna's autobiographical character, acknowledges her fear of writing, yet her fear is not of loneliness but of Paul's judgment and withdrawal. Ella notes parenthetically, "(To Julia she makes bitter jokes about Jane Austen hiding her novels under the blotting paper . . . quotes Stendhal's dictum that any woman under fifty who writes, should do so under a pseudonym)" (208). When Paul, his voice "full of distrust when he mentions her writing," continues to disparage her writing, Ella "begins to hide her work from him" (ibid.). He accuses her of using his "professional knowledge to get facts for her novel" (ibid.), curtailing discussions about her writing. Ella's desire to please Paul inhibits her ability to write; she allows "a black cold fear to enclose her" (207) when she thinks of his leaving her.

When Paul leaves Ella, as Michael leaves Anna, Lessing articulates through Anna's analysis of both the affairs the "theme of naivety" (211) and its effect on a woman and her writing. Blending and doubling autobiographical and fictional discourses, Lessing uses Anna to critique the powerful adversarial effect of romantic and sexual obsessions on a woman's ability to both perceive the truth and write about it. Lessing not only removes her authorial voice by allowing Anna to narrate, Anna uses her fictional characters Ella and Paul to play out the grim specter of a woman writer's struggle to please her lover as well as herself. Like Lessing's women, Hunt writes her *1917 Diary* in a blunt, curtailed style recording the shameful closing down of writing that results when a woman finds herself too caught up in performing for someone threatened by her disclosures.

Anna's and Ella's stories within *The Golden Notebook* examine man's relationship as appositional and stifling to woman's experience and woman's writing. Perhaps Lessing's view helps explain the horror we experience in reading Hunt's dependence on Ford at the expense of her own talent and happiness. Yet Lessing evades any personal relationship to the crippling effect of a male or patriarchal audience. She avoids that kind of "entrapping" by her refusal to be either Ella or Anna, by her refusal to write autobiographical diaries or notebooks that can only be called fictions, by her refusal to expose herself.[8]

Lessing emphasizes through her fictional women the "adjustments women make in order to increase or preserve their portion of praise, love, and comfort" (Sukenick 1973, 106). Indeed, the yellow notebook, which contains Anna's fiction, and the blue notebook, which she perceives as diary, relate the same story—except the names have been changed. Through Anna and Ella, Lessing illustrates the construction of autobiography into fiction as a strategy to deflect the criticism of men whom women invest with the power to hurt them. Women caught between the desire to please and the will to write must struggle to write at all, and when they do, Lessing implies they shape the discourse in response to their ambiguous place in a masculine-dominated culture.

A world that insists on its own definitions of women and resists as unsound and unfair women's depictions that differ from the male view makes women vulnerable to being misunderstood and to misunderstanding others; both are equally dangerous. We see in Violet Hunt's relationship with Ford her vulnerability and the horrible misunderstandings that result. Lessing addresses inequalities and paradoxes within the man/woman relationship within her novel, relegating to fiction, much as Hunt does in *Alien,* the precarious position woman inhabits. This theme surfaces in the first line of Lessing's novel: "The two women were alone in the London flat" (3). In using "women" and "alone" Lessing marks both their vulnerability and their community in defending themselves against masculine imposition, specifically Richard, whose visit is imminent. While waiting for Richard's entrance Anna remarks on the irony of calling themselves " 'Free women,' " noting " 'They still define us in terms of relationships with men, even the best of them'"; Molly reminds Anna, "'Well, *we* do, don't we?'" (4).

Though Anna would like to deny her own complicity in defining herself in terms of a man, she recalls Mother Sugar's reminders of Anna's failed rebellions. Mother Sugar calls her "Electra" or "Antigone," whose strength and subsequent tragedies derive from their attachment to a father and brother, respectively, and their refusal to accept traditional roles as women. The tragedy of Anna's life is that she cannot write; her energy, like Hunt's, has been spent defending her position as a woman in a society where she cannot find the correct designation. Anna can explore with

Mother Sugar but cannot write her explorations. As Tommy says accus-ingly, "You're afraid of writing what you think about life, because you might find yourself in an exposed position, you might expose yourself, you might be alone" (39). This haunting threat recalls Ford's abandoning Hunt when he had no more use for her, after his exposing her to public censure. Mansfield, too, bitterly decries having spent her latter years away from Murry. Only Woolf remained with Leonard, though her suicide sug-gests that she too was alone.

The struggle to write within an alienating culture that upholds the sex-ual dominance and importance of the male partner impinges on a woman's creative process. Anna and Saul explore the equation between sexuality and creativity and the man's need to dominate both spheres. Saul sullenly tells Anna, " . . . Knowing you are here spinning out all these words, it drives me crazy" (604). When Anna responds by saying that "a competitive American shouldn't be with a woman who has written a book" (ibid.), Lessing gives Saul the words that explain masculine resis-tance and hostility to feminine creativity: He says Anna's writing is "a challenge to my sexual superiority, and that isn't a joke" (ibid.). Appropriating Anna's new golden notebook for his own when she refuses to give it to him, he writes: "Whoever he be who looks in this/He shall be cursed,/That is my wish./Saul Green, his book.(!!!)" (607). Saul thus rein-states his "sexual superiority."

But in writing what Anna calls "the old schoolboy's curse" (607), Saul makes Anna laugh. His obvious usurpation releases her from taking the book, or him, seriously. When she throws off Saul's desire to take her book and control its contents, she vows to write "a new notebook, all of myself in one book" (ibid.), and she does so, calling it *The Golden Notebook*. Saul's "naming" of her fears of sexual and creative dominance and possession allows Anna to wrest herself free of his, or any man's, imposition. Anna notes her desire to give the notebook to him, saying, "But I will not, I will not, I will not" (ibid.). Finally free from her fierce desire to please, Anna seizes the notebooks for her own, establishing her discursive independence.[9]

Lessing's tone oscillates between hostility and sympathy concerning the women who measure their achievement against male standards because of emotional dependence. Perhaps what the fictional Anna and Virginia Woolf share is the sense that a gap separates a man's understanding from a woman's—and the dangers that attend the difference. As Anna says, "And yet there's always a point even with the most perceptive and intelli-gent man, when a woman looks at him across a gulf: he hasn't understood; she suddenly feels alone . . ." (214). Anna's repressions and evasions in her diary may, like Woolf's, stem from a sense of loneliness, of misunderstanding, of gendered differences that cannot be breached; Anna-the-diarist represents women stifled and fearful of "institutions rigid and oppressive" (Introduction, xvi). But Lessing's depictions of difference are different from those of Woolf, whose dependence on Leonard was domestic and cultural rather than driven by erotic complicity. Lessing clearly sympathizes with the sexual compulsion of the heterosexual woman, yet she sees this attachment as destructive when it becomes a psychological dependence that interferes with a woman's creative act.

Lessing's sympathies clearly reside with Anna, who in self-mockery speaks impatiently of women who allow themselves to be consumed by male opinion. Often through Ella, Anna speaks of Lessing's understanding of the sexual compacts between men and women that undermine women's own sense of competence. In the yellow notebook Ella "is acutely humiliated, thinking . . . she is dependent on men for 'having sex,' for 'being serviced,' for 'being satisfied' . . . that was not for sex, but . . . all the emotional hungers of her life" (455). In this section, only when Ella feels "completely sexless" can she begin to write "the book which is already written inside her" (459).

Lessing thus forces readers to acknowledge that even in autobiographical writing "no single 'authorial I'" controls perception (Egan 1999, 2). Anna tries to write everything down on September 15, 1954, in order to find a personal pattern of truth. But her perception of the falsity of "this kind of record" and her fear of readers' opinions complicate her project. "I begin to doubt the value of a day's recording before I've started . . ." (Lessing 1973, 340). This humility in recording daily experience and the concern with social propriety and literary value surface in the diaries of Woolf, Mansfield, and Hunt, hinting at the uneasy juxtaposition of woman and writer. Anna, like the others, cannot ignore the problems of cultural convention and audience even in what she perceives as her most private notebook. She talks of James Joyce's description of a man (Bloom) defecating, then writes: "[I]n some review, a man said he would be revolted by the description of a woman defecating. I resented this. . . . But he was right for all that" (ibid.). Caught between cultural taboos and literary tact, diary writers cannot record the sum of experience in a private text. Anna's diary admits to the "problems of being truthful in writing (which is being truthful about oneself)" (ibid.).

Anna's writing block, this writing and nullifying, results from the caution in revealing herself to the peering and peeking of—Tommy, Richard, Michael/Paul, Saul/Milt, Jack—and in part from her internalized audience's expectations about who and what she should be. Her insecurity, especially about relationships, beleaguers her sense of self-worth, subverting her ability to write of the personal except in circumlocution and incomplete fictions. The world that culturally inscribes Anna and the male authorities she courts impose their values on her as she struggles to write. The "invisible enemy . . . the almost tangible shape of malice and destruction" (270) that Tommy embodies when he reads Anna's notebooks resides in Michael when he says, "Ah, Anna, you make up stories about life and tell them to yourself," reducing her feelings to "coldness and dismay" (331). Male mockery makes her feel "as if the substance of the self were thinning and dissolving" (ibid.). Similarly, when Paul leaves Ella after first criticizing her writing, she feels "as if a skin had been peeled off her" (312). Needing man's validation "for the emotional hungers of her life" (455), Anna nevertheless feels the weight of masculine pressure, both culturally and personally, when she begins to write her experience. As she explains to Saul, "[A]t the moment I sit down to write, someone comes into the room, looks over my shoulder and stops me" (639). She describes her intruder in plural figures, presumably masculine: "It could be a Chinese peasant . . . Castro's guerilla fighters . . . an Algerian fighting . . . or Mr. Mathlong. They stand here . . . and say, why aren't you doing something about us, instead of wasting your time scribbling?" (ibid.). Anna's heightened sensitivity about the opinions of others draws attention to the constraint diarists such as Mansfield and Woolf, and Hunt to a lesser extent, feel in presenting versions of themselves to an audience. In anxiously fearing criticism, they seek to place the focus of diary writing elsewhere—not on their own subjectivity.

Lessing's deep suspicion of institutional writing practices and their negative effects on writers indicates the author/narrator's cognizance of audiences that go beyond the personal reader. The dangerous nature of political discourse surfaces early in the novel. Anna's strong philosophical attachment to Marxism informs her thinking and her writing, but she cannot write what she wishes until she releases herself from the contradictions of "truth and lies" (481) the British communist party came to embody. Clearly, Lessing sees the party as a metaphor for all politically imposed systems; her attack is not on the communist party so much as it encompasses all patriarchal systems. Anna, in an ambivalent relationship to the party, struggles to separate the "truth and lies" of her own life. She works to throw off institutionally imposed versions of experience. Early in the novel Anna advises Molly to rip up materials the party had asked for that delineated her "'doubts and confusions'" about party membership. Anna tells Molly she is "mad" to write down what she calls "evidence to hang you" and urges her to destroy her complaints, which Molly does. Anna knows the party's potentially dangerous judgments of her and other members; she struggles to balance the important philosophical underpinnings of communism with the oppression of the actual party.

In the brief vignettes about Anna's work with the party, her joining, her leaving, Lessing explores the institutional silencing of dissent. She draws attention to the tyranny that can destroy a writer's quest for meaning. Anna's descriptions of the party's attempt to control discursive practice and the consequences of disclosure draw attention to the power of artic- ulation and the dangers that await writers within oppressive systems. Anna "jokes" with Jack when arguing their warring political positions: " 'I am essentially the one to be shot—that is traditionally my role'" (341). Anna's awareness of the danger of her rebellion forces her to curtail writ- ing about her political doubts. As Lessing puts it, "Anna's stammer was because she was evading something. Once a pressure or a current . . . start- ed, there was . . . no way of *not* being intensely subjective" (xiii). Cultural institutions promote their own version of "truth" at the expense of indi- vidual renderings.

In embedding harsh critiques in fictions, she ranges from the South African system she writes of in her black notebook, to the British capital- ists who want to change her book for cinema. This look at the imposition of broader, more formalized audiences on discourse may seem far afield from the world of the diary writer. Lessing, however, exposes not herself in the diary but the layers of corrosive ideology on a writer's freedom, illu- minating the oppressive systems within which the women of this study function. Lessing works within a structure of alterity, inducing readers to interrogate diary texts and to use those texts to critique social and politi- cal practices.

Although both men and women write under what Jacques Derrida calls the "fatal necessity" of representation, women are particularly vulnerable to the pressures of audiences holding the power to political and sexual economies. Lessing subverts readers' intentionality to place her, to name her, while she challenges existing modes of experience by creating new dis- cursive practices of her own. Virginia Woolf, Katherine Mansfield, and Violet Hunt each exercise their genius and their remarkably adept use of language to likewise shift such intentions and challenge prevailing custom.

Anna's "invisible projectionist," laughing and jeering, unveiling the script of her life, symbolizes the spectators that so threaten women's dis- closure. In the "Golden Notebook" section, which ends the book, Anna dreams of the projectionist's screening of her experience, *"Directed by Anna Wulf"* (619). He berates her with her "untruth," and Anna, "faced with the burden of re-creating order out of the chaos that [her] . . . life had become," agonizes. Anna confesses that "I was unable to distinguish between what I had invented and what I had known" (ibid.). Neither Anna nor the reader can extricate truth from the dream discourse. Is the projectionist's "sadistically delighted" (620) undoing of Anna's script caused by her own internalized censor casting doubt on its worth or by another's twisted reception? Anna awakens and gives Saul the projectionist's role, telling him, "Do you know, you've become a sort of inner conscience or critic . . . ?" (621).

Saul has become all of the men (Michael, the Pauls, Jack, Willi, and Max) who instructed, criticized, and judged Anna. Yet Anna internalizes Saul, amalgamating a cultural imposition. Always searching, she finds the truth unwinding on the projector of the mind before her, a projector run by a male "projectionist."[10] In her mind Anna names Saul as the purveyor of truth, shifting and subordinating her own keen observations to a masculine sensibility.

Yet, ironically, this recognition of her dependence on Saul liberates Anna. Once she recognizes his influence, she works to reinstate her control of the "critical and thinking Anna" (331) that men have discouraged: "The projectionist now being silent . . . so I leaned out my own hand to switch off the machine" (635). Anna triumphs by writing her book, but at a cost she finds herself unable to measure. Lessing thus contemplates the considerable challenge women writers face in ridding themselves of the "projectionist" to write their own stories—and she illustrates in her own textual strategies the methods they may employ to mediate between the artist and her audience, both internal and external..

Lessing's narrator Anna as well as Woolf, Mansfield, and Hunt face audiences similar to those the Duchess of Newcastle anticipated when she wrote her own diary in 1656: the "carping tongues" and "malicious censurers" (Newcastle, quoted in Jones 1988, 154). The weight of the wedding band or the ache of its absence imposes on these women a deliberate need to negotiate their position in a culture that seeks to diminish them. In their artistry of words, in their arrangement of sentences, they write themselves into text. And, as Bruss points out, "Language . . . offers no way of recording, without also staging" (1976, 302). In staging the performances of their lives, these women diarists write their lines in the presence of audience.

# *Notes*

## Notes to Introduction

1. Elizabeth Bruss's 1976 *Autobiographical Acts* explores the intersections between gender and generic systems; she argues that gender systems are created and sustained in culture and that "outside of social and literary conventions that create and maintain it, autobiography has no features" (6), thus noting the arbitrary definitions of both gender and autobiography. Judith Kegan Gardiner and Irma McClaurin add in a 1998 "Preface" to *Feminist Studies* that "the issue of female resistance to patriarchy has been a continuing feminist theme but until recently scholars have paid less attention to men's experiences as both resisters and reinforcers of patriarchy and to their socialization as specifically masculine subjects." Sherif Hetata notes in a 2003 *PMLA* article the ways in which "men in a patriarchal society divided by class are accustomed to exercising power, to controlling, to constructing, to bringing order to chaos, to concealing weaknesses or replacing it with strength and to mold things to their will. The self is a construction, an image that must be maintained," suggesting that "perhaps women will help men write real autobiography—that is, if literature and art and other beautiful things survive . . ." (125).

2. Simons sees diaries as "a license of uncensored expression" (18) as well as acknowledging a potential readership. She addresses this paradox, saying, "The dividing line between degrees of privacy is a delicate one, and the nature of the implied audience inevitably determines the tone and content of the text" (7). Obviously for Duchess de Praslin, her privacy was breached with disastrous results.

3. I use the term "husband" loosely. Woolf was the only one of the three who was married in a traditional sense. Mansfield lived with John Middleton Murry for more than six years before they finally married in 1918. Whether Violet Hunt and Ford Madox Ford ever did marry is still a matter of dispute, though their affair lasted for almost ten years and they lived together as man and wife much of that time, causing scandal and legal action against them.

4. The terms *diary, journal,* and *notebook* are used interchangeably in this study. Though there are distinctions that can be made between them (the journal generally held to be more complete and organized than diaries or daily notebooks), the texts by Woolf, Mansfield, Hunt, and Lessing's Anna Wulf all share similar characteristics in terms of regular recordings of events, thoughts, and feelings.

5. Barbara Belford found many other Hunt diaries in researching her excellent 1990 biography, *Violet: The Story of the Irrepressible Violet Hunt and Her Circle of Lovers and Friends—Ford Madox Ford, H. G. Wells, Somerset Maugham, and Henry James.* I was able to draw on her published materials. Also of note is Joan Hardwick's 1990 biography, *An Immodest Violet: The Life of Violet Hunt.* Hardwick focuses on Hunt's fiction, which is particularly helpful since so many of Hunt's novels are out of print and difficult to find.

6. I resist a rigid essentialist and gendered reading of diaries, noting that men, too, may write diaries that both conform to and resist patriarchal standards in the presence of audience. John Paul Eakin, for example, argues that men's and women's autobiographical texts share and differ in degrees, not in whole categories. However, cultural power relations that value "subjects" and "selves" differently ideologically and socially dictate that some groups work from within those relations, whereas some struggle against them. Thus, this study emphasizes that "difference" in gendered constructions while acknowledging there are other groups outside the hegemonic power structures that suffer equally, if not more so, from patriarchal devaluation.

7. Domna Stanton in *Autogynography* says, "It will surely come as no surprise that beyond their tacit agreement to exclude women's texts, critics disagreed about the specific nature and substance of autobiography" (1998, 134). Judy Lensink Temple also argues that the diary is "resisted because in both form and content it comes closest to a female version of autobiography . . . emerging as a female text" (1987, 40). Their studies and others in the late 1980s and early 1990s added much to the beginnings of a refiguring of autobiography and diary criticism through a woman's experience: Shari Benstock and her editing of *The Private Self*; Bella Brodski and Celeste Schenck's *Life/Lines: Theorizing Women's Autobiography,* and Mary G. Mason's influential "The Other Voice—Autobiographies of Women Writers." I note especially Sidonie Smith's work, beginning with her *Poetics of Women's Autobiography* and continuing with her several books. These early critical incursions into patriarchal autobiography authority, in addition to poststructural explosions of the canonical, laid additional groundwork for productive and interesting critical queer theory and postcolonial "authorizing" of selves in patriarchal culture. For a more complete reading of the history of diary criticism, see Elizabeth Podnieks's "Blurring Boundaries: Mapping the Diary as Autobiography and Fiction" in *Daily Modernism* (2000, 13–45).

8. The diarists discussed in this study are products of turn-of-the-century British middle- and upper-middle-class cultures. Their personal experiences and geographical place within that culture varied greatly, however, with Virginia Woolf and Violet Hunt primarily urban and independently wealthy—in varying degrees. Both Hunt and Woolf found they had to earn money writing to supple-

ment their income. Katherine Mansfield hailed from a very wealthy New Zealand background but chose a struggling middle-class existence with her literary editor/husband. She too felt the need to write for the salary she would earn. Similar institutions, cultural pressures, and codes of behavior exerted pressures on each. See *Representing Femininity: Middle Class Subjectivity in Victorian and Edwardian Autobiographies* by Mary Jean Corbett (1992).

9. Many critics of autobiography are divided on the importance of audience on the writing, particularly when it comes to diaries. Sidonie Smith, George Gusdorf, and the Personal Narrative Group maintain that the diary is essentially private. Judy Simons holds that women who write diaries often are "secret exhibitionists," though only one chapter, "The Fear of Discovery: The Journals of Fanny Burney," touches on the imposition of a real rather than a fictive audience and its influence on the writer's work (1990, 1). Nancy K. Walker's "Wider than the Sky" does acknowledge the "public presence" (1988, 272) in the diaries of diary writers, specifically Woolf, Emily Dickinson, and Alice James. Shari Benstock and Elizabeth Podnieks share an interest in the ways in which the idea of audience shapes texts. Lynn Z. Bloom creates categories of diary writers: those writing with an audience in mind and those who do not. I concur with Lawrence Rosenwald that "All our utterances are mediated through our sophisticated or imperfect sense of some public, externally given form" (Podnieks 24). I suggest that all diarists know—or find out—that their diaries can be open to scrutiny and are interested in specific audiences of husbands and literary communities as audiences—not in the generalized "idea" of audience.

10. Writing diaries under any oppressive and authoritarian regime, whether domestic or political, can be "downright dangerous," according to Margaret Ziolkowski in her study of Russian diaries (1987, 199).

11. Judy Nolte Lensink Temple uses the artist's metaphor, which I appropriated: "[D]iary writers tell their truth and create female design" (1987, 41).

12. "Modernism" is a term perhaps overly definitive for the tradition-shedding fragmentation of literary genre written at the turn of the century. The modernist author's sense of alienation and rejection of traditional values may parallel many women writer's depictions of themselves in culture; in practice, however, modernism itself limits readings of "modernist" works and authors and, although useful, should be regarded skeptically.

13. Perhaps because of childhood experiences or fear of what Gail Godwin calls "a snooper" (in Lifshin 1982, 17), diaries are often cautious documents. As Maxine Kumin writes to Lifshin, "[V]ery little of my interior is showing. . . . I am too much living a life of mother and wife now to unfold. It is all . . . in the pleats" (ibid.).

14. Thomas Mallon groups Woolf in the category of "Creators" in his book on diaries, and Mary Jane Moffat and Charlotte Painter's *Revelations* categorizes

Woolf's diaries as "Work" diaries. Judy Simons notes the diary "formed a corner-stone for her total artistic undertaking" (1990, 170). H. Porter Abbott provides a close reading of the way Woolf's diary prefigured *Night and Day*. Podnieks's more complete study positions Woolf solidly within the modernist tradition, pro-viding an excellent analysis of Woolf's stylistic method—both in language and diary formats.

15. Hassam invites speculation on the reader's motivation in reading diaries. He argues that although we can no longer sustain the illusion of authenticity with regard to subjectivity, we read "published diaries as if they had not been pub-lished, as if we were not authorized readers" (1987, 442). He suggests that read-ers join in the fiction of their privacy. Gail Godwin seems to agree when she says, "Diarists: that shrewdly innocent breed, those secret exhibitionists and incompa-rable purveyors of sequential, self-conscious life; how they fascinate me and endear themselves to me by what they say and do not say" (in Halpern 1988, 9).

16. In her "Feminist Revision in New Historicism to Give Fuller Readings of Women's Private Writing," Helen Buss provides an excellent reading strategy for reading diaries. She combines close reading in a "consciously interdisciplinary practice in which a 'thick description' and a poststructuralist theory of language is put in the service of a feminist New Historicist agenda" (1996, 100). Using psychology, philosophy, law, and even neuroscience, John Paul Eakin also pro-vides cross disciplinary theories of reading autobiographical texts in his *How Our Lives Become Stories: Making Selves* (1999).

# Notes to Chapter 1

1. Woolf 1980, 239.

2. Virginia Woolf's early diaries (1897–1909) have been collected under the title *Virginia Woolf: A Passionate Apprentice,* Mitchell A. Leaska, editor (1990). Louise DeSalvo, in her *Virginia Woolf: The Impact of Childhood Sexual Abuse on Her Life and Work* (1989), devotes an entire chapter to Woolf's adolescent use of "Miss Jan" in her diary.

3. Virginia Woolf's biographers vary in their opinion of Leonard Woolf and the Woolf marriage. Hermione Lee's *Virginia Woolf* analyzes astutely, concluding that Leonard was a "guardian" and the "marriage made a frame and a space for the work, which was life to her" (1997, 314). DeSalvo (1989) argues that Virginia as an incest survivor invited Leonard's power over her; Mitchell Leaska's *Granite and Rainbow: The Hidden Life of Virginia Woolf* (1998) analyzes the incest narrative differently, seeing Leonard as a "father figure." Roger Poole calls him "despotic" in his *The Unknown Virginia Woolf* (1978) as does Lyndall Gordon, whose *Virginia Woolf* (1984) is critical of the "Master" Leonard. Jeffrey Meyers writes in his *Married to Genius* that Leonard's "code of duty, faith in her

art . . . sustain and even cure her" (1977, 112), a view shared by George Spater and Ian Parsons in *A Marriage of True Minds* (1977). Natania Rosenfeld's *Outsiders Together: Virginia and Leonard Woolf* (2001) sees the two sharing an "outsider" status, a commitment to justice, and a contribution to modernism.

4. "Bunny" is David Garnett, writer and literary editor of the *New Statesman* and *Nation* from 1932 to 1935. He later married Woolf's niece Angelica Bell, though her Aunt Virginia was critical of their relationship. "Duncan" is Duncan Grant, who lived with Woolf's sister, Vanessa, from the year 1915 and fathered Angelica.

5. Male modernist jealousies concerning women writers are discussed at length in Sandra Gilbert and Susan Gubar's *No Man's Land: The Place of the Woman Writer in the Twentieth Century* (1988) and Mary Lynn Broe and Angela Ingram's *Women's Writing in Exile* (1989, 19–41).

6. Rowena Fowler's "Moments and Metamorphoses: Virginia Woolf's Greece" discusses Woolf's use of the "Greek chorus" of collective, anonymous voices in her work (1999). See also Allen McLaurin's "Consciousness and Group Consciousness in Virginia Woolf."

7. Jacques Lacan's phrase "presence in absence" refers to the whole play of Desire; I refer merely to that which we read between the lines, the tensions in Woolf's silences.

8. Woolf's sexuality, or supposed "lack" of sexuality, is seriously discussed by all of her biographers, drawing radically different conclusions. Jane Marcus calls these discussions "a custody battle over her reputation" (1987, xi).

9. "Dady" refers to George Humphrey Wolferstan (Dadie Rylands), "Scholar of Eton and of King's College, Cambridge," one of the "Apostles" (Woolf 1978, n. 258). "Raymond" is Raymond Mortimer, critic and journalist.

10. See Jane Marcus's "Sapphistry: Narration as Lesbian Seduction in *A Room of One's Own,*" in her *Virginia Woolf and the Language of Patriarchy* (1987).

11. Max Beerbohm's *And Even Now* (1920); Aldous Huxley's "The Farcical History of Richard Greenow," a story in his book *Limbo* (1920); and Wyndham Lewis's *The Roaring Queen* (1973) all satirize Woolf's position in the literary modernist world, depicting her power as somehow sexually dominant and emasculating.

12. Jane Marcus's reference to this nightingale image (93) in her essay, "Liberty, Sorority, Misogyny" (1987, 75–95) sparked my own differing analysis.

13. For a thorough analysis of Virginia Woolf's experiences with sexual abuse see Leaska and DeSalvo. For completely different interpretation of events see "Who's Afraid for Virginia Woolf," a review of DeSalvo's book by Quentin Bell in the *New York Review,* March 15, 1990.

14. See Elaine Showalter's *The Female Malady: Women, Madness, and English Culture, 1830–1980:* "It remained to Virginia Woolf, however, to connect the

shell-shocked veteran with the repressed woman of the man-governed world through their common enemy, the nerve specialist" (1987, 192).

15. In *Three Guineas* Woolf redefines the word *feminist* by her hypothesis to rid the world of the word in order to reclaim for everyone the equality and "rights of all" (1936, 102).

## Notes to Chapter 2

1. Boddy 1988, 149.

2. Judy Simons in her study *Diaries and Journals of Literary Women from Fanny Burney to Virginia Woolf* addresses the question of Katherine Mansfield's "naming" of herself: "The very name 'Katherine Mansfield' is a mark of the uncertainties that dogged her. She was born Kathleen Mansfield Beauchamp . . . but throughout her life she was known by different names to her different friends, 'Kathleen,' 'Katherine,' 'Katie,' 'Tig,' 'Kassienska,' 'K.M.,' each one indicting her shift of identity in any particular relationship and her own enjoyment of role-playing" (1990, 152).

3. The complete *Notebooks* "includes everything; even isolated words and sentences . . . the huge, amorphous, nearly illegible mass of material . . .—the whole raft of it—is so rich in reflections of, connections with, roots of, hints at, variations of her best work that to explicate it all would take . . . lifetimes" (Scott 2002, xiv–xv).

4. Mark Gertler, a painter from The Slade, was much a part of Bloomsbury in his relationships with Lady Ottoline Morrell, Dora Carrington, and Virginia Woolf. As Tomalin says of his relationship with Mansfield, "Gertler decided that he liked Katherine, and wanted to know her better. Her journal is discreetly silent about it" (1988, 132).

5. Even after her death D. H. Lawrence had little to say about Mansfield's talent as a writer. He writes to Murry: " 'Poor Katherine, she is delicate and touching—But not Great! Why say great?' (Tomalin 1988, 239). Gilbert and Gubar take Lawrence and other male modernists to task for their arrogance: "[They] were . . . attempting to end the idea of poetry for ladies, and they were often attempting to do so specifically by castigating what they defined as the incoherence or destructiveness of the female language" (1988, 236).

6. Tillie Olsen's seminal work *Silences* delineates what silences women: "[C]ensorship silences: . . . deletions, omissions, abandonment of the medium." They result from "publisher's censorship" or "self-censorship" (1965, 9). Sara Kofman's *The Enigma of Woman* (36–97) draws on Freud's "Three Essays," where she notes his belief that women's "erotic life . . . partly owing to the stunting effect of civilized conditions and partly owing to their conventional secretiveness and insincerity—is still veiled in an impenetrable obscurity" (1985, 151).

7. Recent research on women's diaries (including my own) owes much to earlier theories about the "'unspoken' of femininity" (DeLauretis 1984, 95), the idea that the unspoken in self-narrative marks the text as significantly as the spoken.

8. Mansfield's references to her sexual relationship with Murry were "baldly matter of fact" (Boddy 1988, 42): "Jack & I lay in bed, deeply in love, strangely in love. . . . We have each other our freedom in a strange way" (67). This reticence expresses a repression of sexual language, long a taboo for women. Murry's letters, on the other hand, express a masculine openness and eroticism: "Even now that I begin to imagine our caresses, my hand snuggling against your wonderful breasts, my lips feeling slowly over them till I kiss—it is all so true" (J.M. Murry to K.M., March 29, 1915). These comparisons and many others are in Boddy's *Katherine Mansfield* (1988).

9. Mansfield writes Ida Baker, L.M., expressing a jealousy not to be guessed from the *Journal*: "You're the greatest *flirt,* I ever have met, a real *flirt*. I do wish you weren't. With all my heart I do. It seems so utterly indecent at our age to be still all aflutter at every possible glance . . . I am not going to flirt back, Miss, and say how I want you as part of my life and can't really imagine being without you . . . read as much love as you like into this letter. You won't read more than is there" (K.M. to L.M., 1921; *The Letters of Letters of John Middleton Murry to Katherine Mansfield,* vol. II, 1983, 172).

10. One side effect of pulmonary tuberculosis, which Mansfield may have contracted from D. H. Lawrence in the winter of 1916, is violent mood swings. Mansfield's mood swings make her unpredictable at best. Lawrence suffered from a similar moodiness that critics say bordered on madness.

# Notes to Chapter 3

1. When *White Rose of Weary Leaf* was published in 1908, Hunt received much acclaim. H. G. Wells wrote her: "[I]f you go on you will be a credit to the Fabian Society"; Galsworthy thanked her for writing as "you have let us into many workings of the woman's mind . . ." (Secor and Secor 1983, 15). D. H. Lawrence argued for Hunt "as a novelist, saying that she wasn't at all appreciated" (Secor and Secor 1987, 17). Marie Secor's "Violet Hunt, Novelist" (*English Literature in Transition* 19 [1976]: 25–34) analyzes her literary worth.

2. Until 1918 Ford Madox Ford used his baptismal name, Ford Hermann Hueffer. He called himself Joseph Leopold Hueffer after his German Catholic baptismal name while in Germany. He decided on Ford Madox Ford after World War I. I call him Ford throughout, though I sometimes refer to him as "Joseph Leopold" during the German excursion because Hunt did.

3. Of Ford's six "wives," Hunt, Jean Rhys, and Stella Bowen wrote autobiographies and fictions of their relationship with him.

4. Douglas Goldring decries the fact that "ladies on whom Ford bestowed his affections, and who subsequently nourished grievances against him, were not restrained by these considerations from pursuing their quarrels in public" (1943, 75). Patricia Searles and Janet Mickish counter: "The woman . . . is expected to understand her man's point of view and to accommodate herself to his desires. She is expected to be able to do this in silence" (1984, 269).

5. Ford's German patriot musings in the chapter "Subject Races" can be read with painful retrospective irony after Britain's two world wars with Germany, especially in light of Ford's fighting for Britain in World War I. British colonialism certainly influences *Alien* as the two authors work to praise German aggression while keeping the British Empire intact—rhetorically at least.

6. "Ayenbite of Inwit," a medieval philosophical phrase, describes the poignancy of anxiety coupled with regret.

7. Hunt codes as "H—" or "G—" the small towns and villages whose inhabitants Hunt often describes in much detail and sometimes satirizes. Hunt must have meant to protect the people of the towns and her own legal position.

8. Violet contracted syphilis in an early affair with Oswald Crawfurd, a married man. Just when she discovered it is not clear, but her doctor told Ford of the illness in 1915.

9. In "Marriage and Sex in the Novels of Ford Madox Ford" (*Modern Fiction Studies* 23.4 [1977–1978]), Igor Watt states, "in Ford's novels the love relationship occurs invariably outside marriage, while the marital relationship is experienced as destructive and deathly" (587).

10. In 1914 Ford had an affair with Brigit Patmore, a friend of Hunt's. By 1917 Hunt was still worried about it, writing, "I could love B[rigit]—I suppose if I believed in F & his statements I could not. So—.-. . . F's letter came. I made her read it" (Secor and Secor 1978, 58).

# Notes to Chapter 4

1. Elizabeth Podnieks argues that diary writers such as the ones in this study write with a literary, modernist consciousness of form; if aware of an audience either real or potential (which I hold is nearly always the case) writers are also "concerned with the aesthetic potential of the diary" (2000, 351). Such attention to technique and reception seems to hold regardless of the period in which they write. See Harriet Blodgett's *Centuries of Female Days* (1988).

2. Lessing accuses a myriad of critics of assuming *The Golden Notebook* embodies "The Confessions of Doris Lessing" (Newquist interview 1974, 51). She says in an interview with Florence Howe that the novel "was a detached book" representing what "she took . . . absolutely for granted," the "despicable game" between men and women where "any sort of loaded point sucks in anger or fear" (ibid., 81).

3. Anna mentions the notebook's inclusion of hundreds of newspaper clippings and letters as part of the notebooks, but they are not actually part of this text. In Anna's editing process, she deletes as well as joins materials to create her golden notebook.

4. Patrocinio Schweickart says, "the reader is a visitor and . . . must observe the necessary courtesies. She must avoid unwarranted intrusions—she must be careful not to appropriate what belongs to her host, not to impose herself on the other woman" (1997, 623).

5. By shifting the reader's gaze from the woman writer to the process and effect of writing, Lessing places the discourse, the "structure" as Lessing would have it, at the center of the reader's production of meaning.

6. Anna's "crossed out material" has significance, but "Lessing, Anna's creator, chose not to pursue in her subsequent fiction direct visual presentation of raw worked-over, interpolated, or discarded materials" (Sprague 1987, 81).

7. In *Walking in the Shade*, the second volume of Lessing's autobiography, she writes: "Far from being like George Sand . . . I never put writing before love, or before Jack; . . . [I] was like Jane Austen, writing . . . well, if not under the cover of a blotter, then only when he was not around or expected" (1997, 146).

8. In her interview *Against Utopia* with Suzie Linfield, Lessing admits to writing a diary "now" (she is eighty-one), but when asked if it will be published she says, "Not immediately. Not until the children are all dead. I think the children of well-known people have a terrible time . . . persecuted by journalists" (2001, 69).

9. In this section Anna refuses to give Saul her notebook; this act of refusal empowers Anna sufficiently to give Saul the first line of his novel. It is then that Saul returns her notebook that he has appropriated. Only in refusing to give way to Saul does Anna remain "author, reader, reviewer, parodist, and critic of her own texts" (Franko 1995, 255, 264).

10. In *The Summer before Dark* Lessing writes: "[S]he knew now that . . . all her life she had been held upright by an invisible fluid, the notice of other people" (1983, 176).

# Works Consulted

Abbott, H. Porter. "Old Virginia and the Night Writer: The Origins of Woolf's Narrative Meander." In *Inscribing the Daily,* ed. Susanne L. Bunkers and Cynthia A. Huff, 236–51. Amherst: University of Massachusetts Press, 1996.

Alpers, Antony. *The Life of Katherine Mansfield.* New York: Viking, 1980.

Anderson, Linda. *Women and Autobiography in the Twentieth Century.* New York: Prentice Hall/Harvester Wheatsheaf, 1997.

Ashley, Kathleen, Leigh Gilmore, and Gerald Peters, eds. *Autobiography and Post-Modernism.* Amherst: University of Massachusetts Press, 1994.

Auerbach, Nina. *Romantic Imprisonment.* New York: Columbia University Press, 1986.

Bashkirtseff, Maria. *Journal.* Trans. Mary J. Safford. New York: Dodd, Mead, 1912.

Beerbohm, Max. *And Even Now.* London: Heinemann, 1920.

Belford, Barbara. *Violet: The Story of the Irrepressible Violet Hunt and Her Circle of Lovers and Friends—Ford Madox Ford, H. G. Wells, Somerset Maugham, and Henry James.* New York: Simon and Schuster, 1990.

Bell, Anne Olivier. Introduction. In *The Diary of Virginia Woolf 1915–1919,* vii–xi. Vol. 2. New York: Harcourt, 1978.

———, ed. *The Diary of Virginia Woolf 1915–1919.* Vols. 1–2. New York: Harcourt, 1977.

Bell, Quentin. *Virginia Woolf: A Biography.* New York: Harvest/HBJ, 1972.

———. Introduction. In *The Diary of Virginia Woolf 1915–1919,* ed. Anne Olivier Bell, xiii–xxviii. Vol. 1. San Diego: Harvest/HBJ, 1977.

———. "Who's Afraid for Virginia Woolf?" Review of *Virginia Woolf: The Impact of Childhood Sexual Abuse on Her Life and Work* by Louise DeSalvo. *The New York Review* (1990): 36.

Benstock, Shari. "Women's Literary History to Be Continued: From the Editor's Perspective." *Tulsa Studies in Women's Literature* (Fall 1986) : 5–15.

———. "Authorizing the Autobiographical." In *The Private Self,* ed. Shari Benstock, 10–33. Chapel Hill: University of North Carolina Press, 1988.

———. "Expatriate Modernism: Writing on the Cultural Rim." In *Women's Writing in Exile,* ed. Mary Lynn Broe and Angela Ingram. 1940. Chapel Hill: University of North Carolina Press, 1989.

———, ed. *The Private Self.* Chapel Hill: University of North Carolina Press, 1988.

Blodgett, Harriet. *Centuries of Female Days: Englishwomen's Private Diaries.* New Brunswick: Rutgers University Press, 1988.

Bloom, Lynn. "The Diary as Popular History." *Journal of Popular Culture* 9.4 (1976): 794–807.

———. "'I Write for Myself and Strangers': Private Diaries as Public Documents." In *Inscribing the Daily: Critical Essays on Women's Diaries,* ed. Suzanne Bunkers and Cynthia A. Huff, 23–38. Amherst: University of Massachusetts Press, 1996.

Boddy, Gillian. *Katherine Mansfield: The Woman and the Writer.* Ringwood, Victoria, Australia: Penguin, 1988.

———. "From Notebook Draft to Published Story: 'Late Spring/This Flower.'" In *Critical Essays on Katherine Mansfield,* ed. Rhoda B. Nathan. New York: G. K. Hall, 1993.

Boxwell, D. A. "(Dis)orienting Spectacle: The Politics of Orlando's Sapphic Camp." *Twentieth Century Literature* 44.3 (1998): 306–27.

Bree, Germaine. "Autogynography." *Southern Review* 22 (April 1986): 223–30.

Brodski, Bella, and Celeste Schenck, eds. *Life/Lines: Theorizing Women's Autobiography.* Ithaca: Cornell University Press, 1988.

Broe, Mary Lynn, and Angela Ingram. "Reading the Signs of Women's Writing." *Tulsa Studies in Women's Literature* 4 (1985): 5–15.

———, eds. *Women's Writing in Exile.* Chapel Hill: University of North Carolina Press, 1989.

Brooks, Peter. "Psychoanalytic Constructions and Narrative Meanings." *Paragraph* VII (1987).

Bruss, Elizabeth. *Autobiographical Acts: The Changing Situations of a Literary Genre.* Baltimore: Johns Hopkins University Press, 1976.

Bunkers, Suzanne L. "Midwestern Diaries and Journals: What Women Were (Not) Saying in the Late 1800s." In *Studies in Autobiography,* ed. James Olney, 190–210. New York: Oxford University Press, 1988.

Bunkers, Suzanne L., and Cynthia A. Huff, eds. *Inscribing the Daily: Critical Essays on Women's Diaries.* Amherst: University of Massachusetts Press, 1996.

Buss, Helen M. "A Feminist Revision of New Historicism to Give Fuller Readings of Women's Private Writings." In *Inscribing the Daily: Critical Essays on Women's Diaries,* ed. Suzanne Bunkers and Cynthia Huff, 86–103. Amherst: University of Massachusetts Press, 1996.

Carroll, Berenice A. " 'To Crush Him in Our Own Country': The Political Thought of Virginia Woolf." *Feminist Studies* 4 (1978): 99–131.

Caws, Mary Ann. "Wariness and Women's Language." In *Gender and Literary Voice,* ed. Janet Todd, 26–36. New York: Holmes and Meier, 1980.

———, and Sarah Bird Wright. *Bloomsbury and Friends: Art and France.* Oxford: Oxford University Press, 1999.

Cheng, Vincent. " 'All the Devices of the Prostitute': Sincerity and the Authorial Personae of Ford Madox Ford." *Journal of Modern Literature* 15.4 (1989): 531–40.

Chevigny, Bell Gale. "Daughters Writing: Towards a Theory of Women's Biography." *Feminist Studies* 9.1 (1983): 81–95.

Clausen, Christopher. "Second Thoughts: Victorians and After." *The New Leader* 79.5 (August 12–26, 1996): 14–15.

Conway, Jill, ed. *In Her Own Words: Women's Memoirs from Australia, New Zealand, Canada, and the United States.* New York: Vintage, 1999.

Cooper, JoAnn E. "Shaped Meaning: Women's Diaries, Journals, and Letters— The Old and the New." *Women's Studies International Forum* 10.1 (1987): 95–99.

Corbett, Mary Jean. *Representing Femininity: Middle-Class Subjectivity in Victorian and Edwardian Women's Autobiographies.* Oxford: Oxford University Press, 1992.

Coward, Rosalind. *Female Desires.* New York: Grove, 1985.

Culley, Margo. " 'Introduction' to *A Day at a Time: The Diary Literature of American Women from 1764 to 1984."* In *Women, Autobiography, Theory: A Reader,* ed. Sidonie Smith and Julia Watson. Madison: University of Wisconsin Press, 1998.

Darrohn, Christine. " 'Blown to Bits': Katherine Mansfield's 'The Garden-Party' and the Great War." *Modern Fiction Studies* 44.3 (1998): 514–39.

Davis, Gayle. "Women's Frontier Diaries: Writing for Good Reason." *Women's Studies* 14 (1987): 5–14.

DeLauretis, Teresa. *Alice Doesn't.* Bloomington: Indiana University Press, 1984.

Deppman, Hsiu-Chuang, "Rereading the Mirror Image: Looking-Glasses, Gender, and Mimeticism in Virginia Woolf's Writing." *Journal of Narrative Theory* 31.1 (2001): 31–64.

DeSalvo, Louise. *Virginia Woolf: The Impact of Childhood Sexual Abuse on Her Life and Work.* New York: Ballantine, 1989.

———. "'Tinder-and-Flint': Virginia Woolf and Vita Sackville-West." In *Significant Others: Creativity and Intimate Partnership,* ed. Whitney Chadwick and Isabelle de Courtivron, 83–95. New York: Thames and Hudson, 1993

Dickson, Katherine Murphy. *Katherine Mansfield's New Zealand Stories.* New York: University Press of America, 1999.

Dinnerstein, Dorothy. *The Mermaid and the Minotaur: Sexual Arrangements and Human Malaise.* New York: Harper and Row, 1976.

DuPlessis, Rachel Blau. " 'I' rejected; 'We' Substituted: The Later Novels of Woolf." *Writing beyond the Ending: Narrative Strategies of Twentieth-Century Women Writers,* 162–78. Bloomington: Indiana University Press, 1985.

Duyfhuizen, Bernard. "Diary Narratives in Fact and Fiction." *Novel* 19 (1986): 171–78.

Eakin, Paul John. *Fictions in Autobiography: Stories in the Art of Self-Invention.* Princeton: Princeton University Press, 1985.

———. *How Our Lives Became Stories: Making Selves.* Ithaca: Cornell University Press, 1999

———. "Breaking Rules: The Consequences of Self-Narration." *Biography* 24.1 (2001): 113–27.

Egan, Susanna. *Mirror Talk: Genres of Crisis in Contemporary Autobiography.* Chapel Hill: University of North Carolina Press, 1999.

Evans, Mary. *Missing Persons: The Impossibility of Auto/biography.* London: Routledge, 1999.

Fand, Roxanne. J. *The Dialogic Self: Reconstructing Subjectivity in Woolf, Lessing, and Atwood.* Cranbury, N.J.: Associated University Press, 1999.

Felski, Rita. *Beyond Feminist Aesthetics.* Cambridge: Harvard University Press, 1989.

Flanagan, Anne Marie. "Wor(l)ds within Words: Doris Lessing as Metafictionist and Metaphysician." *Studies in the Novel* 20 (1988): 186–205.

———. "Ford's Women: Between Fact and Fiction." *Journal of Modern Literature* 24.2 (2000/2001): 235–49.

Ford, Ford Madox. *Memories and Impressions—A Study in Atmosphere.* New York: Harper & Bros., 1911.

———. *No More Parades.* London: The Bodley Head, 1962.

———. *Your Mirror to My Times: Selected Autobiographies and Impressions.* New York: Holt, Rinehart, and Winston, 1971.

———. *The Good Soldier.* New York: Knopf, 1991

———, and Violet Hunt. *The Desirable Alien: At Home in Germany.* London: Chatto and Windus, 1913.

———. *Zeppelin Nights.* London: John Lane, The Bodley Head, 1913.

Fowler, Rewena. "Moments and Metamorphoses: Virginia Woolf's Greece." *Comparative Literature* 51.3 (1999): 217–42.

Franklin, Penelope. *Private Pages: Diaries of American Women, 1830s–1970s.* New York: Ballantine, 1986.

Franko, Carol. "Authority, Truthtelling, and Parody: Doris Lessing and 'the Book.'" *Papers on Language and Literature* 31.3 (1995): 255ff.

Friedman, Susan Stanford. "Women's Autobiographical Selves: Theory and Practice." In *The Private Self,* ed. Shari Benstock, 34–63. Chapel Hill: University of North Carolina Press.

Funk, Allison. "A Ribbon of Scenes." *Papers on Language and Literature* 34.3 (1998): 319–26.

Gardiner, Judith Kegan. "On Female Identity and Writing by Women." *Critical Inquiry* 8 (1981): 91–99.

———. "Rhys Recalls Ford: Quartet and the Good Soldier." *Tulsa Studies in Women's Literature* 1.1 (1982): 67–81.

————, and Irma McClaurin. "Female Forms of Resistance." *Feminist Studies* 24.3 (1998): 483.

Gilbert, Sandra, and Susan Gubar. *The Madwoman in the Attic.* New Haven: Yale University Press, 1979.

————. *No Man's Land: The Place of the Woman Writer in the Twentieth Century.* Vol. 1, *The War of the Words.* New Haven: Yale University Press, 1988.

Gillespie, Diane F., ed. *The Multiple Muses of Virginia Woolf.* Columbia: University of Missouri Press, 1993.

Gilmore, Leigh. *The Limits of Autobiography: Trauma and Testimony.* Ithaca: Cornell University Press, 2001.

Goldring, Douglas. *South Lodge: Reminiscences of Violet Hunt, Ford Madox Ford, and the English Review Circle.* London: Constable, 1943.

————. *Life Interests.* London: Macdonald, 1948.

Gordon, Ian. Introduction. In *The Urewera Notebook* by Katherine Mansfield, 11–30. Oxford: Oxford University Press, 1978.

Gordon, Lyndall. *Virginia Woolf: A Writer's Life.* New York: Norton, 1984.

Gordon, Mary. "A Man Who Loved Women, a Womanly Man." *Antaeus* 56 (1986): 206–14.

Gusdorf, Georges. "Conditions and Limits of Autobiography." In *Autobiography: Essays Theoretical and Critical,*" ed. James Olney, 28–48. Princeton: Princeton University Press, 1980.

Halpern, Daniel. "Introduction." In *In Our Private Lives,* ed. Daniel Halpern. New York: Vintage, 1988.

Hankin, C. A. *Katherine Mansfield and Her Confessional Stories.* London: Macmillan, 1983.

Hardwick, Joan. *An Immodest Violet: The Life of Violet Hunt.* North Pomfret, Vt.: Trafalgar Square, 1990.

Harris, Susan C. "The Ethics of Indecency: Censorship, Sexuality, and the Voice of the Academy of the Narration of *Jacob's Room.*" *Twentieth Century Literature* 43.4 (1997): 420–38.

Hassam, A. "Reading Other People's Diaries." *University of Toronto Quarterly* 56 (1987): 435–42.

Heilbrun, Carolyn G. *Writing a Woman's Life.* New York: Norton, 1988.

————. "Non-Autobiographies of 'Privileged' Women: England and America." In *Women Writing in Exile,* ed. Mary Lynn Broe and Angela Ingram, 62–76. Chapel Hill: University of North Carolina Press, 1989.

Henstra, Sarah. "Looking the Part: Performative Narration in Djuna Barnes's 'Nightwood' and Katherine Mansfield's 'Je ne parle pas français.'" *Twentieth Century Literature* 46.2 (2000/2001): 125–49.

Hetata, Sherif. "The Self and Autobiography." *PMLA* 118.1 (January 2003): 123–26.

Hite, Molly. "Doris Lessing's *The Golden Notebook* and *The Four-Gated City:* Ideology, Coherence, and Possibility." *Twentieth Century Literature* 34.1 (1988): 16–29.

———. "(En)gendering Metafiction: Doris Lessing's Rehearsals for *The Golden Notebook.*" *Modern Fiction Studies* 34.3 (1988): 481–500.

Hoff, Molly. "Woolf's Mrs. Dalloway." *The Explicator* 53 (1995): 108–11.

Horney, Karen. *Feminine Psychology.* New York: Norton, 1967.

Howe, Florence. "A Conversation with Doris Lessing." In *Doris Lessing: Critical Studies,* ed. Annis Pratt and L. S. Dembo, 1–19. Madison: University of Wisconsin Press, 1973.

Huff, Cynthia. "Writer at Large: Culture and Self in Victorian Women's Travel Diaries." *a/b: Auto/Biography Studies* 4.2 (1988): 118–29.

———. "Textual Boundaries: Space in Nineteenth-Century Women's Manuscript Diaries." In *Inscribing the Daily,* ed. Susanne L. Bunkers and Cynthia A. Huff, 123–39. Amherst: University of Massachusetts Press, 1996.

———. "Reading as Re-Vision: Approaches to Reading Manuscript Diaries." *Biography* (2000): 504–23.

Hunt, Violet. *Tales of the Uneasy.* London: Wm. Heinemann, 1911.

———. *The House of Many Mirrors.* New York: Brentano, 1915.

———. *I Have This to Say: The Story of My Flurried Years.* New York: Boni & Liveright, 1926.

———. *The Wife of Rosetti: Her Life and Death.* London: John Lane, 1932.

———, and Ford Madox Hueffer. *The Desirable Alien: At Home in Germany.* London: Chatto and Windus, 1913a.

———. *Zeppelin Nights.* London: John Lane, The Bodley Head, 1913b.

Hunter, Diane. *Readings of Gender, Representation and Rhetoric.* Urbana: University of Illinois Press, 1989.

Huxley, Aldous. *Limbo.* New York: Doran, 1920.

Ivask, Ivor, ed. "The Diary as Art: Form and Formlessness, Ephemeral or Timeless?" *World Literature Today* 61.2 (1987): 181–82.

Jauss, Hans Robert. *Question and Answer: Forms of Dialogic Understanding.* Minneapolis: University of Minnesota Press, 1989.

Jeffries, Sheila. *The Spinster and Her Enemies: Feminism and Sexuality, 1880–1930.* London: Pandora, 1985.

Jelinek, Estelle C. *The Tradition of Women's Autobiography: From Antiquity to the Present.* Boston: Twayne, 1986.

———, ed. *Women's Autobiography: Essays in Criticism.* Bloomington: Indiana University Press, 1980.

Jones, Kathleen. *Glorious Fame: The Life of Margaret Cavendish, The Duchess of Newcastle, 1623–1673.* London: Bloomsbury, 1988.

Kaplan, Caren. *Questions of Travel: Modern Discourses of Displacement.* Durham: Duke University Press, 1996.

Kaplan, Deborah. "Representing Two Cultures: Jane Austen's Letters." In *The Private Self,* ed. Shari Benstock, 211–29. Chapel Hill: University of North Carolina Press, 1988.

Kavanagh, P. J. "Good Soldiering On." *The Spectator.* v. 277,iss. 8783 (November 16, 1996): 53–54.

King, Florence. "Violet Hunt: Handmaiden." *The American Enterprise* 6.2 (March 1995): 91.

Kirchhoff, Frederick. "Travel as Anti-Autobiography: William Morris's Icelandic Journals." In *William Morris: The Construction of the Male Self, 1856-1872.* Cleveland: University of Ohio Press, 1990.

Kofman, Sara. *The Enigma of Woman: Woman in Freud's Writings.* Trans. Catherine Porter. Ithaca: Cornell University Press, 1985.

Kolodny, Annette. "Dancing through the Minefield: Some Observations about the Theory, Practice, and Politics of a Feminist Literary Criticism." In *Feminist Criticism: Essays on Women, Literature, Theory,* ed. Elaine Showalter, 144–67. New York: Pantheon, 1985.

Kuhn, Annette. *Family Secrets: Acts of Memory and Imagination.* London: Verso, 1995.

Lacan, Jacques. "The Insistence of the Letter in the Unconscious." In *Structuralism,* ed. Jacques Ehrmann. Trans. Jan Miel. New Haven: *Yale French Studies* 36/37 (1966), reprinted by permission of Doubleday.

———. "The Mirror Stage as Formative of the Function of the I as Revealed in Psychoanalytic Experience." *Ecrits: A Selection* 1–7. *Le moi dans la théorie de Freud et dans la téchnique de la psychanalyse: Le Séminaire II,* 1954–55 (Paris: Seuil, 1978). In *Feminine Sexuality.* Trans. Jacqueline Rose. New York: Norton, 1982.

Law, Joseph, and Linda K. Hughes. *Biographical Passages: Essays on Victorian and Modernist Biography.* Columbia: University of Missouri Press, 2000.

Lawrence, D. H. *Women in Love.* Cambridge: Cambridge University Press, 1987.

Leaska, Mitchell E. *Granite and Rainbow: The Hidden Life of Virginia Woolf.* New York: Farrar, 1998.

Lee, Hermione. *Virginia Woolf.* New York: Knopf, 1997.

Lejeune, Phillipe. "Autobiography in the Third Person." *New Literary History IX* 1 (1977): 27–47.

———. "The Autobiographical Pact." In *On Autobiography,* ed. Paul John Eakin, 3–30. Trans. Katherine M. Leary. Minneapolis: University of Minnesota Press, 1989.

———. "How Do Diaries End?" *Biography* (2001): 99–112.

Lessing, Doris. *The Golden Notebook.* New York: Bantam, 1973.

———. "Introduction." In *The Golden Notebook,* vii–xxii. New York: Bantam, 1973.

———. "Afterword to 'The Story of an African Farm,' by Olive Schreiner." In *A Small Personal Voice,* ed. Paul Schlueter, 97–120. New York: Knopf, 1974.

Lessing, Doris. Interviews on her life and writings by Roy Newquist and at Stony Brook by Jonah Raskin and a talk with her by Florence Howe. In *A Small Personal Voice,* ed. Paul Schlueter, 22–82. New York: Knopf, 1974.

———. *The Summer before Dark.* New York: Random House, 1983.

———. *Under My Skin: My Autobiography to 1949.* New York: Harper, 1994.

———. *Walking in the Shade: Volume Two of My Autobiography, 1942–1962.* New York: Harper, 1997.

———. Against Utopia: An Interview with Susie Linfield. *Salmagundi* 130/131 (Spring/Summer 2001): 59–74.

Lifshin, Lyn. "Introduction." In *Ariadne's Thread: A Collection of Contemporary Women's Journals,* ed. Lyn Lifshin, 1–18. New York: Harper, 1982.

Lewis, Wyndam. *The Roaring Queen.* London: Secker, 1973.

Linde, Charlotte. *Life Stories: The Creation of Coherence.* New York: Oxford University Press, 1993.

Linfield, Susie. Against Utopia: An Interview with Doris Lessing. *Salmagundi* 130/131 (Spring/Summer 2001): 59–74.

Loftus, Brian. "Speaking Silence: The Strategies and Structures of Queer Autobiography." *College Literature* 24 (February 1997): 28–44.

McEldowney, Dennis. "The Multiplex Effect: Recent Biographical Writing on Katherine Mansfield." *Ariel* (1985): 111–24.

McLaughlin, Ann L. "The Same Job: The Shared Writing Aims of Katherine Mansfield and Virginia Woolf." *Modern Fiction Studies* 24.3 (1978–1979): 369–81.

Mallon, Thomas. *A Book of One's Own: People and Their Diaries.* New York: Ticknor and Fields, 1984.

Malone, Anne Richton. "The Power of Shared Stories: Growing Old in the Company of Other Women's Voices." *Frontiers* 19.1 (1998): 64–74.

Mansfield, Katherine. *In a German Pension: 13 Stories.* London: Stephen Swift, 1911.

———. *Bliss, and Other Stories.* New York: Alfred A. Knopf, 1920.

———. "The Garden Party." In *The Garden Party, and Other Stories,* 59–82. New York: Alfred A. Knopf, 1922.

———. *Journal of Katherine Mansfield,* ed. John Middleton Murry. New York: Alfred A. Knopf, 1927.

———. *Journal of Katherine Mansfield,* ed. John Middleton Murry. Definitive edition. London: Constable, 1954. Unless otherwise designated, all citations from the *Journal* are in this edition.

———. *The Urewera Notebook,* ed. Ian Gordon. Oxford: Oxford University Press, 1978.

———. *In a German Prison.* Middlesex: Penguin, 1985.

———. *Selected Letters,* ed. Vincent O'Sullivan and Margaret Scott. Oxford: Oxford University Press, 1990–1996.

————. *The Katherine Mansfield Notebooks, Complete Edition*, ed. Margaret Scott. Vols. 1–2. Minneapolis: University of Minnesota Press, 2002.

Marcus, Jane. "Art and Anger." *Feminist Studies* 4 (1978): 68–98.

————. *Virginia Woolf and the Languages of Patriarchy.* Bloomington: Indiana University Press, 1987.

————. "Invincible Mediocrity: The Private Selves of Public Women." In *The Private Self*, ed. Shari Benstock, 114–47. Chapel Hill: University of North Carolina Press, 1988.

Marcus, Laura. *Auto/Biographical Discourses: Theory, Criticism, Practice.* Manchester: Manchester University Press, 1994.

Martin, Biddy. "Lesbian Identity and Autobiographical Difference[s]." In *Life/Lines: Theorizing Women's Autobiography*, ed. Bella Brodski and Celeste Schenck, 77–103. Ithaca: Cornell University Press, 1988.

Mason, Mary. "The Other Voice: Autobiographies of Women Writers." In *Life/Lines: Theorizing Women's Autobiography*, ed. Bella Brodski and Celeste Schenck, 19–44. Ithaca: Cornell University Press, 1988.

Matthews, William. "Diary: A Neglected Genre." *Sewanee Review* 85 (1977): 286–300.

McLaurin, Allen. "Consciousness and Group Conciousness in Virginia Woolf." In *Virginia Woolf: A Centary Perspective*, ed. Eric Warner, 28–40. New York: St. Martin's, 1984.

Mentzer, Melissa. "Mary Chestnut and the Fiction of Autobiography." Address for Autobiography Session. Philological Association of the Pacific Coast, Claremont Colleges, and California State Polytechnic University, Pomona, November 11, 1989.

Meyers, Jeffrey. *Married to Genius.* New York: Barnes & Noble, 1977.

————. *Katherine Mansfield: A Darker View.* New York: Cooper Square, 2002.

Michie, Helena. "Victorian Honeymoons: Sexual Reorientations and the 'Sights' of Europe." *Victorian Studies* 43.2 (Winter 2001): 229–51.

Miller, Andrew John. "'Our Representative, Our Spokesman': Modernity, Professionalism, and Representation in Virginia Woolf's *Between the Acts*." *Studies in the Novel* 33.1 (2001): 34–50.

Miller, Jane E. "New and Notable: The Edward Naumburg, Jr., Collection of Violet Hunt." *Princeton University Library Chronicle* 51.2 (1990): 210–18.

Miller, Marlowe A. "Unveiling 'the Dialectic of Culture and Barbarism' in British Pageantry: Virginia Woolf's *Between the Acts*." *Papers on Language and Literature* 34.2 (1998): 134–61.

Miller, Nancy K. "Women's Dialectics of Identification." In *Women and Language in Literature and Society*, ed. Sally McConnell-Givet, Ruth Order, and Nelly Furman, 258–69. New York: Praeger, 1980.

————. *Subject to Change: Reading Feminist Writing.* New York: Columbia University Press, 1988.

————. "Representing Others: Gender and the Subjects of Autobiography." *Differences* 6.1 (1994): 1–27.

Misch, George, ed. *A History of Autobiography in Antiquity.* Trans. E. W. Dickes. 2 vols. London: Routledge & Kegan Paul, 1950.

Mizener, Arthur. *The Saddest Story: A Biography of Ford Madox Ford.* New York: Carrol & Graf, 1971.

Modleski, Tania. *Old Wives' Tales and Other Women's Stories.* New York: New York University Press, 1998.

Moffat, Mary Jane, and Charlotte Painter, eds. *Revelations: Diaries of Women.* New York: Vantage Books, 1975.

Monte, Steven. "Ancients and Moderns in *Mrs. Dalloway.*" *Modern Language Quarterly* 61.4 (2000): 587–616.

Morrow, Patrick. *Katherine Mansfield's Fiction.* Bowling Green, Ohio: Bowling Green Press, 1993.

Murry, J. M. *The Letters of John Middleton Murry to Katherine Mansfield,* ed. C. A. Hankin. London: Constable, 1983.

Muske-Dukes, Carol. *Women and Poetry: Truth, Autobiography, and the Shape of the Self.* Ann Arbor: University Michigan Press, 1997.

Nathan, Rhoda, ed. *Critical Essays on Katherine Mansfield.* New York: GK Hall, 1993.

New, W. H. "Mansfield in the Act of Writing." *Journal of Modern Literature* 20 (1996): 51–63.

————. *Reading Mansfield and Metaphors of Form.* Montreal: McGill-Queen's University Press, 1999.

Newey, Vincent, and Philip Shaw, eds. *Mortal Pages, Literary Lives: Studies in Nineteenth-Century Autobiography.* Brookfield, Vt.: Ashgate, 1996.

Nin, Anais. *The Diary of Anais Nin.* Rupert Pole, executor, The Anais Nin Trust. New York: Harcourt, 1983.

Norman, Rose. Review of *Life/Lines: Theorizing Women's Autobiography,* ed. Bella Brodski and Celeste Schenck. *a/b: Auto/Biography Studies* 4.2 (1988): 150–55.

Nussbaum, Felicity A. "Eighteenth-Century Women's Autobiographical Commonplaces." In *The Private Self,* ed. Shari Benstock, 147–71. Chapel Hill: University of North Carolina Press, 1988.

————. "Toward Conceptualizing Diary." In *Studies in Autobiography,* ed. James Olney, 128–39. New York: Oxford University Press, 1988.

————. *The Autobiographical Subject,* 2d ed. Baltimore: Johns Hopkins University Press, 1995.

O'Connor, Frank. "An Author in Search of a Subject." In *Critical Essays on Katherine Mansfield,* ed. Rhoda Nathan, 174–82. New York: GK Hall, 1993.

Olney, James. *Memory and Narrative: The Weave of Life-Writing.* Chicago: University of Chicago Press, 1998.

———, ed. *Autobiography: Essays Theoretical and Critical.* Princeton: Princeton University Press, 1980a.

———, ed. "Some Versions of Memory/Some Versions of Bios: The Ontology of Autobiography." In *Autobiography: Essays Theoretical and Critical,* ed. James Olney, 236–67. Princeton: Princeton University Press, 1980b.

———, ed. *Studies in Autobiography.* New York: Oxford University Press, 1988.

Olsen, Tillie. *Silences.* New York: Delta/Seymour Lawrence, 1965.

Olshen, Barry N. "Subject, Persona, and Self in the Theory of Autobiography." *a/b: Auto/Biography Studies* 10.1 (1995): 5–16.

Olson, Barbara. *Authorial Divinity in the Twentieth Century: Omniscient Narration in Woolf, Hemingway, and Others.* Lewisburg, Penn.: Bucknell University Press, 1997.

O'Sullivan, Vincent. "Finding the Pattern, Solving the Problem: Katherine Mansfield, the New Zealand European." In *Katherine Mansfield: In from the Margin,* ed. Roger Robinson, 9–24. Baton Rouge: Louisiana State University Press, 1994.

———, and Margaret Scott, eds. *The Collected Letters of Katherine Mansfield.* Oxford: Clarendon, 1984.

Ozick, Cynthia. "Mrs. Virginia Woolf: A Madwoman and Her Nurse." In *Women's Voices: Visions and Perspectives,* ed. Pat C. Hoy II, Esther H. Schor, and Robert DiYanni, 249–67. New York: McGraw Hill, 1990.

Parke, Catherine E. *Biography: Writing Lives.* New York: Twayne, 1996.

Perreault, Jeanne. *Writing Selves: Contemporary Feminist Autography.* Minneapolis: University of Minnesota Press, 1995.

Personal Narrative Group. *Interpreting Women's Lives.* Bloomington: Indiana University Press, 1989.

Peterson, Linda. "Audience and the Autobiographical Art." In *Approaches to Victorian Autobiography,* ed. George Landow, 158–74. Athens: Ohio University Press, 1979.

———. "Instituting Women's Autobiography: Nineteenth-Century Editors and the Shaping of an Autobiographical Tradition." In *The Culture of Autobiography: Constructions of Self-Representation,* ed. Robert Folkenflik, 80–103. Stanford: Stanford University Press, 1993.

———. *Traditions of Victorian Women's Autobiography: The Poetics and Politics of Life Writing.* Charlottesville: University Press of Virginia, 1999.

Podnieks, Elizabeth. *Daily Modernism: The Literary Diaries of Virginia Woolf, Antonia White, Elizabeth Smart and Anais Nin.* Montreal and Kingston: McGill-Queen's University Press, 2000.

Ponsonby, Arthur. *British Diarists.* Reprint. Folcroft, Penn.: Folcroft Library Editions, 1974.

Poole, Roger. *The Unknown Virginia Woolf.* Cambridge: Cambridge University Press, 1978.

Porter, Dennis. *Haunted Journeys: Desire and Transgression in European Travel Writing.* Princeton: Princeton University Press, 1991.

Powers, Elizabeth. "The Stain on Vanessa Stephen's Dress." *Commentary* 104 (1997): 43–48.

Pratt, Annis, and L. S. Dimbo. *Doris Lessing: Critical Studies.* Madison: University of Wisconsin Press, 1974.

Prothero, J. K. "Review of *Zeppelin Nights.*" *New Witness* (January 6, 1916): 293.

Putzel, Steven. "Virginia Woolf and 'the Distance of the Stage.'" *Women's Studies* 28.4 (1999): 435–70.

Raoul, Valerie. "Women and Diaries: Gender and Genre." *Mosaic* 22 (Summer 1989): 57–65.

———. "Women's Diaries as Life-Savings: Who Decides Whose Life Is Saved? The Journals of Eugénie de Guerin and Elizabeth Leseur." *Biography* (2001): 140–51.

Reed-Danahay, Deborah E. *Auto/Ethnography: Rewriting the Self and the Social.* New York: Berg, 1997.

Regard, Frederic. "The Ethics of Biographical Reading: A Pragmatic Approach." *Cambridge Quarterly* 29.4 (2000): 394–408.

Rich, Adrienne. *On Lies, Secrets, and Silences.* New York: Norton, 1979.

Robinson, Roger, ed. *Katherine Mansfield: In from the Margin.* Baton Rouge: Louisiana State University Press, 1994.

Rose, Jacqueline. Introduction II. In *Feminine Sexuality* by Jacques Lacan, 27–59. Ed. Juliet Mitchell. Trans. Jacqueline Rose. New York: Norton, 1982.

Rose, Phillis. Introduction. *Woman of Letters: A Life of Virginia Woolf.* New York: Oxford University Press, 1978.

Rosenberg, Beth Carole. "Virginia Woolf's Postmodern Literary History." *Modern Language Notes* 115.5 (2000): 1112–30.

Rosenfeld, Natania. *Outsiders Together: Virginia and Leonard Woolf.* Princeton: Princeton University Press, 2000.

Rosenwald, Lawrence. "Is the Journal Really a Work of Art?" *Emerson and the Art of the Diary,* Part 1: "The Journal as Artifact," 65–83. New York: Oxford University Press, 1988.

Rousseau, Jean-Jacques. *Emile.* New York: Basic, 1979.

Sackville-West, Victoria. *The Letters of Vita Sackville-West to Virginia Woolf.* New York: Morrow, 1985.

Saxton, Ruth, and Jean Tobin, eds. *Woolf and Lessing: Breaking the Mold.* New York: St. Martin's, 1994.

Schenck, Celeste. "All of a Piece: Women's Poetry and Autobiography." In *Life/Lines: Theorizing Women's Autobiography,* ed. Bella Brodski and Celeste Schenck, 281–305. Ithaca: Cornell University Press, 1988.

———. "Exiled by Genre: Modernism, Canonicity, and the Politics of

Exclusion." In *Women Writing in Exile*, ed. Mary Lynn Broe and Angela Ingram, 22–250. Chapel Hill: University of North Carolina Press, 1989.

Schlueter, Paul. *The Novels of Doris Lessing.* Carbondale: Southern Illinois University Press, 1974.

———, ed. *A Small Personal Voice.* New York: Knopf, 1974.

Schweickart, Patrocinio. "Reading a Wordless Statement: The Structure of Doris Lessing's *The Golden Notebook.*" *Modern Fiction Studies* 31 (1985): 263–79.

———. "Reading Ourselves: Toward a Feminist Theory of Reading." In *Feminisms: An Anthology of Literary Theory and Criticism*, ed. Robyn R. Warhol and Diane Price Herndl, 609–34. New Brunswick: Rutgers University Press, 1997.

Scott, Margaret. "The Extant Manuscripts of Katherine Mansfield." *Etudes Anglaises* 26.4 (1973): 413–19.

———, ed. *The Katherine Mansfield Notebooks.* Complete edition. Minneapolis: University of Minnesota Press, 2002.

Searles, Patricia, and Janet Mickish. " 'A Thoroughbred Girl': Images of Female Gender Role in Turn-of-the-Century Mass Media." *Women's Studies* 10.3 (1984): 261–81.

Secor, Robert. "Aesthetes and Pre-Raphaelites: Oscar Wilde and the Sweetest Violet in England." *Texas Studies in Literature and Language* 21.3 (1979): 396–412.

———. "Henry James and Violet Hunt, the 'Improper Person of Babylon.'" *Journal of Modern Literature* 13 (1986): 3–36.

———, and Marie Secor. "Violet Hunt's Tales of the Uneasy: Ghost Stories of a Worldly Woman." *Women and Literature* 6 (1978): 16–27.

———, eds. *The Return of the Good Soldier: Ford Madox Ford and Violet Hunt's 1917 Diary.* University of Victoria: *English Literary Studies Monograph Series*, 1983.

Seidensticker, Edward. "Autobiography." *Biography* 22.1 (Winter 1999): 46–56.

Sellei, Nora. *Katherine Mansfield and Virginia Woolf: A Personal and Professional Bond.* New York: Lang, 1996.

Showalter, Elaine. *The Female Malady: Women, Madness, and English Culture, 1830–1980.* New York: Penguin, 1987.

Simons, Judy. *Diaries and Journals of Literary Women from Fanny Burney to Virginia Woolf.* Iowa City: University of Iowa Press, 1990.

Sinclair, May. "The Novels of Violet Hunt." *The English Review* (1922): 106–18.

Smith, Angela. *Katherine Mansfield and Virginia Woolf: A Public of Two.* Oxford: Clarendon, 1999.

Smith, Marya. "Lessing Is More." *Ms.*, April 1998: 79.

Smith, Sidonie. *A Poetics of Women's Autobiography: Marginality and the Fictions of Self-Representation.* Bloomington: Indiana University Press, 1987.

Smith, Sidonie. *Subjectivity, Identity, and the Body: Women's Autobiographical Practices in the Twentieth Century.* Bloomington: Indiana University Press, 1993.

——. "Performativity, Autobiographical Practice, Resistance." *a/b: Auto/Biography Studies* 10.1 (1995): 17–33.

——. "Women's Autobiographical Selves: Theory and Practice." In *Women, Autobiography, Theory: A Reader,* ed. Sidonie Smith and Julia Watson, 72–82. Madison: University of Wisconsin Press, 1998.

——, and Julia Watson. *Reading Autobiography: A Guide for Interpreting Life Narratives.* Minneapolis: University of Minnesota Press, 2001.

——, eds. *Women, Autobiography, Theory: A Reader.* Madison: University of Wisconsin Press, 1998.

Smith-Rosenburg, Carroll. *Disorderly Conduct: Visions of Gender in Victorian Americans.* New York: Knopf, 1985.

Spacks, Patricia Meyer. "Selves in Hiding." In *Women's Autobiography: Essays in Criticism,* ed. Estelle C. Jelinek, 112–32. Bloomington: Indiana University Press, 1980.

——. "Female Rhetorics." In *The Private Self,* ed. Shari Benstock, 177–91. Chapel Hill: University of North Carolina Press, 1988.

Spater, George, and Ian Parsons. *A Marriage of True Minds.* New York: Harvest/HBJ, 1977.

Sprague, Claire. *Rereading Doris Lessing: Narrative Patterns of Doubling and Repetition.* Chapel Hill: University of North Carolina Press, 1987.

Stanley, Liz. *The Auto/Biographical I: The Theory and Practice of Feminist Auto/Biography.* Manchester: Manchester University Press, 1992.

Stanton, Domna C. "Autogynography: Is the Subject Different?" In *Women, Autobiography, Theory: A Reader,* ed. Sidonie Smith and Julia Watson, 131–44. Madison: University of Wisconsin Press, 1998.

Stone, Wilfred. "Some Interviews with E. M. Forster, 1957–1958, 1965." *Twentieth Century Literature* 43 (1997): 57–74.

Stout, Janis. "A Quest of One's Own: Doris Lessing's *Summer before Dark.*" *Ariel* 21 (1990): 5–19.

Sukenick, Lynn. "Feeling and Reason in Doris Lessing's Fiction." In *Doris Lessing: Critical Studies,* ed. Annis Pratt and L. S. Dembo, 98–118. Madison: University of Wisconsin Press, 1973.

Swanson, Diana L. " 'My Boldness Terrifies Me': Sexual Abuse and Female Subjectivity in *The Voyage Out.*" *Twentieth Century Literature* 41 (1995): 284–309.

Swindells, Julia. *The Uses of Autobiography.* London: Taylor and Francis, 1995.

Taylor, Jenny. Introduction, "Situating Reading." In *Notebooks/Memoirs/Archives: Reading and Rereading Doris Lessing,* ed. Jenny Taylor, 3–42. Boston: Routledge and Kegan Paul, 1982.

Temple, Judy Nolte Lensink. "Expanding the Boundaries of Criticism: The Diary as Female Autobiography." *Women's Studies* 14 (1987): 39–53.

Tomalin, Claire. *Katherine Mansfield: A Secret Life*. New York: Knopf, 1988.

Vandivere, Julie. "Waves and Fragments: Linguistic Construction of Subject Formation in Virginia Woolf." *Twentieth Century Literature* 42 (1996): 221–33.

Voss, Norine. "Saying the Unsayable: An Introduction to Women's Autobiography." In *Gender Studies: New Directions in Feminist Criticism*, ed. Judith Spector, 218–33. Bowling Green: Bowling Green State University Popular Press, 1986.

Waldron, Philip. "Katherine Mansfield's Journal." *Twentieth Century Literature* (1974): 11–18.

Walker, Nancy K. " 'Wider than the Sky': Public Presence and Private Self in Dickinson, James and Woolf." In *The Private Self*, ed. Shari Benstock, 272–303. Chapel Hill: University of North Carolina Press, 1988.

Walters, Anne. "Self-Image and Style: A Discussion Based on Estelle Jelinek's *The Tradition of Women's Autobiography from Antiquity to Present*." *Women's International Forum* 10.1 (1987): 85–93.

Watson, Julia. "Writers' Autobiographies and the Other." In *Studies in Autobiography*, ed. James Olney, 140–49. New York: Oxford University Press, 1988.

Webb, Igor. "Marriage and Sex in the Novels of Ford Madox Ford." *Modern Fiction Studies* 23.4 (1977–1978): 586–92.

Westman, Karin E. "The Character in the House: Virginia Woolf in Dialogue with History's Audience." *Clio* 28.1 (1998): 1–27.

Whitlock, Gillian. *The Intimate Empire: Reading Women's Autobiography*. London: Cassell, 2000.

Wilson, Elizabeth. "Yesterday's Heroines: On Rereading Lessing and de Beauvoir." In *Notebooks/Memoirs/Archives: Reading and Rereading Doris Lessing*, ed. Jenny Taylor, 57–73. Boston: Routledge and Kegan Paul, 1982.

Wilson, Sonia. "Making an Exhibition of Oneself in Public: The Preface to Marie Bashkirtseff's Journal Intime." *French Studies* (2001).

Wollstonecraft, Mary. *A Vindication of the Rights of Women, with Strictures on Political and Moral Subjects*, ed. Charles W. Hagelman Jr. New York: Norton, 1967.

Woolf, Leonard. *The Wise Virgins: A Story of Words, Opinions and a Few Emotions*. London: Edward Arnold, 1914.

———. *Beginning Again: An Autobiography of the Years 1911 to 1918*. New York: Harcourt, Brace and World, 1964.

———. "Introduction." *A Writer's Diary: Virginia Woolf*, ed. Leonard Woolf. San Diego: Harvest/HBJ, 1981.

Woolf, Virginia. *To the Lighthouse*. San Diego: Harvest/HBJ, 1927.

———. *A Room of One's Own.* New York: Harcourt, Brace, 1929.

———. *The Waves.* San Diego: Harvest/HBJ, 1931.

———. *Three Guineas.* San Diego: Harvest/HBJ, 1936.

———. *The Years.* San Diego: Harvest/HBJ, 1937.

———. *Mrs. Dalloway.* San Diego: Harvest/HBJ, 1953. Originally published by Harcourt, 1925.

———. "Phases in Fiction." In *Granite and Rainbow Essays,* 93–145. New York: Harvest/HBJ, 1958.

———. "A Terribly Sensitive Mind." In *Granite and Rainbow Essays,* 73–76. New York: Harvest/HBJ, 1958.

———. *Between the Acts.* New York: HBJ, 1969. Originally published by Hogarth, 1941.

———. *Moments of Being: Unpublished Autobiographical Writing,* ed. Jeanne Schulkind. New York: HBJ, 1976.

———. *The Diary of Virginia Woolf.* Vol. 1, ed. Anne Olivier Bell. San Diego: Harvest/HBJ, 1977.

———. *The Diary of Virginia Woolf.* Vol. 2, ed. Anne Olivier Bell, assisted by Andrew McNeillie. San Diego: Harvest/HBJ, 1978.

———. *The Diary of Virginia Woolf.* Vol. 3, ed. Anne Olivier Bell, assisted by Andrew McNeillie. San Diego: Harvest/HBJ, 1980.

———. *The Diary of Virginia Woolf.* Vol. 4, ed. Anne Olivier Bell, assisted by Andrew McNeillie. San Diego: Harvest/HBJ, 1982.

———. *The Diary of Virginia Woolf.* Vol. 5, ed. Anne Olivier Bell, assisted by Andrew McNeillie. San Diego: Harvest/HBJ, 1984.

———. "The Decay of Essay Writing." In *The Essays of Virginia Woolf.* Vol. 1, 24–27. New York: HBJ, 1986.

———. *The Complete Shorter Fiction of Virginia Woolf,* ed. Susan Dick. San Diego: Harvest/HBJ, 1989.

———. *A Passionate Apprentice: The Early Journals of Virginia Woolf,* ed. Mitchell Leaska. London: Hogarth, 1990.

Ziolkowski, Margaret. "Diaries of Disaffection: Some Recent Russian Memoirs." *World Literature in Review* 61.2 (1987): 199–202.

# Index